The Newspaper Indian

The History of Communication

Robert W. McChesney and John C. Nerone, editors

A list of books in the series appears at the end of this book.

The Newspaper Indian

NATIVE AMERICAN IDENTITY

IN THE PRESS, 1820–90

John M. Coward

UNIVERSITY OF ILLINOIS PRESS

Urbana and Chicago

© 1999 by the Board of Trustees of the University of Illinois
Manufactured in the United States of America
1 2 3 4 5 C P 5 4 3 2 1

This book is printed on acid-free paper.

Library of Congress Cataloging-in-Publication Data
Coward, John M.
The newspaper Indian : Native American identity in the
press, 1820–90 / John M. Coward.
p.   cm. —(The history of communication)
Includes bibliographical references and index.
ISBN 0-252-02432-X (cloth : alk. paper)
ISBN 0-252-06738-X (pbk. : alk. paper)
1. Indians—Press coverage—United States.
2. Journalism—United States—History—19th century.
I. Title.
II. Series.
PN4888.I52C68   1999
070.4'4997—ddc21   98-19663
CIP

CONTENTS

Illustrations follow page 124

ACKNOWLEDGMENTS

T HIS book began many years ago as a doctoral dissertation in the Department of Journalism at the University of Texas at Austin. I am grateful to my professors at Texas for the inspiration and ideas they contributed to this research. I especially thank my dissertation committee: Pam Shoemaker, Jim Tankard, Gene Burd, and my advisor Marvin Olasky, who was extraordinarily encouraging during the sometimes painful research and writing of the dissertation. The final member of my committee, Shelley Fisher Fishkin of the American Studies Department, was particularly helpful and I thank her as well.

I am grateful to John Nerone of the University of Illinois for his interest in this project as well as his insightful criticism. I also wish to acknowledge two anonymous reviewers, one from the University of Oklahoma Press and the other at the University of Illinois Press. Their ideas improved this work. I also thank Barbara Cloud, editor of *Journalism History,* and Wallace Eberhard, editor of *American Journalism,* for permission to publish portions of articles that appeared in their journals. For help with illustrations, I appreciate the assistance of Sandy Barnard of the Department of Communication at Indiana State University, Terre Haute.

At the University of Tulsa, I have learned much from my colleagues. Joli Jensen in communication, Jim Ronda in history, Garrick Bailey and Richard Grounds in anthropology helped me clarify my ideas. Former communication colleagues John Pauly, now at St. Louis University, and Steve Jones, now at the University of Illinois, Chicago, were also helpful in shaping this book. I also appreciate the diligence of Jody Brown, a former student, who read reel after reel of microfilm for me during one long semester at Tulsa.

I owe a special debt to my family for their support over the many years I worked on this manuscript. My wife, Linda, has kept me grounded and sane during the many times the "Undertoad" threatened to drown me. My children, Ian and Rachel, gave meaning and purpose to the many hours I spent completing this research. As an imperfect parent, I see more clearly now the gifts my own parents bestowed on me. I thank my mother, Loretta Mason Coward, for the example of energy and drive she provided. Finally, I dedicate this book to the memory of my father, George Edmond Coward, a history major (Carson-Newman College, class of 1949) from whom I learned more about history—and life—than I knew.

The Newspaper Indian

INTRODUCTION:
INDIANS, IDEOLOGY, AND THE PRESS

HORACE Greeley was forty-eight years old when he decided to take his own advice and "Go West." Although he had been promoting western expansion and opportunity for years, the popular editor of the New York *Tribune* had lived his entire life in the East. By 1859, with a transcontinental railroad to promote, Greeley began his much-anticipated journey across the plains to the Pacific. Along the way, he filed a series of dispatches so that *Tribune* readers everywhere could follow his adventures. These reports, collected the following year in a book, were superficial and incomplete, Greeley admitted. Nevertheless, Greeley believed his firsthand reporting had merit: "The value of such a work . . . must be sought in the unstudied simplicity of narration, in the freshness of its observations, and in the truth of its averments as transcripts of actual experiences and current impressions."[1]

The trip provided Greeley a chance to see people and places he had long imagined. As a self-made editor and American idealist, Greeley saw the West as a place for ambitious young men to seek their fortunes. As a leading nineteenth-century reformer, Greeley saw the West as a safety valve, a place where eastern laborers could avoid the excesses of factory life and urban squalor. As a champion of American nationalism, Greeley also imagined the West as God's gift to the United States, a nearly empty wilderness that Americans were destined to tame and civilize. Now, in middle age, the famous editor would see for himself the land that held such promise.

But Greeley's experiences with western Indians soon challenged his buoyant spirit. Bumping his way across the grasslands of eastern Kansas, Greeley met his first "real" Indians—Delaware, Kaw, Ottawa, Osage, Kickapoo, and Potawatamie all lived nearby. Visiting Lawrence, Greeley noted the town's potential for growth, but added that "a large Indian reservation (the Delaware) impedes its progress."[2] Indian reservations, Greeley concluded, were "heavy drawbacks" to Kansas prosperity.[3] At a place called Prairie Dog Creek on 31 May, Greeley described some Arapahos who, though not hostile, were "intent on begging or stealing, and stopping wagons peremptorily till [sic] their demands [were] complied with." The Arapahos were fighting the Pawnees, Greeley noted, though it was a pitiful conflict. "Indian wars with each other are, in our day, cruel and cowardly plundering forays, fitted only to excite disgust," Greeley concluded.[4] In Denver some days later, he had a long meeting with Left-Hand, a southern Arapaho chief who spoke English. Greeley found the chief "shrewd in his way," though Left-Hand's traditionalism was too much for the progressive editor, who failed to convince the chief to support a tribal farm. Left-Hand was, Greeley concluded, "every whit as conservative as Boston's Beacon street or our Fifth Avenue."[5]

Greeley stayed in Denver long enough to reflect on his Indian experiences. He was largely disappointed. For one thing, these were not the idealized, literary Indians he had imagined all these years. Indeed, Greeley's experience with Native Americans quickly convinced him that they were major obstacles to western expansion. "I have learned to appreciate better than hitherto . . . the dislike, aversion, contempt, wherewith Indians are usually regarded by their white neighbors, and have been since the days of the Puritans," Greeley wrote. "[One] needs but little familiarity with the actual, palpable aborigines to convince any one that the poetic Indian— the Indian of Cooper and Longfellow—is only visible to the poet's eye," he wrote.[6]

Greeley's harsh and paternalistic evaluation of Native Americans represents more than one man's misunderstandings and prejudice. Greeley was, after all, one of the most popular and famous editors of the nineteenth century, widely read and respected. Greeley was also a leading reformer and life-long abolitionist, an idealist who wrote that the chief purpose of life was to make the world a better place. How was it, then, that Horace Greeley, a defender of rights for African Americans, viewed Native Americans in such hostile and racist terms? The answer, I suggest, lies in an ideology of progress that animated nineteenth-century America, a set of ideas embraced by Horace Greeley and many other Americans, ideas that helped fix the place of Indians in the American mind. According to this ideology, America was destined for greatness through Christian self-improvement, economic opportunity, and western expansion. Such greatness also involved America's moral improvement, which meant the abolition of slavery. The slaves should be freed and even educated as proof of America's success in the community of nations.

But Native Americans fell into a somewhat different category. As "barbaric" and apparently uncivilized people, most Native Americans seemed to be on the margins of the ordinary moral universe, unworthy of respect or justice. As original tenants of desirable land, Native Americans were also obstacles to economic development and growth in the West. Finally, as cultural outsiders, Native Americans had been cut off from blessings of the Enlightenment and most of them were now incapable of advancing at an appropriate pace. Greeley was clear on this point. The future belonged to those who used education and hard work to make their way in the world. With appropriate charity and training, some Indians might be guided from darkness to light, Greeley conceded. But there was no way of stopping the spread of civilization; Indians had to join the march or risk extinction. In short, the standards and characteristics of Euro-American life—individualism, capitalism, democracy, Christianity—were used to explain and understand Native Americans in the nineteenth century. Measured by such standards, Native Americans were clearly found wanting. For a reformer like Greeley, a man who very much wanted to do the "right thing," the choice was clear. Push them to become civilized, or watch them waste away and disappear. This was the ideology that motivated Greeley and a host of other nineteenth-century journalists for decades, an ideology that created and sustained an elaborate, useful, and highly mythologized set of understandings of Native Americans and their place in American life.

Greeley's ideology revealed itself in his judgments of Native American life. An ambitious, pull-yourself-up-by-your-bootstraps New Englander, Greeley could find only contempt for what he saw as native laziness. The Kansas bottom lands were extraordinarily fertile—"the very best corn-lands on earth," Greeley wrote—yet the Indians were "sitting around the doors of their lodges at the height of the planting season." The sight caused Greeley to quote himself: "I could not help saying, 'These people must die out—there is no help for them. God has given this earth to those who will subdue and cultivate it, and it is vain to struggle against His righteous decree.'"[7]

To Greeley, Indian men were especially troublesome. As "braves"—a word he always put in quotation marks—native men, like white soldiers, were given to play and unsuited for farming or steady work. Besides, Greeley noted, their traditions and habits were far too powerful to expect change. "Squalid and conceited, proud and worthless, lazy and lousy, they will strut out their existence, and at length afford the world a sensible relief by dying out of it."[8]

Greeley found more to praise in Indian women. Though they were "degraded and filthy," Greeley wrote, "they are neither too proud nor too indolent to work."[9] Indeed, by Greeley's lights, the women did *all* the work, pitching the tents, chopping the firewood, dressing and cooking the game, sewing, and more. Always the reformer, Greeley saw dutiful native women as the salvation of the race. To that end, he proposed a formal training program:

> A conscientious, humane, capable christian trader, with a wife thoroughly skilled in household manufactures and handicraft . . . can do more good than a dozen average missionaries. Let them keep and sell whatever articles are adapted to the Indians' need and means, and let them constitute and maintain an Industrial School, in which the Indian women and children shall be freely taught how to make neatly and expeditiously not only moccasins, but straw hats, bonnets, and (in time) a hundred other articles combining taste with utility.[10]

Greeley thought such schools could combine "trade with instruction, thrift with philanthropy," thereby teaching some Indians "the blessings of civilization." In twenty years, Greeley concluded, such schools would "silently transform an indolent savage tribe into a civilized christian community."[11]

To Greeley and like-minded Americans, the Indians had somehow missed the march of progress and squandered their chance to advance. In fact, they were far down the evolutionary scale, Greeley believed, little more than children. "Their arts, wars, treaties, alliances, habitations, crafts, properties, commerce, comforts, all belong to the very lowest and rudest ages of human existence."[12] Although there were individual exceptions such as Pontiac or Tecumseh, "this does not shake the general truth that they are utterly incompetent to cope in any way with the European or Caucasian race. Any band of schoolboys, from ten to fifteen years of age, are quite as capable of ruling their appetites, devising and upholding a public policy, constituting and conducting a state or community, as an average Indian tribe."[13] Unless good Christian men and women stepped in to help, Greeley noted, "the aborigines of this country will be practically extinct within the next fifty years."[14]

Greeley's judgment of Native Americans was influenced by American Christianity; he used the Bible to support his ideas about native life. But Greeley's judgments extended beyond religion to a world view that was thoroughly and powerfully progressive. That is, Greeley understood the world generally and Native Americans specifically within the social, economic, technological, and scientific accomplishments of Enlightenment Europe. From this perspective, Native Americans were indisputably "backward" and uncivilized; they lacked a work ethic, a reasonable or effective government, an interesting or defensible culture, and almost all kinds of technology. In short, Native Americans lacked most of what it took to be modern and civilized and this, of course, was why they were vanishing. Fair or not, civilization was advancing—that was the way of the world, Greeley thought—and all humankind had to keep up or suffer the consequences.

The Press and the "Indian Problem"

To say that Native Americans received "bad press" during the nineteenth century is to state the obvious. Of course they did. From the "treacherous" Seminoles of the Florida swamps to the Sioux "camp of cut throats" along Montana's Little Bighorn River, the occasions for misunderstanding and conflict between whites and Native Americans during the 1800s were plentiful and frequently violent. Newspapers across the nation often reported these outbreaks in sensational and graphic detail. Typically, a short telegraphic report from the frontier described "hostile" Indians maiming, mutilating, kidnapping, and killing white men, women, and children as they traveled south and west across the continent. "We cannot open a paper from any of our exposed States or Territories, without reading frightful accounts of Indian massacres and Indian maraudings," said the New Orleans *Picayune* in 1866.[15]

The cultural and territorial conflicts between whites and Indians were often complicated, building on years of mutual mistrust and fear concerning land, trade, and other issues. But in the papers, these critical conflicts as well as stories of cooperation and mutual respect were often obscured by reports of violence, stories rich in drama and easily understandable to journalists and readers alike. This emphasis on violence ensured that a major theme of Indian news would be inflammatory and consciously anti-Indian, the press solving the "Indian problem" by advocating and justifying white revenge and genocide. "Self preservation demands decisive action," wrote William N. Byers of the *Daily Rocky Mountain News* in 1864, "and the only way to secure it is to fight them their own way. A few months of active extermination against the red devils will bring quiet, and nothing else will."[16]

The "Ignoble Savage" also served the nation's expansionist ideology. Manifest Destiny, after all, required that Americans tame the wilderness and spread Christian civilization to the shores of the Pacific. In this great national drama, Indians were obvious and necessary villains and a series of popular figures emerged as new, uniquely American heroes: the rugged mountain man draped—like an Indian—in buckskin, the eternally optimistic Forty-Niner, the prairie Madonna westward-bound in a covered wagon, and, most importantly, the tough but romantic cowboy. This story also required that real people be transformed into legendary types and that these legends serve as powerful myths for a growing nation. Following this pattern, Daniel Boone and Davy Crockett—men who combined both "civilized" and "Indian" qualities—became larger-than-life folk heroes, representing not mere men against the wilderness but the strength and determination of a unique breed of triumphant Americans, destined to build a great nation. Such ideas helped propel George Armstrong Custer to instant glory after the Little Bighorn and made native leaders such as Sitting Bull and Geronimo into subhuman (yet widely admired) savages. Over the course of the nineteenth century, the story of western expansion became part of a celebrated national myth where heroes rose to their civilizing task and Indians were worthy—and exotic—impediments to progress and empire.

Yet not every Indian was a "bad Indian." In fact, there were many peaceful native people on the continent, most of whom wanted nothing more than to be left alone. Sometimes these "good Indians" emerged in the press in honest and sympathetic terms, especially when correspondents looked beyond their expectations and discovered the humanity of the natives.[17] More often, however, "good Indians" were imagined as "Noble Savages," exotic but primitive creatures who might be "saved" if, as Greeley and other idealists suggested, enough civilization and Christianity could be applied. In dozens of eighteenth- and nineteenth-century stories, poems, plays, and novels—including, most prominently, the *Leatherstocking Tales* of James Fenimore Cooper—the virtuous but nevertheless doomed Indian was celebrated and then, in the words of Roy Harvey Pearce, "sentimentally or melodramatically ennobled out of existence."[18] Like the "bloodthirsty savage," this idealization was a popular and "natural" way of representing Indians in the nineteenth century. Some Americans, in fact, embraced the Noble Savage as an idealized other, a model for some vital and "authentic" qualities that could reinvigorate an over-civilized society and counteract the growing effects of urbanization and industrialization. This was a morally ambiguous position—though it was rarely seen that way at the time—because it offered praise for presumed Indian qualities but took no responsibility for the welfare of actual native people. Sadly, so the thinking went, these people were destined to disappear. Thus the "Noble Savage," like the "Ignoble Savage," was a false and misleading stereotype, incorporating a host of ideas about native people that owed more to the Euro-American imagination than to Native Americans themselves.

The competing Indian identities imposed on Native Americans reveal a persistent ambiguity in nineteenth-century America. In the popular imagination, Indians were most often known and understood in a "doubleminded" or "either-or" fashion: either they were sensitive, proud, peaceful children of the forest or they were sneaky and cruel barbarians, a race of naturally violent and warlike people. Both identities were oversimplified stereotypes and both conceived of Indians as markedly different from Euro-Americans. Nevertheless, these stereotypes proved incredibly useful and durable in the business of building a nation and creating a distinct national identity. Through the Ignoble Savage, Americans could imagine nation-building as a great triumph over savagery. Christian civilization would conquer heathen barbarity, a development believed to be sanctioned both by God and the laws of history and nature. The uncivilized Indian also allowed eighteenth- and nineteenth-century Americans to know themselves better by observing a savage past that they believed they had outgrown. In this sense, Americans needed Indians in order to measure their success; the blessings of progress and civilization were more sharply drawn against the backdrop of the savage.

But the romantic Indian was also useful, perhaps more so. These "good" Indians—though still very different from Euro-Americans—were also redeemable, an obvious project for American religious and philanthropic leaders. In addition, eighteenth- and nineteenth-century Americans used the Noble Savage to link themselves to the imagined attributes of this "New World," a place of natural men and earthly abundance, free from the class conflicts of European history. Native women could be praised for their gentleness and closeness to nature; native men could be admired for their skill as hunters, for their strength and virility, their apparent autonomy, and their freedom from the restrictions of conventional society. In this idealized role, the Indian symbolized political independence, social mobility, and economic opportunity, qualities not widely available in Europe. In America, the Noble Savage was available as a symbol of natural virtue, a superior being whose idealized identity helped make the case for American abundance and optimism.

On a more psychological level, the Noble Savage was also an object of desire, a strange, exotic, and satisfyingly romantic figure. Romantic Indians, after all, were romantic precisely because they appeared to possess qualities highly desired by pioneering Americans: strength, dignity, boldness, and freedom. From colonial times onward, these ideals became exaggerated in the American psyche, a fact that reveals a deep-seated envy of Indians and Indian ways. Some eighteenth- and nineteenth-century Americans came to love the Indian. That is, they loved the idea of the Indian as a Noble Savage and they sought to save this figure and possess these superior, primitive qualities, even as actual native people were being killed and their cultures undermined. Despite this inconsistency, the characteristics of the exotic, "orientalized"[19] Indian were symbolically embraced in the folklore of the pioneer and the mountain man, in Cooper's fictional Hawkeye and Natty Bumppo, and later in Buffalo Bill Cody's Wild West show and even in news accounts of the celebrated Indian fighter himself, Custer, always imagined in buckskin as he rode the western range. In the twentieth century, this desire for things authentically Indian (and thus authentically American) was evident once again, this time as a symbol for back-to-nature hippies, mainstream environmentalists, war protesters, New Age apostles, and others. In short, the Noble Savage has been a durable symbol of romance, integrity, and simplicity, celebrated by generations of Americans eager for alternatives to conventional social and political norms.

Yet this embrace of the noble Indian could only go so far. It was one thing to admire Indian qualities in the abstract or to "play Indian" for amusement or even enlightenment, but it was quite another to "go native" and attempt to become Indian. That is, a full and unrestrained love for Indians, even romantic Indians, was never fully acceptable in mainstream American society; to reject Euro-American values and celebrate Native American ways would risk losing oneself in an uncertain and alien culture. As colonial historian John Demos has shown, early Americans were concerned about the lure of Indianness, a fear that whites would somehow forget civilization and revert to a cruder form of existence.[20] Thus the desire for Indianness in eighteenth- and nineteenth-century American life was—as it had to be—repressed. Americans might love the freedom and dignity that Indians seemed to possess, but they hated what they saw as Indian barbarity, a quality sometimes assigned to the immigrant and laboring class in nineteenth-century America. In other words, the idea of the Indian in eighteenth- and nineteenth-century America was bound up in a complex love-hate relationship whose extremes were more complementary than contradictory. Indians were embraced or despised—often embraced *and* despised—as cultural, political, and economic conditions changed. Thus Indian identity in the American psyche was fundamentally ambiguous, so much so that it is more accurate to think not of a single Indian identity but of several related and connected identities, all created within the bounds of Euro-American culture and all readily available for use by that culture. In this way, Native Americans were turned into Indians, people whose identities could be created, controlled, and manipulated at the convenience of the dominant culture. Thus constituted and positioned, Indian identity was effectively circumscribed and seemingly complete: Americans knew—or thought they knew—all they needed to know about Indians and Indian life, a fact that repeatedly undermined attempts to reconsider or enlarge native identity.

On a more theoretical level, I argue that the creation of the Indian "other" was a function of Euro-American knowledge and power. As Edward Said has noted, the very collection and structure of Western knowledge itself has been the source of considerable power, making the objects of this knowledge "inherently vulnerable to scrutiny." Thus the Western creation and organization of knowledge has profoundly shaped ideas about the non-Western world, Said points out, because such knowledge allows the West to dominate this "other" and deny its autonomy.[21] In this fundamental way, Indians were "produced" by Western epistemology and made meaningful in Euro-American culture within this frame of understandings. This was a highly unequal process, of course, and it allowed few opportunities for native people to speak for themselves or to control the manner in which their lives and cultures were understood or interpreted.

Communication theorist James Carey offers a useful link between the formation of knowledge and the process of communication. The real power of communication, Carey notes, is not the transmission of messages from one source to another, but the ritualistic offering of "a situation where nothing new is learned but in which a particular view of the world is portrayed and confirmed."[22] Thus mass communication—in this case news about Indians—is "not pure information but a portrayal of the contending forces in the world."[23] In other words, news about Indians was created, organized, and received in ways that supported Euro-American ideas and challenged or ignored native ones. In this way, Carey argues, mass media "also tend to block out . . . those values, attitudes, and groups which threaten the tenuous basis of social order."[24] Social actors (such as Indians) who deviate from social norms, Carey continues, are punished or degraded by the media.

Sociologist Todd Gitlin has put this power in ideological terms. By creating and organizing the news based on dominant values and assumptions, Gitlin writes, the media has ideological power—the power to define the terms of everyday life. Moreover, Gitlin argues that even "non-ideological" media assumptions and reporting practices have an ideological dimension that influences the way news is defined and made. Thus Gitlin sees the media as a major force in the establishment and maintenance of an ideological hegemony over the interpretation and meaning of events in American life. As such, Gitlin argues, the media define and limit the boundaries of our social world, confirming some groups of people and some kinds of practices, but condemning or marginalizing those people and practices that lie outside the boundaries.[25]

These perspectives suggest deeper and more powerful ways of thinking about Indian news in the nineteenth century. Indian representations in the papers helped create and confirm a social order as well as a racial hierarchy—a powerful belief, in Richard Slotkin's words, "that economic, moral, and spiritual progress are achieved by the heroic foray of civilized society into the virgin wilderness, and by conquest and subjugation of wild nature and savage mankind."[26] English culture and values formed the basis of American social norms; typically, native cultures and values were deviant. As a result, Indians were explained in the press ethnocentrically; that is, not by their own standards (a twentieth century ideal), but by those of the press and its readers. Thus editors and correspondents in the field usually emphasized familiar romantic and savage Indian identities by relying on a conventional set of Indian myths, stories, and images—tropes, we might call them—that met the "civilized" public's expectations and progressive ideas. For example, horse-stealing between plains tribes dependent on the horse or Indian raids on frontier settlements were not presented or understood as justifiable acts of native self-preservation but as evidence of the vengeful and irrational nature of a savage race. As the nineteenth-century press developed and expanded, its patterns of news gathering and interpretation became even more standardized, so that the papers automatically and inevitably reinforced the ideas and norms of the powerful—mostly white, Protestant, Anglo-Americans—and undermined individuals and groups who departed from those norms—Native Americans, African Americans, Chinese, Irish and Italian Catholics, and many others.

Despite this power, the press's role in creating Indian identities has not been well studied. A number of important scholars, including Robert Berkhofer and Roy Harvey Pearce, have examined Indian identities within the "myth and symbol" tradition of American history and have done much to determine the origins and effects of these identities.[27] But the newspapers remain largely unexamined in the scholarly literature. Even Slotkin's *The Fatal Environment,* a useful and persuasive explanation of the meaning of the frontier myth in the nineteenth century, did not fully explore the newspapers' role in the creation of popular Indians. This study, unlike most others, places newspapers at the center of nineteenth-century debates over race, progress, and civilization. I argue that newspapers themselves—organizations with their own practices, assumptions, and values—were a significant force in the creation and promotion of a powerful set of Indian representations that dominated the nineteenth-century imagination and endure in popular culture today. This means that I am interested in more than merely locating factual errors and condemning "bad" reporting—though there's plenty to condemn—because the problems of popular Indian identities were never simple matters of "getting the facts" or "telling the truth." Indeed, following Carey and Gitlin, I argue that news should not be evaluated against some external (and problematic) notion of "reality" but analyzed as a particular form of reality itself. This approach opens the news-making process for an interrogation of its forms and practices. Who decides which Indians are newsworthy? Which facts "count" in Indian stories? Which ones don't? For Native Americans, such questions recognize that the "facts" and "truth" about popular Indian identities are themselves products of a meaning-making process that was created daily on the pages of America's newspapers.

This book investigates the creation, uses, and meaning of Native American identities as produced by the nineteenth-century press. Specifically, this work examines the ways that newspapers conceived of, explained, and made sense of Native Americans at particular historical moments. The shift in the significance and meaning of Indians across the decades highlights the fact that Indian news, like all news, is a complex, culturally constructed product, more relative than absolute. Thus a major goal of this study is to identify and critique the political, economic, social, and cultural forces that produced Indian news, determined its structure, and defined its popular understandings. Beyond the "good Indian-bad Indian" stereotypes, I also examine the ideological and cultural contradictions in the news in order to reveal the role of the papers in controlling and resolving the "Indian problem" in nineteenth-century America. This emphasis highlights the ways the press turned actual Native Americans into ideologically useful Indians, flexible but potent symbols by which Americans could measure themselves as well as the progress of their civilization.

The book is organized chronologically, an arrangement that helps retain the historical context of Indian news representations across the seven decades under review here. That is, I argue that the patterns of Indian identity ebb and flow across the century for a variety of reasons, many of which can be explained by the particular historical circumstances. I believe the essential elements of specific Indian identities—the persistent themes as well as the subtle shifts in meaning and tone—can be better understood when they are more firmly tied to specific historical moments. But a caveat should be noted: this study is not a comprehensive history of all newspaper representations of all native tribes, a task so large as to be impractical. Instead, I chose to study a variety of newspapers, including influential eastern dailies in New York, Philadelphia, and Washington—papers often studied by historians—as well as growing midwestern papers in Chicago and Cincinnati, and small weeklies in the rural South and the frontier West—papers often overlooked by scholars.[28] These papers were selected for their political and geographic diversity and, in some cases, for their interest in or proximity to particular native news events. By casting a wide editorial net, I sought to identify the major as well as minor themes of native identity across a broad spectrum of the American press.

Another caveat: this analysis is limited to a number of representative encounters between Indians and whites. Although few in number, these encounters—often controversial, always "newsworthy"—demonstrate the power of progressive ideology over press representations of Native Americans. That is, the language, themes, and patterns of Indian news are analyzed here for the ways they represent the expansionist, evolutionary ideas of nineteenth-century American progress. Specific Indian representations were created to mark social and cultural boundaries, symbolic lines that nineteenth-century Americans used to define themselves and identify those who were different and "un-American." Although Native Americans were obviously different from Euro-Americans in many important ways, the newspapers created popular identities that oversimplified and overemphasized these differences. As a result, Indians in the papers sometimes seemed much more threatening and violent than actual Indians, a fact noted by some western travelers but one rarely acknowledged in the press.[29] In addition, journalists usually portrayed cultural and technological differences as racial differences, a view that tended to widen the cultural gap between natives and whites. Finally, this emphasis on Indian differences was politically and economically useful in the nineteenth century, producing "deviant" native identities that served the needs of a land-hungry nation and its expanding economy. This "newspaper Indian" took on a number of guises over the years, but in almost all cases the newspapers helped foster Indian identities that were outside of "normal" civilized society, identities that could be idealized, admired, and loved even as actual native people were losing both their lands and, in too many cases, their lives.

The Powers of the Press

Richard Slotkin has pointed out that American culture was transformed in the nineteenth century by the rise of the mass media, especially popular newspapers.[30] Cities and towns grew, literacy expanded, technology and transportation improved, and newspaper circulation soared. In the penny press "revolution" of the 1830s, urban newspapers reached out to the common reader with an emphasis on crime, scandal, and other topics designed for mass appeal. James Gordon Bennett, the flamboyant editor of the New York *Herald*, founded his penny paper in 1835. Within a year, the *Herald's* circulation reached 20,000. Horace Greeley was even more successful. His New York *Tribune*, founded in 1841, reached over 10,000 readers in just seven weeks and topped 40,000 readers by 1860.[31] The Civil War also spurred newspaper growth as both civilians and soldiers sought the latest reports. Using its fast new press, the Philadelphia *Inquirer* sold 25,000 copies of a single Civil War issue in nearby army camps.[32] Two illustrated weeklies, *Frank Leslie's Illustrated Newspaper* and *Harper's Weekly,* carried vivid battle scenes to many thousands more, making the war more realistic—and creating a profitable market for dramatic images. By 1890, the United States had more than 1,600 daily newspapers with a combined circulation of nearly 8.4 million. In addition, almost every town and village in America had its own weekly paper—almost 9,000 in 1880.[33] The rise of the mass circulation newspaper, Slotkin points out, shifted the nation's ideological focus from works of literature and history to the pages of the popular press. Indeed, as Slotkin notes, the nineteenth-century press was especially significant as the place "in which the raw material of history was immediately processed, conflated with ideology and legendry, and transformed into myth."[34] The newspapers' myth-making process and its effects on Native American representations are central themes of this work.

This study begins in the 1820s, when news was loosely defined and news gathering was tied to the post office. Early antebellum papers printed many items recognizable today as news: government reports, political announcements, commercial developments, and the like. But the papers also printed private letters, tall tales, anecdotes, poems, and other literary items, materials that would not necessarily make the papers in later years. The relative openness of this process meant that antebellum news making was an idiosyncratic affair, largely dependent on an editor's needs or interests. Without strong professional norms, antebellum editors, especially those in small cities and towns, were relatively free to print (or refuse to print) all manner of "unofficial" and contradictory information, including hearsay and hoaxes. This process was not necessarily logical or consistent, but it did allow a variety of editorial voices to emerge in the antebellum papers and helped broaden the Indian identity for a time.

The newspaper exchange system was also an important part of antebellum news. In the days before the telegraph (and well into the telegraph era), news circulated largely through the mails. Editors used the post office to establish exchanges with editors in distance cities. By clipping items from exchange papers, antebellum editors could obtain regular accounts of national and international news, material otherwise difficult to obtain. As one editor put it, "Who could edit a paper ten minutes without scissors!"[35] Newspaper exchanges were free, thanks to Congress, and many editors filled their columns with exchange material. The news flow was two-way: political and business news traveled from New York, Washington, and the state capitols to regional cities and small towns, while the smaller papers fed their news to the urban dailies. This system was so popular that it continued even after the telegraph became the preferred information channel. Mailed news, after all, was almost free compared to the high cost of the telegraph. Moreover, exchanges and private letters were capable of longer and more detailed reports than brief wire dispatches. As media historian Richard Kielbowicz has noted, the two channels were used in a complementary way. The telegraph provided a brief summary of the facts;

letters filled in the details and added commentary and opinion. Mailed news, Kielbowicz adds, also had another advantage: redundancy. The same news could come from several sources, minimizing (slowly but surely) the distortions of the news-gathering system.[36] The telegraph, as we shall see, tended to homogenize the news, promoting a standardized set of facts and a more "official" form of news.

The informal and relatively slow business of collecting news began to change in the 1830s, when the penny press emerged in New York. In contrast to the six-cent papers aimed at business owners, traders, and merchants, the penny papers were designed to reach the urban artisan and working classes by emphasizing police and crime news, unusual human interest stories, and the like. In addition, the penny press promoted a more vigorous form of news gathering. Editors who had once been content merely to collect the news now hired reporters to search for it. Benjamin Day, who started the New York *Sun* in 1833, hired George Wisner to cover the daily police court at 4:00 A.M.[37] More famously, James Gordon Bennett of the New York *Herald* scandalized New York in 1836 with his sensational accounts of the murder of prostitute Ellen Jewett and her suspected killer, Richard Robinson. From the scene of the crime, Bennett observed the victim's body and reconstructed the crime. "She died without a struggle; and the cold blooded villain deliberately threw off his cloak, cast the lifeless body upon the bed *and set fire to that*," Bennett concluded.[38] Bennett's persistent reporting on this and other stories marked a change in news gathering, promoting the power of journalistic observation and investigation.[39] In New York at least, a more aggressive, more reader-oriented form of journalism was dominating the marketplace.

But the editorial energy and sensationalism of the penny press did not immediately change all antebellum newspapers. In fact, as John Nerone has argued, the news-gathering developments of the penny press were less revolutionary than evolutionary and were largely confined to New York and several other eastern cities.[40] In contrast to the penny press, smaller papers across the East, West, and South worked in a less competitive environment and for most of the antebellum era they had few reasons to change either their news-gathering practices or their content. At many smaller papers, in fact, the editor was also the owner as well as the printer and primary editorial employee. At these papers, there was neither the energy nor the means to locate news sources, investigate the news, or hire correspondents to produce routine stories. Thus small-town and rural journalism in the early nineteenth century was relatively unaffected by the developments of the penny press and these papers continued to practice an informal brand of journalism well into mid-century, printing a variety of news and other reports in order to fill a variety of editorial needs.

The Civil War changed American journalism in important ways. First, the war dramatically increased newspaper readership and stimulated new competition between urban newspapers. Editors quickly discovered that they could increase their profits when they published stories about major battles. Thus newspapers had an economic incentive to improve both their news-gathering and their production processes. Stereotyping and the web-perfecting press were both introduced in the United States during the war years.[41] With circulation gains—and profits—at stake, newspapers were driven not only to improve their machinery but to get the story first, a goal that had a number of significant social consequences. Soon, the best reporter was the fastest reporter, someone capable of overcoming all manner of natural and human-made obstructions to get a dispatch on the wire. In this way, the Civil War and the telegraph made speed a critical aspect of news gathering and affected the time-cycle of American journalism. As Phillip Knightley put it: "For the first time in American history, it was possible for the public to read what had happened yesterday, rather than someone's opinion of what had happened last week."[42]

Yet the speed of the telegraph had several less beneficial effects. The telegraph helped put speed ahead of accuracy. J. Cutler Andrews, who did a two-volume study of press performance during the Civil War, wrote that "editors were more likely to censure a reporter for being scooped . . . than for including items of doubtful authenticity."[43] Thus Civil War reporters had a professional incentive to beat the competition, even when that meant stretching the truth or inventing details of news stories. Even after the war, some editors recognized that telegraphic speed was a liability. *The Round Table,* a New York literary journal, stressed this point when it criticized Washington dispatches in 1867: "Hasty news is necessarily imperfect, and the telegraph was always a liar. But one shining source of lying rumors— one which we do not scruple to call a nuisance in metropolitan newspapers—might be removed with benefit to everybody, namely, Washington correspondences per the wires."[44] With regard to the Washington "specials," the magazine added, "Even if they were true, they would still be so grossly partisan as to be utterly worthless; but they are not true." *The Round Table* also commended Horace Greeley's New York *Tribune* for admitting that it was "'strongly tempted to forgo all Washington telegraphy.'"[45]

In the post–Civil War West, the telegraph was used primarily to transmit short news bulletins. These dispatches provided essential facts of Indian-white conflicts but rarely supplied the full context of such events, a practice that affected the nature of Indian news. As James Carey has noted in a more general context, "the telegraph eliminated the correspondent who provided letters that announced an event, described it in detail, and analyzed its substance, and replaced him with a stringer who supplied the bare facts."[46] By reducing the amount and variety of routine western news, the telegraph contributed to the one-dimensional nature of Indian war reporting.

The high cost and increased importance of the telegraph also changed the structure of nineteenth-century news gathering. The formation of the New York Associated Press by six New York publishers in 1846 marked the beginning of cooperative news gathering.[47] This arrangement helped defray telegraph and other costs of gathering news from around the nation and the world. For Indian news, the formation of the AP meant a geographic enlargement of the Indian news network. With the AP in operation, individual newspapers were no longer dependent on reports in exchange papers or on the haphazard system of volunteer and official correspondence. With AP newspapers throughout the nation, Indian news could be collected and distributed more efficiently and consistently.

Unfortunately, this improved news-gathering system helped standardize American news. As business historian Menahem Blondheim has argued, "Whereas the mailbag could carry numerous communications simultaneously, the telegraph transmitted only a single copy of one message at a time."[48] In addition, the AP soon became the most powerful force in American journalism, promoting a normalized set of ideas and themes about many topics in the news, including Native Americans. As early as the 1850s, most major American newspapers were running two columns of identical AP news.[49] Because they were widely distributed, AP reports could set the tone for coverage of particular events, reinforcing stereotypes, repeating clichés, and generally offering the most popular interpretations of news events. By the same token, errors in AP reports were of greater significance because they turned up in so many newspapers. In short, the Associated Press had tremendous power over Indian representations in the postwar period because of its unchallenged ability to portray Indians in conventional ways in hundreds of papers every day.

The Civil War also fostered the rise of the on-the-scene reporter, a newsman who could get the latest details from the front and get these details on the wire first. Following the war, a new corps of fact-driven, professional newsmen displaced private letter writers and occasional correspondents as major producers of news. But the twentieth-century notion of the disinterested, objective journalist—the "independent interpreter of events"[50]—had yet to evolve and most postwar journalists were far from independent. In fact, many newsmen were openly suspicious of Indians or plainly racist; they saw few similarities between Indians and themselves and had little reason to consider the native side of issues. In addition, most Indian war reporters were unapologetically sympathetic to government and business sources whose culture and ideology they shared. Similarly, publishers and editors were (and are) members of an elite or would-be elite class of businessmen, industrialists, politicians, and bureaucrats who were usually aligned with powerful institutions, especially government and business interests. In the last half of the nineteenth century, this meant that news and editorials tended to reproduce an "official" point of view—dominated by mainstream American ideals of moral improvement, economic growth, and western expansion. Unofficial and idiosyncratic views of Indians turned up in the press too, but such reports often fell outside the increasingly narrow news-gathering channels and, in any event, such perspectives were no match for the unending stream of government proclamations, army reports, expansionist propaganda, and boosterism that dominated newspapers large and small.

The dependence on government sources and the empathy between reporters and official sources were especially influential in coverage of the Indian wars. Press historian Oliver Knight found that many western correspondents openly identified with the army and happily fired at Indians whenever they had the chance. "Because of the nature of Indian warfare—a war that was not a [civilized] war, a war that had no rear echelon—the correspondent traveled with the troops, lived with the troops, ate with the troops, fought with the troops, and shared the dangers of the troops," Knight wrote.[51] Under such circumstances, there was little chance for "independent" or "objective" news from the Indian frontier.

More important than the reporter-source relationship, however, was the growing romance of journalism and the economic impact of sensational news. Reporters in the last half of the nineteenth century began to see themselves as adventurers, seeking the news in exciting and dangerous places. As a result, Indian war reporters were less interested in balanced reporting of facts—a twentieth-century ideal—than with the creation of colorful adventure stories. Charles Sanford Diehl, an Indian war correspondent for the Chicago *Times,* stressed "action" as a theme of his time in the field. "Journalism and the army have a certain relationship," Diehl wrote. "They both represent action."[52] Oliver Knight also found excitement as a motivating force in Indian war news. "Adventure and the hero rated high in reader appeal, and war correspondents contributed their bit through accounts of their own adventures as well as the adventures of others," Knight wrote.[53] Readers liked war news and were willing to pay for it; the Civil War had made that very clear. The Civil War had also taught editors and publishers that war news could boost circulation and profits. All this helped foster a more vigorous brand of Indian reporting in the last half of the century, promoting stories with dramatic power, colorful details, and exciting characters. In short, reporters and editors became more interested in good stories than in accuracy or truth. One modern journalism critic has called this the "artistic bias" of news, an emphasis on compelling narratives that "fit the standards of familiarity, simplicity, drama."[54] This artistic "fit" promoted a standardized set of Indian narratives that the reading public could recognize and understand. Although some reporters overcame their biases and wrote about Indians honestly and compassionately,[55] Indian news often emphasized action, danger, and treachery because it was an essential aspect of the "Indian formula." In short, the "artistic bias" of Indian news had a cultural force that shaped the newspaper Indian throughout the century.

Complementing its interest in drama and adventure, the Civil War and postwar public wanted more facts in the news. While the collection and dissemination of facts seemed to offer greater certainty in the papers, fact gathering itself had ideological consequences. For one thing, the "facts" themselves were not necessarily neutral; they were identified and selected according to *some* point of view. In addition, no arrangement of facts is ever fully complete; some facts are necessarily emphasized more than others. For Native Americans, this new emphasis on "facts" and a movement toward journalistic "objectivity" did not mean more thoughtful or balanced news; it meant, instead, that their cultures and their lives were more clearly positioned on the wrong side of history, cut off from the blessings of liberty, civilization, and economic progress. In sum, the "facts" about Indians emphasized in the press were those that confirmed native differences and most of those differences—in cosmology, language, religion, food, dress, and the like—provided clear evidence of native deficiencies.

The rising power of facts also involved a dangerous assumption. Journalists and readers alike began to equate the collection of facts with the attainment of truth. Collect enough facts and, lo and behold, "the truth" would emerge. As noted above, this assumption was always problematic. Nevertheless, it was widely believed and, more importantly for Native Americans, it was easily and routinely applied to people who fell outside the mainstream. To put it more directly, nineteenth-century journalists often assumed that Indians and their cultures could be easily known and explained by simple observation and (limited) experience. The "facts" gathered by such reporting were often "true," but they were also incomplete and superficial, tied more to standard assumptions, cultural clichés, and stereotypes than to deeper or more thoughtful assessments of native life. Thus a simplified notion of "truth" and a continuing assumption of superiority by the press worked against more sensitive understandings of native life and helped limit the range of Indian representations. Various ideas about Indians emerged in the press over the years, but the most dominant ones were the most obvious ones, the ones that were already sanctioned by popular ideology.

These ideological, organizational, and technological forces shaped popular Indian identities in the nineteenth-century press. These forces demonstrate, in fact, how Indian identities were less the intentional result of overt newspaper bias or editorial personalities than of a fundamental interaction between the major ideologies of nineteenth-century American life—individualism, capitalism, Protestantism, Manifest Destiny, and social progress—and an evolving set of news-making practices. Thus the ideological and cultural assumptions of conventional news, the embrace of "official" views over alternative explanations, the need for profits and the appeal to the masses, the rise of the adventure-seeking reporter, and the standardization of news-gathering practices all operated to ensure that journalism would interpret Native Americans in particular ways, most of them harmful to native people.

Notes

1. Horace Greeley, *An Overland Journey from New York to San Francisco in the Summer of 1859* (New York: C. M. Saxton, Barker & Co., 1860), "Preface," no page numbers.
2. Ibid., 43.
3. Ibid., 61.
4. Ibid., 91–92.
5. Ibid., 152.
6. Ibid., 151–52.
7. Ibid., 152.
8. Ibid., 153.
9. Ibid.
10. Ibid., 154–55.
11. Ibid., 155.

12. Ibid., 151.

13. Ibid.

14. Ibid.

15. New Orleans *Evening Picayune,* 31 Dec. 1866, 2.

16. *Daily Rocky Mountain News,* 10 Aug. 1864, 2.

17. See, for example, the reporting of Frederic E. Lockley and John Hanson Beadle in Charles E. Rankin, "Savage Journalists and Civilized Indians: A Different View," *Journalism History* 21.3 (Autumn 1995): 102–11.

18. Roy Harvey Pearce, *Savagism and Civilization,* rev. ed. (Berkeley: University of California Press, 1988), 175.

19. Edward Said, *Orientalism* (New York: Pantheon Books, 1977).

20. John Demos, *The Unredeemed Captive: A Family Story from Early America* (New York: Alfred A. Knopf, 1994).

21. Said, *Orientalism,* 32.

22. James W. Carey, "A Cultural Approach to Communication," *Communication* 2 (1975): 8.

23. Ibid.

24. James W. Carey, "The Communications Revolution and the Professional Communicator," *Sociological Review: Monograph 13* (January 1969): 31.

25. Todd Gitlin, *The Whole World Is Watching* (Berkeley: University of California Press, 1980), 2–10.

26. Richard Slotkin, *The Fatal Environment* (New York: HarperPerennial, 1994), 531.

27. See, for example, Robert F. Berkhofer Jr., *The White Man's Indian* (New York: Vintage Books, 1979); Pearce, *Savagism and Civilization;* Brian W. Dippie, *The Vanishing American* (Middletown, Conn.: Wesleyan University Press, 1982); and Bernard W. Sheehan, *Seeds of Extinction* (Chapel Hill: University of North Carolina Press, 1973).

28. Traditional media historians have emphasized eastern urban papers and personalities, especially those in New York. Even Slotkin, who does look beyond New York, devotes most of his attention to the New York press. Small dailies and rural weeklies have received only scattered attention from media scholars.

29. Glenda Riley, *Women and Indians on the Frontier, 1825–1915* (Albuquerque: University of New Mexico Press, 1984), 92–100. Also see Lillian Schlissel, *Women's Diaries of the Westward Journey* (New York: Schocken Books, 1982), 145. Schlissel examines the accounts of 103 women who traveled west and found that only 7 percent recorded Indian attacks.

30. Slotkin, *Fatal Environment,* xiv.

31. Michael Buchholz, "The Penny Press," in William David Sloan, James G. Stovall, and James D. Startt, eds., *The Media in America: A History* (Worthington, Ohio: Publishing Horizons, 1989), 125–34.

32. J. Cutler Andrews, *The North Reports the Civil War* (Pittsburgh: University of Pittsburgh Press, 1955), 32.

33. John J. Pauly, "The Press and Industrial America," in Sloan et al., eds., *Media in America,* 201.

34. Slotkin, *Fatal Environment,* xiv.

35. Quoted in Richard B. Kielbowicz, *News in the Mail: The Press, Post Office, and Public Information, 1700–1860s* (Westport, Conn.: Greenwood, 1989), 147.

36. Ibid., 142.

37. Jean Folkerts and Dwight L. Teeter Jr., *Voices of a Nation,* 2d ed. (New York: Macmillan, 1994), 125.

38. New York *Herald,* 11 Apr. 1836, quoted in Calder M. Pickett, *Voices of the Past* (Columbus, Ohio: Grid, 1977), 93.

39. Mitchell Stephens, *A History of News* (New York: Viking, 1988), 242.

40. John C. Nerone, "The Mythology of the Penny Press," *Critical Studies in Mass Communication* 4.4 (Dec. 1987): 392–94.

41. J. Cutler Andrews, *The North Reports the Civil War* (Pittsburgh: University of Pittsburgh Press, 1955), 33.

42. Phillip Knightley, *The First Casualty* (New York: Harcourt Brace Jovanovich, 1975), 20–21.

43. Andrews, *North Reports the Civil War,* 644.

44. *The Round Table,* 5 Jan. 1867, 5.

45. Ibid.

46. James W. Carey, "Technology and Ideology," *Prospects* 8 (1983): 311.

47. Menahem Blondheim, *News over the Wires* (Cambridge: Harvard University Press, 1994), 47–52. Other scholars date the beginning of the NYAP in 1848. See Oliver Gramling, *AP: The Story of News* (New York: Farrar and Rinehart, 1940), 19–25.

48. Blondheim, *News over the Wires,* 4.

49. Ibid., 6.

50. Carey, "Communications Revolution," 32.

51. Oliver Knight, *Following the Indian Wars* (Norman: University of Oklahoma Press, 1960), 316.

52. Charles Sanford Diehl, *The Staff Correspondent* (San Antonio: Clegg Co., 1931), 89.

53. Knight, *Following the Indian Wars,* 29.

54. Max Ways, quoted in J. Herbert Altschull, *From Milton to McLuhan* (New York: Longman, 1990), 287.

55. Rankin, "Savage Journalists and Civilized Indians," 110.

O · N · E

Discovery, Destiny, and Savagery: Imagining Indians in America

THE contemporary Native American stereotype—a horse-mounted plains warrior in war bonnet and buckskin—has its roots in the romantic images of nineteenth-century popular culture. But the ideas that shaped this familiar figure were created in the European imagination centuries earlier when old ideas about the nature of the world interacted with the wonder and speculation surrounding America and its "barbarous" inhabitants. Medieval folklore was full of exotic beasts and half-human monsters, some of whom might turn up in America. No less than St. Augustine himself had speculated in *City of God* as to "whether the descendants of Adam or of the sons of Noah produced the monstrous races of men."[1] Long before 1492, Europeans imagined strange worlds inhabited by "giants, pygmies, dragons, griffins, white-haired boys, bearded ladies, human beings adorned with tails, headless creatures with eyes in their stomachs or breasts, and other fabulous folks."[2]

Unfortunately, such speculation did not improve much after Columbus and other explorers encountered Native Americans. Having imagined strange lands and exotic people, some Europeans saw America in just those terms. As Lewis Hanke has noted, early Spanish explorers looked at America "through medieval spectacles"[3] and many European descriptions of Native Americans centered on the fantastic. Columbus and other early explorers believed they were close to Asia and they extended the ideas of Marco Polo and Sir John Mandeville to the land and people before them. "The strange, the fantastic, and the unreal were familiar and to that extent real," historian David Quinn has noted.[4] As evidence, Quinn cites Columbus's reports that he had found rhubarb, aloe wood, cinnamon, and other spices in America; such sightings, Quinn writes, "were derived from the names and concepts of the earlier literature and not from the actual plant species of the New World: they were the product of wishful thinking."[5]

Later explorers searched for the Seven Cities of Gold, another fantasy of medieval Europe. Although they imagined this city, called Cibola, to have houses ten stories high with turquoise-studded doors, they found only adobe buildings and Indians who were, in their eyes, poor and uncivilized.[6] Again, medieval ideas affected European views of the native people. Columbus had read both Polo and Mandeville and he expected to find man-eating people in this part of the world.[7] Reporting on his first voyage, Columbus wrote, "In these islands I have so far found no human monstrosities, as many expected." But Columbus heard a story about a nearby island, Carib, "which is inhabited by a people who are regarded in all the islands as very fierce and who eat human flesh."[8] Quinn has pointed out that the name of the islanders, *Caribes,* and the word for cannibalism, *Canibales,* came to Europe through Columbus "and were interchangeable at the outset." Quinn concludes: "This constitutes the simplest and clearest case in which classical and medieval tales reinforced what was seen or heard of in the New World. The idea [of cannibalism] was old, only the name was new: the new name became the thing."[9] Unfair though it was, this focus on the sensational marked Native Americans as distinct from Europeans and this emphasis on difference became a primary way that sixteenth-century Europeans came to know and understand Native Americans.

Yet some Europeans recognized that even these "heathens" seemed to have some redeeming qualities, an early sign of the Western ambivalence about Indian identity. In describing the island of Hispaniola, for instance, Peter Martyr stressed the gentle nature of the people: "So that if we shall not be ashamed to confesse the truthe, they seeme to lyue in that goulden worlde of whiche owlde wryters speake so much: wherin men lyued simplye and innocentlye without inforcement of lawes, without quarrellinge Iudges and libelles, contents onely to satisfie nature, without further vexation for knowelege of things to come."[10] Martyr's primitivism offered a positive characterization of Native Americans, but—like the emphasis on the sensational—it too separated the natives from the civilized Europeans. In Martyr's writing, America is a marvelous but mysterious Eden— a "goulden worlde" abundantly rich in gold, silver, and other resources—

inhabited mostly by innocents, people who "haue byn euer soo vsed to liue at libertie, in play and pastyme."[11] Martyr knows, however, that the so-called New World is not Eden and the natives are not as innocent as they appear: "Yet these naked people are also tormented with ambition for the desyre they haue to enlarge their dominions: by reason wherof they kepe warre and destroy one an other: from which plage I suppose the golden world was not free."[12] This ambivalent view of America and its people was produced by the contradictory atmosphere of the "fabulous" that permeated sixteenth-century Europe, "an atmosphere supercharged with dreams—dreams of Indian souls to convert and Indian gold to exploit," as historian George Hammond put it.[13]

From the very beginnings of exploration, then, Native Americans were identified as different from, and mostly inferior to, Europeans. Columbus's own words are revealing. In his *Diario,* the first mention of Native Americans was a reference to their nakedness, a sign of their incivility.[14] The *Diario* also shows that Columbus immediately assumed a superior position toward the indigenous people, seeing them as natural subjects of Spanish power and religion. He gave the first Americans he met red caps and glass beads "because I recognized that they were people who would be better freed [from error] and converted to our Holy Faith by love than by force."[15] The people were "very poor in everything," he noted; they were also primitive, never having seen iron weapons.[16] Although Columbus sometimes praised the native people and even recognized their intelligence, he did so—and this is telling—as part of his evaluation of their potential to be servants.[17]

Columbus's ideas illustrate the unequal nature of early encounters between Europeans and Americans. Europeans clearly and automatically assumed a superior position toward the Americans—not surprising given the technological and organizational superiority of the Europeans. But the consequences of this superiority were far-reaching and were structured into the language and ideology of European discovery in fundamental ways. As Stephen Greenblatt has noted, the first wave of European explorers "shared a complex, well-developed, and, above all, mobile technology of power: writing, navigational instruments, ships, war-horses, attack dogs, effective armor, and highly lethal weapons, including gunpowder."[18] Little wonder that Europeans felt superior to Native Americans, people who were, in their eyes, obviously deficient. But the European "prejudice of superiority"[19] extended beyond technology, for Europeans tended to view

Native Americans as inferior even when they recognized their achievements. The Aztecs, for instance, people whose technical and organizational skills impressed many Europeans, were an interesting and clever people but they were not seen as the equal of Europeans. Peter Martyr, for instance, recognized the advanced nature of Aztec society in Mexico, referring specifically to the contents of several books made from tree bark: "In these books are furthermore comprehended their laws, rytes of ceremonies and sacrifyces, annotations of Astromie, accompts, computations of tymes, with the maner of grassynge, sowyng, and other thynges perteining to húsbandry."[20] Martyr could see the strength and refinement of Aztec society but, like most Europeans, he was repulsed by reports of human sacrifice, cannibalism, and even the Aztec practice of piercing the lower lip to wear pieces of gold. About the latter practice, Martyr wrote, "I cannot remember ever to have seen anything more hideous; but they think that nothing more elegant exists under the human circle."[21] Martyr and other observers saw that the Aztecs were advanced in some ways, but neither he nor most other Europeans had much doubt about the superiority of European civilization and culture.

A major part of this attitude was religious; as Greenblatt has noted, the explorers believed the "Christians' conviction that they possessed an absolute and exclusive religious truth."[22] But the power of writing itself was also a major element of the European attitude. Indeed, writing was seen as a divine gift that marked the difference between civilized people and the rest. As Samuel Purchas wrote in the seventeenth century: "God hath added herein a further grace, that as Men by the former exceed Beasts, so hereby one man may excell another; and amongst Men, some are counted Civill, and more both Sociable and Religijous, by the Use of letters and Writing, which others wanting are esteemed Brutish, Savage, Barbarous."[23] Literacy, then, marked Europeans as high in God's order for humankind, just as illiteracy marked Native Americans as low and uncivilized.

In sum, Europeans imagined and then set about creating Native Americans who had specific virtues but also glaring weaknesses, both of which marked Indians as different. The emphasis on difference shaped the idea of the Indian. For example, Columbus's name for the natives, *los Indios,* suggested to fifteenth- and sixteenth-century Europeans (and then Americans) that Native Americans were a single group of native people who could be understood largely through their differences from European peoples. As Robert Berkhofer has noted, "By classifying all these many peoples as *Indians,* Whites categorized the variety of cultures and societies as a single entity . . . thereby neglecting or playing down the social and cultural diversity of Native Americans then—and now—for the convenience of simplified understanding."[24] Thus the seemingly simple act of naming the inhabitants of America proved to have enormous significance because it oversimplified native people and their cultures. In European language and thought, vastly different Native American cultures began to merge into a generalized Indian culture characterized most prominently by its peculiar differences from European cultures. Colonial discourse also reinforced a language of difference that marked Indians as distinct from Europeans: native people were "savages" and "barbarians" because they were not "civilized" Europeans, they were "heathens" and "infidels" because they were not Christians, and so on.[25]

The power of language also helped Europeans organize and make sense of their New World, another process that had important consequences for Native Americans. In a careful examination of early writings from America, Wayne Franklin has shown how European explorers and travelers used language to subdue and domesticate America and its inhabitants. By giving familiar names to people and places in the American wilderness, Franklin notes, European adventurers and settlers asserted their continuing faith in the "correctness of Old World Culture."[26] The explorers also used their letters, journals, and official reports to celebrate their successes, justify their decisions, and glorify their conquests. Moreover, Franklin writes, such language "provide[d] voyagers just departing for America with a set of articulated goals and designs by which the course of Western events actually might be organized beforehand. This ability to 'plot' New World experience in advance, was, in fact, the single most important attribute of European language."[27] From the fifteenth century on, America and its peoples were known to Europeans through language, a language that served the ends of the explorers and their sponsoring nations. Hernán Cortés, for example, knew what Charles V wanted to hear about New Spain and his colonial reports were constructed in those terms. In such a setting, Franklin has noted, language develops a special power, exerting "a subtle influence on how life in the colony is conceptualized, even perceived or carried on."[28] Franklin concludes, "The special languages of colonial order, of Old World government, of Christianity, of, finally, perception itself—all these dialects surrounded Cortés like a series of expanding yet constraining rings, each of them forcing on him a decorum of act and word."[29] The result of this language was an image of America based less on the actual American experience than on the need to protect the explorers and fulfill the empire-building desires of the European nations. "The voyager was converted into a conscious hero of European order, and the ideal sketch of his future career became a romantic allegory of victory in the West," Franklin writes.[30] But if European explorers were the conquerors, Native Americans were assigned the opposite role: the conquered.

Another historian, Patricia Seed, has pointed out how Spain, France, England, and Portugal used language and ceremony to take "possession" of the "New World." Such acts—solemn words, the planting of flags and crosses—demonstrate the power Europeans attached to symbols in America. For Ferdinand and Isabella, Seed writes, "Columbus was required to make a grave declaration of the intent to remain [in the New World] and to record those words for posterity by writing them down."[31] This act enabled the Spanish crown to claim rightful power in America and to seek legal title from the pope. The crown and Christianity thus combined to establish Spanish authority in America.

The English made a similar claim in patent letters created for Humphrey Gilbert and Walter Raleigh. These letters, Seed writes, invoked "the authority of the Crown and the eminent domain of Christian princes" to rationalize the possession of new lands. Moreover, the authority of Elizabeth I was based on the medieval English idea "that royal authority derives from God and comes to the Crown by grace."[32] In short, God had provided this "New World" for English use; the land was theirs to take and to name, its people were theirs to convert and dominate. For all the European explorers and their sponsor nations, language helped create an America—and an American Indian—subject to European domination and control.

The words of Richard Hakluyt the younger confirm the popularity of this view in England. Writing in 1584 as Raleigh was preparing to colonize Virginia, Hakluyt contended that American colonization would give England the opportunity for "inlargeing the glorious gospell of Christe, and reducinge of infinite multitudes of these simple people that are in errour into the right and perfecte way of their salvacion."[33] Hakluyt believed that the English were better equipped to do this than the Spanish, people who practiced a false religion sullied by "filthie lucre" and "vaine ostentation." In contrast to the Spanish—already infamous across Europe for their mistreatment of native people—Hakluyt argued that the English could convert the Indians "without cruelties and tyrannie."[34] But Hakluyt was promoting more than conversion. He advocated large-scale agriculture, using the supposedly "gentle and amyable" Indians as a plantation work force.[35] Profitable trade between England and the colonies would soon follow, providing greater prosperity both for the colonies and the mother country. It was a pleasing vision for sixteenth-century Englishmen, but it was also a highly imperialist one. The basic image of America in Hakluyt's writing, historian Jack Greene concluded, was "as a large and fruitful country available for the taking by the enterprising and the bold." As for Hakluyt's image of Native Americans, they, "like the land and other resources of America, were essentially passive objects who had no integrity or selfhood of their own and whose priorities and objectives ordinarily demanded no consideration," Greene writes.[36] For the English, America was imagined as a free and open land, a place they could manage and control for their own economic and political ends.

Beyond language, European philosophy and religion were instrumental in the European conception of Native Americans. Both Christian and Aristotelian ideas were said "to explain everything from the first and last ticks of history to what happens to the egg prior to the hatching of the chick," writes Alfred W. Crosby Jr.[37] But the New World generally—and Native Americans specifically—fell outside of European explanations of the world, leaving Native Americans without legitimate standing in the eyes of Europeans. Thus, as Crosby notes, Europeans found it easy to conclude that the natives, with their unusual customs and behavior, were agents of the Devil. "The Europeans had either to conceive of the naturalness of cultural diversity and invent cultural toleration to go along with it, or to assume that Indians were in league with Hell."[38] Aristotle was also used to explain Native Americans. In the early days of conquest, historian Lewis Hanke notes, America was seen as a strange and exotic place, inhabited by mysterious people. It is not surprising, Hanke concludes, "that even the ancient theory of Aristotle, that some men are born to be slaves, was borrowed from antiquity and found conveniently applicable to the Indians from the coasts of Florida to far-distant Chile."[39]

Two centuries later, the French naturalist, Comte de Buffon, echoed such views from a more "scientific" perspective. Noting that there were few large animals in America, Buffon concluded that other natural features in America were also diminished, including the Indian. To Buffon and other Europeans, Native Americans were "inferior in technology, political organization, military prowess, resistance to disease, intelligence and—most important of all—in 'ardor for women,'" writes Crosby.[40] In European eyes, then, Native Americans were so different from Europeans that they warranted both military domination and—once domination was achieved—sympathy. "Again and again during the centuries of European imperialism, the Christian view that all men are brothers was to lead to persecution of non-Europeans—he who is my brother sins to the extent that he is unlike me—and to the tempering of imperialism with mercy—he who is my brother deserves brotherly love," Crosby writes.[41] This ambiguity was unified through what Hanke has called the "standard cliché of Indian nature"—native deficiencies.[42] Whether Indians were perceived as virtuous or evil, Europeans rarely imaged them as equals, an inequality that justified the European domination of native life and inspired repeated attempts to "save" the Indian through religion, education, and other blessings of Western civilization. Yet as James Axtell has noted, this was not a benign process, since both Catholic and Protestant missionaries believed that unschooled "savages" could not be trusted with the holy ordinances of the church until they had adopted European ideas of order, industry, and manners.[43] Not surprisingly, this civilizing process was frequently destructive of native traditions. "At its most extreme," Axtell writes, "the civilization process entailed the wholesale substitution of a European lifestyle for the natives' own, beginning with material artifacts—clothing, weapons, tools—and ending with deeply ingrained habits of thought and feeling."[44] By such means, the colonizing Europeans used both religion and the trappings of Western civilization to position Native Americans as generally unworthy people, desperately in need of European guidance and salvation.

Creating the American Other

European ideas came to dominate American views of Native Americans. But colonial Americans had their own need to subdue Native Americans and control their destiny. Although Europeans sometimes saw the complex variety of native life[45]—as did Americans—Native Americans were, over time, reduced to two broad categories: the bloodthirsty barbarian and the romantic, sentimental Indian. Unfortunately for Native Americans, neither of these identities was an adequate conception of their cultures. But these rough portraits were useful for Americans, providing apparently natural categories of difference between Indians and whites and ensuring they were perceived and understood as fundamentally different from and opposed to American life and its ideals. This "otherness," in turn, provided intellectual and moral support for the ongoing usurpation of Indian lands and a host of other anti-Indian policies to come.

Colonial journalists did not merely reflect such racial sentiments; like European and colonial writers, they created Indian representations in language and then used their papers to amplify and promote these representations throughout the colonial period. American newspapers, in fact, had trouble understanding Native Americans from the very beginning. The first newspaper published in colonial America, Benjamin Harris's *Publick Occurrences, Both Forreign and Domestick,* discovered both good and bad Indians in colonial Massachusetts. In spite of hostilities between New France and their Indian allies (King William's War) and an ongoing conflict between colonists and the Abenaki (the second Abenaki war),[46] Harris identified some Indians who warranted praise. He singled out the "Christianized Indians in some parts of Plimouth" for their decision to worship God with a day of Thanksgiving. One paragraph later, however, Harris pointed out that "barbarous Indians were lurking about Chelmsford" about the same time that two children were reported missing and that "both of them supposed to be fallen into the hands of the Indians."[47] Harris published his paper—which was unauthorized and quickly suppressed—on 25 September 1690. Thus the first American journalist to write about Indians praised those who were most like the colonists and criticized—without direct evidence—those Indians who appeared "barbarous." Like European explorers and other early writers on America, Harris identified two kinds of Indians, and, in so doing, effectively labeled both as "outsiders."

The dominant Indian figure in colonial writing was the barbaric savage. Given the increasing competition for land and resources that marked the colonial expansion toward the Appalachians, this was an entirely predictable response. Like European explorers, most early American colonists believed that they, not the native people, had the God-given right to occupy and improve the land—an attitude that ignored ongoing agricultural practices among the Native Americans.[48] If this taking of Indian lands meant the removal or destruction of a few seemingly unproductive heathens, so be it. This mixture of Christian superiority and racial hostility was popularly expressed in a series of colonial-era captivity narratives, tales of sensational violence and redemption that were widely read in colonial America.[49] The first and most famous of the early captivity narratives, *Soveraignty & Goodness of God . . . Being a Narrative of the Captivity and Restauration of Mrs. Mary Rowlandson,* carried this anti-Indian ideology. Published in 1682, Mary Rowlandson's message about God's grace and the cruelties of the Indians proved popular with New England readers.[50] The story affirmed Mrs. Rowlandson's faith in God, but it also created a graphic and terrible portrait of native barbarities. The backdrop for the attack on Lancaster, Massachusetts, where Rowlandson lived, was a war between the Puritans and the Wampanoag tribe led by chief Metacomet, or King Philip.

The origins of the "King Philip's War" were obscure and complex, but Mrs. Rowlandson's story was not—it was as gripping as it was terrifying. The attack began about sunrise on 10 February 1676:

> Hearing the noise of some guns, we looked out; several houses were burning and the smoke ascending to heaven. There were five persons taken in one house; the father and the mother and a suckling child they knocked on the head; the other two they took and carried away alive. . . . Another there was who running along was shot and wounded and fell down; he begged of them his life, promising them money (as they told me), but they would not hearken to him but knocked him in [the] head, stripped him naked, and split open his bowels.[51]

The Wampanoag attackers soon came to Rowlandson's house, where they succeeded in catching it afire, forcing family members into the arms of the natives:

> No sooner were we out of the house, but my brother-in-law (being before wounded, in defending the house, in or near the throat) fell down dead; whereat the Indians scornfully shouted, hallooed, and were presently upon him, stripping off his clothes. The bullets flying thick, one went through my side, and the same (as would seem) through the bowels and hand of my dear child in my arms. One of my elder sister's children, named William, had then his leg broken, which the Indians perceiving, they knocked him on the head. Thus were we butchered by those merciless heathen, standing amazed, with the blood running down to our heels.[52]

Violence on this order made a dramatic impact in Puritan New England. Even for those who had not witnessed such actions firsthand, such sensational tales ensured that Indian barbarities would be known and discussed throughout the colonies. The theme and language of violence made it all the more plain to colonial Americans that native people were inhumane heathens very much in need of Christian virtue and English law.

Not surprisingly, reports of Indian violence dominated colonial news of Native Americans in the eighteenth century.[53] Relations between natives and settlers were often strained and conflicts over land produced important and often sensational news in the colonies. John Campbell's Boston News-Letter, founded in 1704, provided regular and graphic accounts of Indian attacks on whites from all across the eastern seaboard. The Indians were portrayed as "the Sculking Indian Enemy," a phrase used repeatedly by Campbell and other colonial editors.[54] This characterization symbolized the very real differences that editors perceived between civilized Englishmen and uncivilized natives. These differences were nowhere more apparent than in the reports of native barbarity and torture that appeared regularly in the colonial press. In 1729, Benjamin Franklin carried this gruesome item of "Shawnese" torture in his Pennsylvania *Gazette:*

> They made the Prisoner Sing and Dance for some Time, while six Gun Barrels were heating red hot in the Fire; after which they began to burn the Soals of the poor Wretches Feet until the Bones appeared, and they continued burning him by slow Degrees up to his Privites, where they took much Pains. . . . This Barbarity they continued about six Hours, and then, notwithstanding his Feet were in such a Condition, they drove him to a Stake . . . and stuck Splinters of Pine all over his Body, and put fire to them. . . . In the next Place they scalp'd him and threw hot Embers on his Head. . . . At last they ran two Gun Barrels, one after the other, red hot up his Fundament, upon which [he] expired. . . . P.S. They cut off his Thumbs and offer'd them him to eat and pluck'd off all of his Nails.[55]

If these actions weren't savage enough, a 1745 report in the Boston *Evening-Post* resurrected cannibalism as a Native American practice: "The Enemies had 2 kill'd and as many wounded in the Engagement, which being over, the Indians cut open Capt. Donahew's Breast, and suck'd his Blood, and hack'd and mangled his Body in a most inhuman and barbarous Manner, and then eat a great part of his Flesh. They also suck'd the Blood and mangled the Bodies of the other Slain."[56] This was the oldest and most malicious charge against Native Americans and it was especially effective propaganda in the war against Indian land rights. As Axtell has noted, "The logic of dispossession was inexorable: Indians are animals; animals do not own land; therefore we, God's Chosen People, may 'increase and multiplie'. . . as the Bible directs."[57] With a steady stream of torture and cruelty appearing in the press, colonial readers had powerful reasons for hating Native Americans and their barbaric ways.

Even when relations with Native Americans were friendly, the colonial press made important distinctions between Indians and whites. Good Indians, as Benjamin Harris made clear, were "Christianized Indians." These Indians could sometimes be praised in the papers, though of course the basis of this praise was the surrender of their own religious beliefs—"heathen" beliefs—in favor of Christianity. The point is that "good" Indians, like the "bad" ones, were portrayed in the press as different from the English in significant ways. Indians were uncivilized and heathen, differences that made all the difference in the public's ability to see them as a legitimate part of colonial society. Thus separated, all Indians—even "good" ones—were destined to be treated in the press as different from—and generally inferior to—Euro-Americans.

If the Indian as "murdering savage" was the product of sensational language and ethnocentric logic, the romantic Indian was even more fantastic, based as it was on an unrealistic assessment of Indians as natural children of the forest. This idealized figure appealed to a range of European and American beliefs about the virtues of the "natural" man—honest, virtuous, and unsullied by the corruption of the civilized world. In this role, the horrors of Indian life were replaced by notions about their childlike innocence and their special relationship with nature. Significantly, the Noble Savage was a creature more fictional than real. Colonial poet and journalist Philip Freneau, for example, created an imaginary Creek Indian named Tomo-Cheeki in the 1790s in his quest to critique civilized life in Philadelphia. Freneau has Tomo-Cheeki describe the idyllic Creek life in the forest: "In the morning early we rise from the bed of skins to hail the first dawn of sun. We seize our bows and arrows—we fly hastily through the dews of the forest—we attack the deer, the stag, or the buffaloe, and return with abundance of food for the whole family. Wherever we run it is amidst the luxuriant vegetation of Nature, the delectable regale of flowers and blossoms, beneath trees bending with plumb and joyous fruits."[58] Freneau's Indians live naturally and happily in an American Eden, which Freneau imagined to be more pure and serene than civilized city life. Like other European and American writers, Freneau used idealized natives to criticize civilized society, though Pearce notes that he stopped well short of imagining "an Indian society to which whites should go to school."[59]

Although superficially benign, the romantic Indian involved a variety of assumptions and ideas about Native Americans and their place in the world. "Most romantic of all," Berkhofer has noted, "was the impression of the Indian as rapidly passing away before the onslaught of civilization."[60] The "vanishing Indian" theme was especially popular in the nineteenth century, when native cultures did seem to be fading before the westward rush of white settlement. Thus early American writers and artists used the romantic Indian as a central symbol for the mystery and glory of the life in the New World. The tragedy of the dying Indian was a staple of early American literature, appearing in the poems and essays of Freneau, and, more popularly, in the novels of James Fenimore Cooper.[61]

But the romantic Indian represented more than a sentimental attachment to an idealized native past. In fact, romantic Indians were seen as romantic precisely because they were assumed to be a vanishing breed, a noble race now destined to disappear from the earth. The effect of this romantic identity was the glorification of their inevitable disappearance, a position that tacitly aided in native destruction. Nineteenth-century romantics such as Lydia Maria Child in *Hobomok* (1824) and Henry Wadsworth Longfellow in *The Song of Hiawatha* (1855) "portrayed the Noble Savage as safely dead and historically past."[62] One prominent advocate of the "vanishing Indian" ideology was George Catlin, best known for his paintings of native life in the West. But Catlin also wrote extensively about his motives, making clear his belief in the vanishing Indian. Catlin traveled West in 1832 in order to produce, as he put it, "a literal and graphic delineation of the living manners, customs, and character of an interesting race of people, who are rapidly passing away from the face of the earth—lending a hand to a dying nation, who have no historians or biographers of their own to portray with fidelity their native looks and history; thus snatching from a hasty oblivion what could be saved for the benefit of posterity."[63] Catlin admired and respected the Native Americans he encountered in the West, but he could not help romanticizing their lives. He referred to native men as "red knights of the prairie" and "red sons of the forest."[64] Indian boys, Catlin wrote, were "graceful youths, without a care to wrinkle, or a fear to disturb the full expression of pleasure and enjoyment that beams across their faces—their long black hair mingling with their horses' tails, floating in the wind, while they are flying over the carpeted prairie."[65]

Catlin also made frequent classical allusions, another way of ennobling the Indian. The wilderness of our country, Catlin wrote, has "afforded models equal to those from which the Grecian sculptors transferred to the marble such inimitable grace and beauty."[66] The Blackfeet carry their shields on the "outside of the left arm, exactly as the Roman and Grecian shield was carried, and for exactly the same purpose."[67] In a Mandan village on the upper Missouri, Catlin was greatly impressed by Mah-to-toh-pa, or Four Bears, and again a classical reference came to mind: "No tragedian ever trod the stage, nor gladiator ever entered the Roman Forum, with more grace and manly dignity than did Mah-to-toh-pa enter the wigwam. . . . He took his attitude before me [for a portrait], and with the sternness of a Brutus and the stillness of a statue, he stood until darkness of night broke upon the solitary stillness."[68] Catlin and other nineteenth-century American writers perpetuated the romantic Indian ideal, a creature who was free, noble, and unsullied by the evils of civilization. But this view also encompassed the idea that Native Americans were a "doomed" race, destined to disappear before the advance of civilization. Such ideas undermined a more realistic public assessment of the native future while at the same time relieving whites of responsibility for their fate. In time, as we shall see, these ideas influenced government policy about a host of Indian issues.

The effect of both the savage and romantic Indian identities was to maintain and reinforce the idea of the Indian as an enemy of the new American civilization. Whether romantic or savage, most colonial Americans understood Indians as literal outsiders, people who were cut off from the traditions and principles of American life. This conception supported the idea of the Indian as cultural "other," an image of the Native American "whose life was to be comprehended by the idea of savagism," in the words of Roy Harvey Pearce.[69] Like the European idea of the Indian, this identity emphasized the differences between Indians and whites—and their cultures. Indians were viewed as outside the sweep of progress and civilization. More specifically, they were seen as diametrically opposed to the main principles of American life. "Whether evaluated as noble or ignoble, whether seen as exotic or degraded, the Indian as an image was always alien to the white," Berkhofer writes.[70] This made Indians useful to whites, because Indians were a vivid example of the contrast between civilization and savagery. In this view, Pearce continues, the Indian "lived as an example of the savage life out of which civilized Americans had long grown. He was, in fact, a means of measuring that growth."[71]

Thomas Jefferson also saw Native Americans as fundamentally different, though he recognized their humanity and their complexity in ways the colonial press did not. In *Notes on the State of Virginia,* Jefferson defended America against Comte de Buffon, who had charged that the environment in America produced inferior plants, animals, and people. But the American Indian, Jefferson argued, was stronger, smarter, and more sensitive than Buffon knew. Replying to the French critic, Jefferson asserted that the Indian was "neither more defective in ardor, nor more impotent with his female, than the white reduced to the same diet and exercise."[72] Jefferson argued that native men were fully human creatures, brave, affectionate toward their children, loyal, and kind. As for their intellect, their "activity of mind is equal to ours in the same situation," Jefferson wrote. The differences were not due to any deficiency in America, Jefferson argued, but to the "barbarous" nature of Indian life.

Even as Jefferson defended Indian men, he noted that Indian women "are submitted to unjust drudgery," an aspect of life with every "barbarous people." He continued, "It is civilization alone which replaces women in the enjoyment of their natural equality."[73] Here Jefferson was making clear the advantages of civilization and the distinctions between civilized and uncivilized societies. Jefferson did not believe (and did not argue) that Native American culture had produced men and women the equal of civilized Europeans or Americans. For all his willingness to see Indians as humans, Jefferson too saw major differences between Native Americans and Euro-Americans. His solution to Indian deficiency was to seek more information about Indians—this, in fact, was one of the goals he set out for Lewis and Clark—so that Indians could be gently guided to civilization and Christianity. But as historian James Ronda has noted, Jefferson's optimistic view was "based more on Enlightenment faith than American reality."[74]

American artists, too, emphasized the differences between whites and Indians. George Catlin, for one, illustrated his idea of the vanishing Indian in a remarkable "before" and "after" portrait of an Assiniboine chief named Wi-Jun-Jon. In the "before" picture, Catlin painted a serene and proud chief, adorned in all his buckskin finery. But the "after" picture showed an Indian much reduced by his visit to Washington. "The colonel's uniform, the umbrella, the fan, the cigarette, and the clownish, foppish strut in the 'after' picture all reveal in Catlin's opinion how civilization corrupted the natural nobility and manner of the Indian," Berkhofer said of this portrait.[75]

The outsider status of Indians was especially apparent in the American West. As the telegraph and the railroad spanned the continent, the Indian seemed all the more anachronistic. This image of the Indian was explicit in Fanny Palmer's 1868 print "Across the Continent. 'Westward the Course of Empire Takes Its Way.'" The foreground was dominated by a group of hearty pioneers, busy constructing a new town. The most prominent building was labeled "PUBLIC SCHOOL." The scene was diagonally bisected by a railroad, the tracks stretching West to the far horizon. All this was the very picture of American progress in the West. But Palmer also imagined two warriors watching the train from a small bluff beside the tracks, which separated them from the new village. More pointedly, the Indians stood in a cloud of smoke from the train's engine, swept away by the technological prowess of the advancing civilization. Here, in unmistakable terms, was a vision of Manifest Destiny, a painting that emphasized mythic American themes—building a school in a new town in the wilderness and linking that town to a whole continent of such towns. The time and place for Indians had passed; they were helpless.

Such an image was based on an apparent "fact" of nineteenth-century American life: Indians were in no position to counter advancing whites materially or militarily. But the assignment of the Indian to a no-man's-land helped justify white injustice and domination. That is, the image of the Indian as an inferior and hapless "other" made it easier to justify policies that removed Indians from their land or punished them for attacks on whites. By promoting Indian "otherness," eighteenth- and nineteenth-century journalists, writers, and artists created Native American representations that undermined native status and provided support for a language and culture of domination. For the natives, the choices became increasingly stark. By the waning years of the century, they had given up most of their land. All that was left was their culture—and that too was under siege, both symbolically and in fact.

The outsider status had important and continuing consequences for Indian-white relations. For one thing, it positioned Indians as impediments to American ideas of progress, expansion, and national destiny. In the march across the continent, the Indian was something to be removed, exterminated, or otherwise subdued. Thus the American belief in Manifest Destiny was openly hostile to Indians and unsympathetic to their culture and their interests. Historian Reginald Horsman has connected nineteenth-century American Anglo-Saxon ideology with national expansion. Speeches and debates early in the century contained a sense of national destiny, Horsman writes, but they did not have the "jarring note of rampant radicalism that permeates the debates of mid-century."[76] By then, Horsman concludes, "the American public and American politicians had for the most part abandoned any belief in potential Indian equality. They now believed that American Indians were doomed because of their own inferiority and that their extinction would further world progress."[77] In Horsman's view, neither the romantic nor the savage Indian could stand up to the pervasive racism of nineteenth-century American thought.

American newspapers drew their images of Indians from centuries of racism, stereotypes, and misinformation. But the papers did more than simply repeat these themes. Indeed, it is my argument that the nineteenth-century press contributed to the native identity in several powerful ways. As suggested earlier, the press helped give form and substance to the long-standing "doublemindedness" about Indians in American culture. That is, Indians had two clear but contradictory identities, one romantic and one savage. Within these categories, the press represented Indians in a variety of ways, but almost always as people distinctly different from Euro-Americans and outside the blessings of Western civilization. Occasionally, as Jefferson's views demonstrate, more empathetic and balanced views of Indians surfaced in popular discourse. But such views remained rare in the nineteenth-century press because the practical and professional forces that shaped the news had important ideological consequences. As the following chapters will make clear, the newspaper Indian was a product of newspapers aligned with both government and business interests, a view that saw Indians as obstacles to economic growth and national expansion. Indian representations were also shaped by the fact that newspapers themselves were economic entities, seeking to please both advertisers and readers with colorful and exciting stories that confirmed the correctness of American values and goals. As the decades passed, these stories were produced by journalists who were increasingly conscious of the need to please editors and impress readers with heroic deeds and sensational copy. In addition, journalists routinely represented Indians through standard formulas and clichés, easily understood themes that seemed to explain Indians and their place in American life. Finally, the changing technology of news gathering and the new organizational power of the Associated Press promoted a fact-filled but narrow native identity and helped further standardize the Indian image in newspapers across the nation. For all these reasons, a harsh and paternalistic Indian identity dominated American newspapers for decades.

Notes

1. Quoted in Lewis Hanke, *Aristotle and the American Indians* (Bloomington: Indiana University Press, 1959), 3–4.

2. Ibid., 3.

3. Ibid.

4. David B. Quinn, *Explorers and Colonies: America, 1500–1625* (London: Hambledon Press, 1990), 72.

5. Ibid., 74.

6. George P. Hammond, "The Search for the Fabulous in the Settlement of the Southwest," *Utah Historical Quarterly* 26.1 (1956): 6.

7. Quinn, *Explorers and Colonies,* 75.

8. Quoted in Robert F. Berkhofer Jr., *The White Man's Indian: Images of the American Indian from Columbus to the Present* (New York: Vintage Books, 1979), 7.

9. Quinn, *Explorers and Colonies,* 75.

10. Quoted in Franklin T. McCann, *English Discovery of America to 1585* (New York: King's Crown Press, 1952), 131.

11. Quoted in ibid.

12. Quoted in ibid.

13. Hammond, "Search for the Fabulous," 6.

14. Christopher Columbus, *The Diario of Christopher Columbus's First Voyage to America, 1492–1493,* trans. Oliver Dunn and James E. Kelley Jr. (Norman: University of Oklahoma Press, 1989), 63.

15. Ibid., 65.

16. Ibid., 65, 67.

17. Ibid., 67–68.

18. Stephen Greenblatt, *Marvelous Possessions: The Wonder of the New World* (Chicago: University of Chicago Press, 1991), 9.

19. Tzvetan Todorov, *The Conquest of America: The Question of the Other* (New York: Harper and Row, 1984), 33, 165.

20. Quoted in McCann, *English Discovery,* 130.

21. Quoted in Benjamin Keen, *The Aztec Image in Western Thought* (New Brunswick: Rutgers University Press, 1971), 65.

22. Greenblatt, *Marvelous Possessions,* 9.

23. Quoted in ibid., 10.

24. Berkhofer, *White Man's Indian,* 3.

25. The language and ideology of colonialism remains embedded in a host of other terms still used to describe the European exploration and settlement of America. Such terms as "New World" and "frontier," for example, assume and privilege a European perspective. America was not "new" to its aboriginal inhabitants and, as my colleague Richard Grounds has written, "One culture's 'frontier' is another's homeland." Many other widely accepted terms are also problematic. I am indebted to Professor Grounds for bringing these matters to my attention. See Richard A. Grounds, "Tallahassee and the Name Game" (Ph.D. diss., Princeton Theological Seminary, 1994).

26. Wayne Franklin, *Discoverers, Explorers, Settlers: The Diligent Writers of Early America* (Chicago: University of Chicago Press, 1979), 5.

27. Ibid.

28. Ibid., 4.

29. Ibid.

30. Ibid., 5.

31. Patricia Seed, "Taking Possession and Reading Texts: Establishing the Authority of Overseas Empires," in Jerry M. Williams and Robert E. Lewis, eds., *Early Images of the Americas* (Tucson: University of Arizona Press, 1993), 112.

32. Ibid., 114.

33. Richard Hakluyt, "Discourse of Western Planting," quoted in Jack P. Greene, *The Intellectual Construction of America* (Chapel Hill: University of North Carolina Press, 1993), 36.

34. Quoted in ibid., 37.

35. Quoted in ibid., 38.

36. Ibid., 44.

37. Alfred W. Crosby Jr., *The Columbian Exchange: Biological and Cultural Consequences of 1492* (Westport, Conn.: Greenwood Press, 1972), 9.

38. Ibid., 10.

39. Hanke, *Aristotle and the American Indians*, 11.

40. Crosby, *Columbian Exchange*, 20.

41. Ibid., 12.

42. Hanke, *Aristotle and the American Indians*, 99.

43. James Axtell, *The Invasion Within: The Contest of Cultures in Colonial North America* (New York: Oxford University Press, 1985), 133–37.

44. Ibid., 4.

45. Thomas D. Matijasic, "Reflected Values: Sixteenth-Century Europeans View the Indians of North America," *American Indian Culture and Research Journal* 11.2 (1987): 31–50.

46. Ian K. Steele, *Warpaths: Invasions of North America* (New York: Oxford University Press, 1994), 140–46.

47. Benjamin Harris, *Publick Occurrences, Both Foreign and Domestic,* 25 Sept. 1690, quoted in Calder M. Pickett, *Voices of the Past: Key Documents in the History of American Journalism* (Columbus, Ohio: Grid, 1977), 20.

48. Native people in seventeenth-century New England regularly cleared fields with fire and planted a variety of crops including maize, beans, and squash. See Neal Salisbury, *Manitou and Providence* (New York: Oxford University Press, 1982), 30–34.

49. Roy Harvey Pearce, *Savagism and Civilization,* rev. ed. (Berkeley: University of California Press, 1988), 58.

50. Alden T. Vaughan and Edward W. Clark, eds., *Puritans among the Indians: Accounts of Captivity and Redemption, 1676–1724* (Cambridge, Mass.: Belknap Press, 1981), 3.

51. Mary Rowlandson, *The Sovereignty & Goodness of God,* quoted in ibid., 33.

52. Rowlandson, *Soveraignty & Goodness of God,* quoted in ibid., 34.

53. David Copeland, *Colonial American Newspapers: Character and Content* (Newark: University of Delaware Press, 1997), 45, 67.

54. Ibid., 46–56.

55. *Pennsylvania Gazette* (Philadelphia), 24 Feb. 1729, 3, quoted in ibid., 42.

56. *Boston Evening-Post,* 29 July 1745, 2, quoted in ibid., 49.

57. James Axtell, "Through a Glass Darkly: Colonial Attitudes toward the Native Americans," *American Indian Culture and Research Journal* 1.1 (1974): 18.

58. Quoted in Pearce, *Savagism and Civilization,* 144.

59. Ibid.

60. Berkhofer, *White Man's Indian,* 88.

61. Ibid.

62. Ibid., 90.

63. George Catlin, *Letters and Notes on the Manners, Customs, and Conditions of the North American Indians,* 2 vols. (New York: Dover, 1973), 1:3.

64. Ibid., 23, 34.

65. Ibid., 15.

66. Ibid.

67. Ibid., 32.

68. Ibid., 145–46.

69. Pearce, *Savagism and Civilization,* 199.

70. Berkhofer, *White Man's Indian,* xv.

71. Pearce, *Savagism and Civilization,* 200.

72. Thomas Jefferson, *Writings* (New York: Library of America, 1984), 184.

73. Ibid., 185–86.

74. James P. Ronda, *Lewis and Clark among the Indians* (Lincoln: University of Nebraska Press, 1984), 4.

75. Berkhofer, *White Man's Indian,* following p. 138.

76. Reginald Horsman, *Race and Manifest Destiny* (Cambridge: Harvard University Press, 1981), 1.

77. Ibid., 207.

Romance and Rumor:
The Indian in the Antebellum Press

IN 1836, the *State-Rights' Sentinel* of Augusta, Georgia, published a letter from an unidentified writer who was concerned about the treatment of the Cherokees in his state. The writer went to some lengths to defend the Cherokees against the aggressive Georgians. But the most notable aspect of the letter was the writer's acceptance of a Cherokee religious ceremony known as the "New Corn Dance": "This dance . . . is held sacred by them and is held in religious reverence; and however ridiculous their ceremonies on such occasions may appear to the white man, they hold them in reverence, and offer them as a thanksgiving to that God who looks upon the red as he does upon the white man, for his kindness in providing the products of the season to supply their hunger."[1] This newspaper passage was rare in the 1830s because it openly acknowledged the value of Indian religious observances. Usually newspapers treated Indian religions as curious but decidedly heathen practices, in no way comparable to Christianity. This writer, however, recognized that the Cherokees were sincere in their religious beliefs and that even though such beliefs might appear "ridiculous," they deserved the respect of the whites.

The rarity of such a passage in American newspapers in the early nineteenth century highlights the pervasive ethnocentrism of the antebellum era. In society and in the press, Indians were routinely judged by Anglo-American standards, a practice that emphasized their perceived weaknesses and slighted their achievements. Racial prejudice, of course, helps explain such treatment. But prejudice alone does not account for the contrasting Indian identities found in the press in the antebellum era. On one hand, Indians were regularly represented in the press as strange and exotic people, worthy of white attention—and even praise—precisely because they were so different. On the other hand, Indians were often explained as dangerously different, prone to irrational behavior and violence. Both identities were based on a popular racial determinism that assumed *cultural* differences between Indians and whites were inherently racial differences. Thus Indians were regularly and automatically placed in a different category than Euro-Americans; they were people trapped by a set of predetermined "Indian" characteristics—a unique set of qualities that caused them to be sometimes dignified, virtuous, and brave but also unreliable and violent. In other words, Indian identities in the early nineteenth century were arbitrary and unselfconscious, shaped by the racial ideology of the age as well as the particular historical circumstances that brought Indians into popular consciousness.

Making sense of Indians in the antebellum era was a complex ideological endeavor and newspapers approached this task from a variety of positions. Eastern urban dailies had little contact with Indians and were only occasionally interested in Indian news; the stories they did publish tended to emphasize the violence of Indian-white encounters. Other papers, including small-town and frontier weeklies, reported on Indians more frequently, but they too were quick to highlight Indian violence. Yet the romantic Indian and antebellum sentimentalism sometimes slowed or disrupted the stream of violent images. On occasion, both urban and rural papers were open to a range of ideas about Indians, including positive and sympathetic portraits. These representations were fostered by the relatively open nature of antebellum news, practices that allowed a diverse set of Indian images to emerge during this period.

Antebellum News and Indian Identities

The most common way for antebellum papers to gather national and other non-local news was through the mails. As outlined in the Introduction, the post office and a free, informal system of newspaper exchanges provided an effective means of disseminating information in the pre-telegraph era. Mailed news was, of course, a relatively slow method for the distribution of information. But mailed news helped unify the nation. Through the mails, small town papers were linked to government officials at the county, state, and federal levels, a connection that promoted the publication of government announcements and other "official" documents. Even after the telegraph, as Richard Kielbowicz has noted, the exchange system proved useful. The telegraph was quick but expensive, promoting brevity and a corresponding lack of context. The post office, on the other hand, "accommodated discursive, complex, colorful and opinionated articles sent either as exchanges or as letters."[2] In short, the mails provided a variety of "unofficial" news sources, adding diversity to the news and opinion columns. Thus most antebellum newspapers were unlike the penny press in their news-gathering methods; their news came largely from exchange papers and a variety of other "official" and "unofficial" sources. "Official" sources were government proclamations, military correspondence, political announcements, business and commercial news, and the like. "Unofficial" sources included private letters and an assortment of literary and human interest items such as anecdotes, poems, tall tales, gossip, and hearsay. Taken together, this informal news-gathering system ensured a certain openness in Indian representations.

The case of private letters is instructive, especially since such letters were a common source of Indian news. These documents appeared in the press only after they were judged to be interesting by their recipients, who turned them over to local editors, who also judged them newsworthy. These letters often had the singular advantage of direct observation. In the days before the widespread use of correspondents or professional reporters, letter writers could describe Indians and Indian life firsthand. But the motives and interests of writers varied widely, of course, and letters could be highly prejudiced or inaccurate, matters generally not challenged by editors. In addition, many such letters repeated information and ideas that lent support to familiar stereotypes and readers' expectations, not to a reliable understanding of Indians or their concerns. Thus despite their reliance on observation and experience, private letters about Indians were filtered through the personal motives of individual writers and selected haphazardly by editors with various political and social interests. Sometimes these letters yielded thoughtful, complete, or empathetic portraits of specific Indians or tribes, but other times the letters were highly partisan, incomplete, or wrong. With few professional or occupational rules in place, writers were free to report hearsay, rumor, or whatever else they found of interest. Editors, too, could publish what they saw fit, whether or not it met some external definition of news. Thus Indian news in the antebellum press was varied and contradictory, in contrast to the narrowing of Indian identities after professional news-making practices became more firmly established.

The reminiscences of Gen. Thomas S. Woodward illustrate how private correspondence about Indians became news in the South. General Woodward, a prominent citizen of Alabama, had many encounters with Seminoles and Creeks in the early nineteenth century. In 1857, while retired in Louisiana, Woodward wrote about his experiences in a series of letters, which soon found their way into the Montgomery *Mail,* the Columbus [Ga.] *Sun,* and the Union Springs [Ala.] *Gazette.*[3] An editor at the *Mail,* J. J. Hooper, was given one of Woodward's letters and was impressed enough to request additional reminiscences from the general. These were published in the *Mail* in 1858. In 1859, Hooper brought out a collection of the general's letters under this self-explanatory title: *Woodward's Reminiscences of the Creek, or Muscogee Indians, Contained in Letters to Friends in Georgia and Alabama.* In the book's "Introduction," Hooper explained that the original letters "were not expected to be published, at all."[4] Nevertheless, Hooper expressed enormous faith in Woodward, primarily because his experiences were firsthand: "Few men have had better opportunity for studying the Indian character and investigating their customs, than Gen. Woodward."[5] Woodward himself was less confident. In one letter to Hooper, he closed with this remark: "There is too much of this to publish, even if it were worth publishing. Read it, show it to Col. Pickett, burn it and send me his History of Alabama."[6] Despite his own misgivings, General Woodward at least formed his images of the Creeks from personal experience, more than can be said of Fenimore Cooper and many antebellum newspaper writers.

Personal experience of another kind moved many writers to report on Indian life. Diseases—especially the dreaded smallpox—were a popular subject of western travelers. In 1838, for example, the *Western Weekly Review* in Tennessee included this item among a series of news briefs: "100,000 of the Western Indians have died of the small pox since the prevalence of the disease amongst them—so says a traveller from the Rocky Mountains."[7] Despite this alarming message, the paper provided no other information about the epidemic nor did it explain how this information came to the paper. But by publishing this information without explanation, the paper added further credence to the belief in the biological inferiority of the Indians, a race apparently doomed to extinction by disease.

This same point was made explicit in a more extensive account of smallpox in the West. This story, composed of several letters from traders on the Upper Missouri, appeared in *The United States Gazette,* and filled about a column and a half. The letters expressed genuine remorse for the fate of the tribes, though the point of view was very much that of the white trader. The writer noted, for example, that he had tried to warn the Indians about smallpox: "I represented to the Indians that they would if they went near it, be infected by it, but I might as well have talked to the winds. The survivors however are now sorry for their obstinacy, and are as humble as poor dogs who seek in vain for their dead masters."[8] But trade was never far from this writer's mind. Thus the "humble survivors" are seen in terms of economics in the very next sentence: "Our trade in this section is utterly ruined for years to come, nor can all the peltries pay the expenses of the Fort."

The second and third letters in this report turned the natives over to the hands of fate. The second said: "These unfortunate beings have been fast disappearing before our advances; and Providence has at last threatened to sweep them from the earth. . . . The ways of heaven are just, yet mysterious, and nations must bow before its will, as the reed before the storm."[9] Such conclusions shifted responsibility for the epidemic from whites—who, after all, brought smallpox to the Indians—and assigned it to heaven. Again, this shift reinforced the idea of the vanishing Indian, doomed to disappear no matter what the actions of the advancing whites. And by publishing such letters without comment, the *Gazette* promoted the disappearance of Indians as inevitable, even natural.

Of course, it is unreasonable to expect such writers to compose balanced or sympathetic reports, especially in their private letters. Most likely, they simply wrote the "truth" as they saw it. Thus the smallpox epidemic, which they saw firsthand, could be explained as something more than the ravages of a white disease; it was evidence of racial inferiority and confirmation of the vanishing native.[10] Firsthand observations, then, sometimes helped tell a more complete story about Indians in the antebellum era, but these observations, like other forms of antebellum news, were rarely able to transcend the idea of the deficient Indian.

The cultural position of Indians, combined with the haphazard news-collection process of the day, also meant that Indians were often invisible in the papers. Despite occasional letters from the frontier and a flurry of violent news from the Seminole Wars (discussed later in this chapter), Indians were not the stuff of everyday journalism in most newspapers in the 1820s and 1830s. This is hardly a surprise, of course, since most newspapers were founded by and edited for the Anglo-American population, whose information needs were directed toward such news items as international affairs, business, and state and national politics. By the early years of the nineteenth century, most Indians had been pushed out of eastern population centers and were of little interest to newspaper editors or their readers, many of whom were merchants and tradesmen with no connection to Indians. In addition, New York and other East coast papers looked for news in England and on the continent, where American merchants and traders had continuing commercial ties.[11] This fact helps explain why American newspapers frequently carried news about politics and change in Europe and elsewhere. In 1823, for example, the Providence *Gazette* ran page-one articles on such exotic places as Egypt, Madagascar, and China.[12] The continuing hostilities between France and Spain were also much in the news that year, but Indians made few appearances in the *Gazette*.[13] In the 1830s, the Charleston [S.C.] *Mercury* was a highly commercial newspaper with regular reports on the money and cotton markets. The paper also published news and features from Europe, including adventure and romantic pieces from *Chamber's Edinburgh Journal* and the *Royal Gazette*. In short, a reader of the *Mercury* could find more information about the actions of European royalty than about the lives of Native Americans.[14]

The presence of the Indians was ignored even by some of those writing about the American West. In June 1835, for example, the Augusta *State-Rights' Sentinel* published a long piece on western emigration taken from Hall's *Western Monthly Magazine*. The article was explicit about the desire of Americans for western lands: "We have already suggested that although every part of the Western country is good, and some of it surpassingly excellent, a large portion of our people are continually looking for better land."[15] The West was described both as "Eden" and as a "newly discovered Eldorado." In another passage, the writer speculated about the number of "Alexanders among us, who having overrun every known field of ambition, are sighing for new worlds to conquer." Despite this military language, the writer makes no mention of Indians or the dangers they might present on the frontier. Indeed, the conquest of the West was taken as a natural and inevitable goal of American progress: "Our steamboats have ascended the Mississippi to the falls of St. Anthony; . . . our traders pass annually over vast deserts to Santa Fe, and the adventurous trapper has sought the haunts of the beaver beyond the Rocky Mountains; and yet the lust for newer lands, and for novel scenes of commercial enterprise, is undiminished."[16] Perhaps this image was just wishful thinking, a bold vision of the West as uninhabited land, ripe for the taking. But this vision also provides a clue into the ideological positioning of Indians in the West. That is, in the inevitable conquest of the continent, Indians were of marginal significance. Destiny, after all, was believed to be driving the new nation; the eventual expansion of the United States from Atlantic to Pacific was just a matter of time. Little wonder, then, that this antebellum writer overlooked the Indian as he imagined the rising American empire in the West.

Romancing the Indian

Although Indian identity was bounded by the "good" and "bad" extremes, there were some variations within these boundaries. These included some of the most common ideas about Indians of the day, ideas that became part of the standard press explanation of Indians and Indian life. These themes coalesced into a loose formula used to describe Indians in the antebellum press. Describing several of these themes helps explain how the news-gathering process affected these images.

The portrayal of the Indian as Noble Savage goes back to the European *philosophes* and to pre-revolutionary America.[17] But the romantic Indian gained its greatest popularity following the publication of James Fenimore Cooper's *The Last of the Mohicans* in 1826. In this embodiment, the Indian male was a brave and fearless warrior as well as a natural aristocrat and child of nature. Such ideas appealed to many Americans and—absent hostilities that might break the spell—idealized natives often turned up in the press.

One example was published in a Tennessee weekly in 1834. Under the headline "Indian Eloquence," the story recounted the mourning of an Indian woman over the twin graves of her husband and child. According to the story, the woman was eloquent: "The father of Life and Light has taken from me the apple of my eye, and the core of my heart, and hid him in these two graves. I will moisten the one with my tears, and the other with the milk of my breast, till I meet them in that country where the sun never sets."[18] The paper gave no source for the speech and it seems unlikely that anyone at the newspaper ever witnessed such a scene. It seems more likely that the account was written by a white author for an eastern periodical and then reprinted in Tennessee. But whatever its origin, this account appears to owe more to white ideas of the Noble Savage than to the actual grief of a specific native woman. Like many antebellum accounts of native life, this story reinforces the vanishing Indian idea by portraying native life as marked by tragedy and by suggesting that Indian happiness comes only when their lives have ended, in "that country where the sun never sets."

The same paper also reprinted an exchange story from the Washington *Telegraph* in 1838. According to this account, a private captured by Seminoles reported that as the Indians prepared to execute him, he was saved by a seventeen-year-old Indian girl who rushed to him at the last minute and won his release. The paper concluded that the private's story related "a singular development of noble feeling and humanity upon the part of the Indians."[19] The private's story may be true, though it seems suspiciously similar to the Pocahontas–Capt. John Smith legend of colonial Virginia:

> Then the maiden Pocahontas
> Rushes forward, none can stop her,
> Throws her arms about the captive
> Cries,—"oh spare him! Spare the Paleface!"[20]

In both stories, Indian women display a touch of nobility and show that they can be as humane and sympathetic as whites, at least under some conditions. Yet the Florida story concluded by separating Indians from whites under everyday conditions: "we only introduce the adventure here to show how much different their conduct under ordinary circumstances from that of the white men's."

In practice, then, the romantic "good Indian" had some important limitations; it could not be applied to any native in any situation. For example, an 1830 report in *The United States Gazette* discussed one of the most sensitive areas of Indian-white relations: intermarriage. Was an Indian man good enough to marry a white woman? The *Gazette* writer thought so, though he expressed doubts about proponents of the Indian Removal Bill then under discussion. According to the *Gazette,* a Cherokee man named Riggs had married a white woman from Connecticut, an act that caused "considerable excitement." The success or failure of the marriage also aroused great local interest. Said the paper: "His wife has been observed, by visiters [*sic*], to be melancholy; and it appears that her husband has given her sufficient cause, inasmuch as he has taken several squaws into his house, in consequence of which, I understand, she has been made seriously unhappy, that she has more than once made attempts on her own life."[21] But this tale proved nothing, the *Gazette* reporter claimed. After all, "There is as much vice among us, as among the Indians; and if we are to be acquitted or condemned from the aggregate of vice, we shall probably be in a worse condition than the Cherokee." Despite his optimism, the reporter noted that these facts "will probably be used to show that the Indians have not benefitted by our christianizing efforts."[22] This treatment of Indian-white marriage reveals the superficiality of the Noble Indian idea. It was one thing to praise the Indian in nature or in the abstract, but it was quite another to actually accept an Indian as a marriage partner, in effect admitting Indian equality with whites. The *Gazette* writer was prepared to do so in this case, but there were many in Connecticut and elsewhere who were not. In any event, the *Gazette* correspondent recognized that Riggs was being judged not simply as a bad husband, but as a representative of all Indian men. In other words, the "good Indian" was a limited and fragile construct that could be easily attacked and destroyed. It was, in fact, a concept that was valid only when it was useful to the dominant society. In the case of Riggs, any sign of weakness—true or not—could be used to puncture the good Indian identity. The best the *Gazette* writer could do was to state plainly the unfairness of such judgments.

One of the ways Indians made news in the informal world of antebellum journalism was in anecdotes and jokes, many of them based on perceived cultural differences and some openly racist. Thus the image of a generic Indian turned up in a bit of doggerel printed in a Tennessee weekly. Wrote an unidentified poet:

> Tobacco is an Indian,
> It was the d[evi]l sowed the seed;
> It drains your pockets—scents your clothes,
> And makes a chimney of your nose![23]

Even as a joke, this poem is obviously unflattering, linking Indians to the devil and suggesting comparisons between them and several distasteful aspects of smoking. More importantly, this representation emphasizes the "otherness" of Indians, separating them from the more "civilized" ways of whites, who, after all, were less likely to "drain your pockets" or "scent your clothes." The poem, in short, was a small confirmation of native difference and inferiority.

This theme was repeated in a sketch published in a Georgia paper in 1835. The topic of this story was not Indians but their dogs: "Their [*sic*] are no greater thieves in existence than Indian dogs; not even excepting the old squaws. . . . With the last, it is a matter of habit, and practice; but with the former, it is instinct."[24] This statement is significant not so much because it is prejudicial but because of the way it conveys this prejudice.

Indian dogs, like Indian women, are summed up in a sweeping statement that is less fact than hyperbole. The purpose of the sketch, then, is not to provide information but to entertain the reader by poking a little fun at Indians. A single such comment might be considered harmless. But the Indian identity in these anecdotes reveals a popular way of thinking about Native Americans that turned up in the antebellum press again and again. For that reason, such comments had a cumulative power, operating across the decades to make plain the idea that Indians were, by "habit" and "practice," deficient when compared to whites. It is also significant that neither of these anecdotes names an individual Indian or identifies a specific tribe. The Indians represented in these stories are not real individuals, not identifiable members of actual tribes, but types. In other words, the anecdotal Indian was open for criticism because he or she was, in some essential way, an Indian, a racial category that was both different from and inferior to another "racial" category, Anglo-American.

Even anecdotes meant to praise Indians often included elements of condescension. For instance, a report published in an Arkansas paper cited the patriotism of a Creek chief known as Little Turtle. According to the report, the chief was impressed by Kosciuszko, the Polish-American Revolutionary War hero, but he could not pronounce the Polish name. Instead, the chief called him "Kotcho," which was, the paper said, "the nearest approach to Kosciuszko that his unpracticed organs could accomplish." The chief was also described as an excitable man. When he spoke, he "walked rapidly about the room, with angry gesticulations, and swinging his tomahawk."[25] Without saying so directly, such an account supported the notion that civilized men were educated, rational, and calm while uncivilized men, such as Little Turtle, were illiterate, highly emotional, and perhaps dangerous.

Other anecdotes were vehicles for the "good Indian." A newspaper story published in the mid-1830s played up the wit of John Sequashquash, an Indian from Connecticut. According to the report, Sequashquash got drunk—a common negative image—and found himself before a justice of the peace. But Sequashquash

> would only tell the JP, "Your honor is very wise—y-y-your honor is very wise. . . ."
> The next day (after a night in jail) the JP tells him what he said. The Indian says:
> "Did I call you wise?" said the Indian, with a look of incredulity.
> "Yes," answered the magistrate.
> "Then," replied John, "I must have been drunk true enough."[26]

In this story, the Indian, privileged by his outsider status, gets to demonstrate his cleverness at the expense of white authority. Such cleverness helps reveal this Indian as a more fully developed character because it assigns him a sophisticated verbal skill, the same kind of skill assigned to whites. In this way, Sequashquash is used as a social critic, a "good Indian" representation worthy of white attributes. On the other hand, the positive image is offset by the Indian's drunkenness, a sign here of racial inferiority. Finally, the literal truth of this anecdote is open to question. Indeed, the story appeared in the paper not as a news report but under the heading, "Indian Anecdote," a signal that its value was entertainment, not information. In this context, Sequashquash was an example of both cleverness and irresponsibility, yet still positioned as an object of public amusement.

Sequashquash can also be seen as a useful "pretend Indian," a fictional native figure who, because he is outside the normal social structure, is free to critique that society. If we assume, as I do, that this story is more fiction than fact, it can be read as a small—but safe—jab at local authority. In this way, Indian identity was expropriated for use in political and social criticism, a role not unique to the antebellum period. Indeed, revolutionary Americans "played Indian" to great effect at the Boston Tea Party, disguising themselves as Mohawk Indians when they dumped 342 chests of tea into Boston Harbor to protest a new British tax. After the revolution, the Delaware chief Tamanend, famous in the seventeenth century for his kindness, was expropriated as a symbol for the Tammany Society (or Columbian Order) of New York City. The association between Tamanend and the New York political machine was slight, but the native image remained a useful and popular symbol. An 1837 political cartoon, for instance, illustrated the Tammany's political woes by imagining the death of Tamanend and his wife "Loco Foco," who, along with a fallen James Gordon Bennett and a group of Whig politicians, were retreating before a group of attacking New York editors.[27] Again, Indians were useful political symbols, more so because they were assumed to be simple people whose virtues (or vices) could be attached to whatever cause the writer or cartoonist desired.

Rumors, Exchanges, and Indian News

A significant amount of news about Indians during the first decades of the nineteenth century was not firsthand, but second- or thirdhand, courtesy of the post office and its system of newspaper exchanges. These exchanges served as a primitive news service and editors were not shy about reprinting Indian information they found interesting or compelling, with or without attribution.[28] This system allowed a range of Indian images to be circulated in the antebellum press, a fact that helped enlarge the native identity. But exchanges could be confusing; until new, more authoritative letters arrived, it was difficult to know which report might be correct. As a result, a great many antebellum Indian news stories were confusing or contradictory.

The Albany [N.Y.] *Argus* discovered this problem when it reported on the disturbances by Creek Indians in the South in 1829. Wrote the *Argus,* "The following statement from the last Macon *Telegraph,* contradicts the report which we published from the Columbus *Enquirer."* The *Argus* then published this complicated statement from the *Telegraph:* "We have received from Col. John Crowell, agent for the Creek nation, a letter . . . in which he authorizes us to say, that the statement from the Columbus Enquirer is, in many of its important facts, incorrect; and that great alarm has been *unnecessarily* and *improperly* produced by it on the frontiers."[29] It is clear from this explanation that the original information about the Creeks in the *Enquirer* had alarmed their agent, Colonel Crowell, and that he then used the *Telegraph* to help set the record straight. A careful reader of the Albany paper could probably follow this story but there is no guarantee that less careful readers—or other exchange papers—would make this correction.

The Seminole Wars of the 1820s and 1830s provided many examples of confusion and rumor in the news. Newspapers throughout the country reported the story, but few had reliable sources of information. Instead, news reports slowly made their way back from travelers, soldiers, and sailors who told what they knew to newspapermen in Florida or neighboring states. Such stories were subject to exaggeration, misstatement, and a host of other errors. Once published, however, these stories could be picked up by exchange papers, repeating whatever errors appeared in the original published accounts. And in the news-gathering era before the telegraph, editors had no timely way of verifying such reports.

The problem was serious enough to confound some editors. The editor of the Cincinnati *Whig* once made an issue of the confusion by publishing these two statements one after the other:

The Florida war is ended.—Gen. Jesup.

The Florida war is not ended.—Oceola.

And then he added this commentary: "Such are the contradictory accounts we constantly receive from Florida. There appears to be no possibility of obtaining accurate information from that quarter. We should not be surprised to hear tomorrow, for the fortieth time, that Gen. Jesup had captured Oceola . . . and on the next day have the whole story contradicted, with this addition—Gen. Jesup and his army have been captured by Osceola [*sic*]."[30] Confusion, then, was a regular part of the news from Florida. For readers, such confusion was probably so common that they discounted much of what they read about the war. If so, this further undermined the credibility of antebellum news.

At their worst, war reports were based on speculation and rumor. Thus the *Western Weekly Review* in Tennessee reprinted a dispatch from the Milledgeville *Journal* that began with an honest admission of its source: "We hear it rumored that the Creek Indians are exhibiting indications of a turbulent and hostile spirit."[31] At the end of the article, the *Journal* writer revealed his own misgivings about the report: "Such is the story that has reached here. We hope it is exagerated [*sic*]." Yet the very next paragraph contained new information. "A letter received in this city conffirms [*sic*] the above and states the Indians were assembling in large bodies with hostile intentions, and that the whites were becoming alarmed."[32] Perhaps so—but the facts presented here do not inspire confidence. No direct evidence on the intentions of the Indians was presented in either report and it is at least plausible that the Indians intended no harm.

With Indian rumors—some of them quite alarming—coming in from the frontiers, newspapers sometimes attempted to distance themselves from the messages they printed. When the Albany *Argus* published a rumor about Indians gathering for an attack in Missouri, the editor inserted this disclaimer: "As to the verity of this, we cannot speak—but we feel it a duty we owe to the public to publish all the information which has been put in circulation relative to this important subject."[33] In other words, the information was not verified and may not have been true, but the paper was publishing it anyway—a journalistic practice that continues to this day. In any case, given such standards of news, it is little wonder that Indians were often portrayed in exaggerated and hostile terms. What this—and stories like it—reveal about Indian news is the uncertain nature of antebellum war reporting and the tendency of the press to assume the worst and print whatever information it had.

In sum, newspaper exchanges on Indian information in the pre-telegraph era were a useful technique for journalists as well as readers because the exchange system functioned like a primitive wire service. The system wasn't fast, but it did convey some sense of the news from the scene. Yet the exchange system could be wildly inaccurate and unreliable, since first reports from the scene—especially a battle scene—had a tendency to be exaggerated. Moreover, many frontier reports assigned the worst possible characteristics to the Indians. Thus the newspaper exchanges were far from reliable when it came to Indian-white conflicts, a fact that distorted the Indian identity in the antebellum press.

Making the Evil Indian

The most vivid press portrayal of Indians in the 1830s was the bad Indian, a creature of violence and certain cruelty. This was largely due to the Second Seminole War in Florida, where tales of torture and death quickly became staples of reporting about the war. The evil Indian was also a frequent theme of reporting from the western frontier, where conflicts with white settlers caused additional news reports. Unlike the Indian who was romantically vanishing or the anecdotal Indian who was a useful social critic, the evil Indian was very much alive. He was also the obvious product of an event-driven news-making process. As long as there were Indian-white conflicts in Florida and the West, the papers made sure that the Indians were identified by a host of unfavorable characteristics.

An example from the Albany *Argus* shows how the scales were tipped against "hostile" Indians on the frontier. The Albany story was taken from the Fayette County [Mo.] *Western Monitor* in July 1829. The *Argus* headlined the story, "Bloodshed on the Frontier" but the original title was also published: "Indian Murders in Missouri." The story opened on a serious note: "We have to perform the melancholy duty of announcing the murder of three most respectable citizens of this county." The paper then described the confrontation between the Indians and the whites in terms that blamed the Indians: "The whites then finding it was useless to reason further with them, and seeing that some of the Indians had their guns to their faces, discharged one of their guns upon the Indians."[34] The whites shot first, but the Indians were assigned the blame, both for their perceived stubbornness and their apparent threats to the whites.

The southwestern frontier was also threatened by Indians. In an unsigned but official letter, an Arkansas newspaper described the exploits of the feared Comanches, emphasizing their contempt for authority: "Free as the buffalo themselves, they acknowledge no superior—depreciating upon the Mexicans of the interior States, ravaging and burning their towns[,] murdering their people, sometimes taking prisoners, which they either torture to death or make slaves of, carrying off immense herds of mules and horses."[35] This writer seemed most concerned about the Indians' superior attitude and he was not content to let the idea slip by without comment: "Their impunity heretofore prompts these wandering hordes to look upon themselves as the most powerful of nations." Clearly, the Comanches were a threat to white society and the writer was doing his duty by reporting this fact officially. The newspaper was doing its duty too, alerting the public to the danger and assigning the Comanches a position as the evil raiders of the Southwest. If there was a humane aspect to this tribe, or if factions of the tribe were peaceful, it was not evident in such stories.

In Florida, alarmist reporting was the order of the day. In early 1836, for example, the Jacksonville *Courier* appealed for immediate military aid and claimed that "the whole of East Florida is in danger." The editor put the point in emotional terms: "We must not only abandon our property to destruction, but, stripped of all our hard earnings, must fight for our lives, our women and our children."[36]

In other stories, the Seminoles became notorious for their methods of murder. The papers often reported the exact number of bullet or arrow wounds in the victims as well as the details of the scalping or other mutilations of the bodies: "Through Gen. Thompson were shot fifteen bullets, and sixteen through Rogers."[37] Such information might be taken as merely descriptive and, presumably, it satisfied the public's curiosity about death. Nevertheless, such reports also emphasized the apparent blood lust of the Seminoles.

Another example of sensational reporting followed the defeat of Major Francis L. Dade's troops in late 1835. A Mobile *Chronicle* report published in *The United States Gazette* carried an alarming headline—"Horrid Massacre"—and pointed out that 112 men were killed while only three survived the Seminole ambush. The paper also noted that numerous scalps were taken. The story ended with an editorial comment: "We do not remember the history of a butchery more horrid, and it stands without an example in the annals of Indian warfare. Our citizens we are sure, will meet together and send some relief to the suffering and defenceless inhabitants of Florida."[38] Unfortunately this story was wrong both in its particulars and its implications. The actual number of casualties was too high,[39] though it should be said that such information is difficult to confirm even under the best of circumstances. The report also failed to mention that the scalps were probably not taken by the Seminoles but by a band of former slaves who were their allies and who arrived shortly after the battle.[40] More importantly, both the *Gazette*'s headline and the *Chronicle*'s closing commentary framed the ambush as a "massacre," a term the press used to stigmatize Indian victories against whites and put the violence in its most alarming light. For example, the *Chronicle* did not "remember the history of a butchery more horrid," and said this massacre was "without example in the annals of Indian warfare." Such conclusions, however, overstated the truth. The Mobile editor overlooked the annihilation of 634 soldiers—including 68 officers—under the command of Gen. Arthur St. Clair in 1791.[41] In that forgotten battle, Chief Little Turtle and his band of Miamis killed *six times* the number killed in the Dade ambush.

In any event, the *Chronicle* advocated relief for the "defenceless inhabitants of Florida." But in this story, such a phrase implied that the massacre involved ordinary citizens who had no chance to defend themselves. But if a massacre is defined as "the indiscriminate killing in numbers of the unresisting or defenseless," as a modern dictionary suggests,[42] then this battle was not a massacre. No women, children, or defenseless men were involved.[43] Major Dade and his troops were well armed—they even hauled a six-pound cannon along on their fatal march. When the Indians ambushed them, the soldiers put up a gallant defense, even building a makeshift breastwork from trees they cut when the Indians temporarily withdrew.

Such details, however, did not come through in the *Chronicle*'s account. There the fight was a "massacre," an inflammatory term readily applied by the contemporary press to incidents in which every soldier was killed by Indians. But there were three survivors of this attack. Was it, then, a massacre? Perhaps—because the Indians intended to kill every soldier. In any case, the *Chronicle* was less interested in a precise definition of the word than in conveying a sense of outrage and alarm over the utter defeat of Major Dade and his troops. Significantly, "massacre" was rarely applied when whites successfully killed a band of Indian warriors. In other words, the ambush of Dade's men was a massacre not because innocent people were involved or because every soldier was killed but primarily because the Indians won. If Dade had successfully destroyed the attacking Seminoles, no newspaper would have called it a massacre. By using language in this way, the *Chronicle* protected the interests of its readers—the white population—reporting the battle in highly emotional terms and emphasizing the dangers to the larger population.

Three days later the *Gazette* published a Congressional report that apparently confirmed the savagery of the Seminoles. Mr. Benton, a Congressman, told his colleagues that the Seminoles were naturally a bad race and that even other Indians thought so, as "signified by their name *Seminole,* which, in Indian, means 'wild,' 'runaway.' "[44] In this way, war news produced not only sensational details of violence and death at the hands of the Seminoles but also racial bigotry and hatred.

Perhaps the most unfair reporting from the war consisted of stories that attempted to demonstrate the treachery and inhumanity of the Seminoles. In 1837, for example, the New Orleans *Picayune* explained that the removal of the Seminoles was necessary because they could not be trusted: "Their fate *seems* to be a hard one, but their treachery, and the safety of our white population require it." Then the paper explained the main flaw in the native character: "When once the Indian is aroused to revenge and war, his spirit will never be subdued. They cannot—must not be trusted." An editorial in the *Picayune* echoed this judgment when discussing Seminole chief Osceola (also spelled Oceola): "This fellow is possessed of great daring—and we shall not be surprised to hear further of his tricks and treachery."[45]

In other reports, the Indians were shown to be subhuman because they did things—desperate things under great duress—that presumably no (white) human would do. Thus a report from a Florida paper told of some Seminole women and children who had been captured. "In the evening one of the squaws was observed to give her children a drink from a coffee pot," the story said. The woman soon escaped, but her three children remained in captivity. The report concluded: "Her children were all found dead, from *poison* administered by their unnatural mother."[46] This was a terrible and desperate act, of course, but it was presented in the press as evidence of the cruelty and inhumanity of the Seminoles, who, like animals, had no moral standards and no genuine feelings toward their young. The report made no attempt to understand the mother's motives or to speculate on her fears or feelings—or, indeed, the emotional strength required to kill one's children in these circumstances. In short, this Seminole woman was portrayed as incapable of genuine human emotion. She was defined by her apparent weaknesses, weaknesses made glaring by the drama of war. The same Florida report included a second incident of Indian cruelty. After a fight in a swamp, the story said, the Indians retreated in defeat. "Before their flight they strangled their children by stuffing their mouths and nostrils with *mud moss.* The children were found in that condition after the battle was over."[47] Assuming this event actually occurred, it was presented as another example of Seminole cruelty and, again, was published without any regard for the terror and pain that must have driven the Seminoles to commit these acts. The Seminoles were defined once more by their callousness and cruelty, not by their pain or suffering.

Such characterizations contrast with the reporting of similar cases among whites in one important detail: explanation. Unlike the Seminoles, whites who committed terrible crimes were frequently provided a disclaimer by the papers. Thus the Augusta *State-Rights' Sentinel* in 1834 reported the murder of two sailors by one James M. Hardy, a fellow shipmate. The headline itself provided the sailor's excuse: "Effects of Intemperance."[48] Another story, this one a suicide report from an 1837 Newark *Daily Advertiser,* explained the woman's action in three words: "She was deranged."[49] The New York *Journal of Commerce* followed a similar pattern when reporting the suicide of a well-known music publisher: "His affairs were not embarrassed, but he had some time ago lost his wife and daughter also, which had so much preyed upon his mind as to break down his spirits."[50] This explanation—extreme depression—could have been applied to the Seminole woman above. Significantly, it was not.

Newspaper stories of white cruelty to children also followed this explanatory pattern. When a young woman abandoned an infant in Ohio, the New Orleans *Picayune* explained that she had left a note with the baby "alleging all sorts of distresses as the cause of her conduct." But the townspeople had a more complicated explanation: "The child did not belong to the woman; but she was the hireling of a *higher* power, and the child the innocent offspring of shame."[51] Either way, the woman's actions warranted an explanation in the press.

Drunkenness was the explanation for maternal cruelty in two other 1837 stories from the *Picayune.* One involved a woman who fell into a drunken stupor while holding her child before a fire. "The still drunken mother never awoke until the child was burnt to death," the paper reported.[52] Still another drunken mother was stopped before she could stuff her baby down the "sluices of the Canal street sewer, New York."[53] The editors of the *Picayune* printed many stories about the evils of strong drink. Liquor is not a satisfactory explanation for these cruelties, of course, but at least it made the actions of these whites understandable. The Seminoles got no explanation at all.

Such reporting reduced the Seminoles and other tribes in conflict with whites to one-dimensional creatures. Their tribal life, their social organization, their religious practices—all important aspects of native life—were of little interest during wartime. On the battlefield and in the papers, Indians had a more dramatic role to play. Indians were, after all, the enemy and the enemy was evil by definition. Under such circumstances, it is not surprising to find anti-Indian themes in the papers. But such reporting served a more important ideological function as well. By overemphasizing the treachery and cruelty of Indians, underplaying their human qualities, and denying their motives, news from the Second Seminole War reinforced the identity of these Indians as ruthless, subhuman savages, resistant to progress and incapable of civilization. Unfortunately for American Indians generally, this image persisted in one form or another throughout much of the nineteenth century.

Competing Indian Identities

In the absence of violence or conflict, the antebellum press was not especially interested in Indians. Along the eastern seaboard especially, Indians were not an important part of daily life and neither editors nor readers had compelling reasons to follow Indian news. But in the borderlands of the South and West, Indians were often newsworthy by their very presence. In a growing frontier economy, Indians were usually seen as a political and economic problem, a fact that ensured a certain level of news coverage, much of it focused on conflict. But the newspaper Indian in the antebellum period was not universally condemned. "Good" Indians were identified too. These were gentle natives who were graciously giving way to progress and civilization. These Indian representations were inspired by the imagination of colonial writers such as Philip Freneau and the contemporary novels of James Fenimore Cooper. These Indians were "safe," easy to praise because they seemed to be vanishing and presented no threat to expansion on the frontier. In other instances, Indians were used in jokes and anecdotes. In this role, Indians were useful vehicles for social and political criticism since the outsider status of the Indian provided a convenient way of criticizing official power. Even the "bad" Indian could be praised in some instances. Osceola, the Seminole leader who was widely condemned for his treachery, was also admired for his military skills. Writing in 1836, one Florida observer noted that there were "many extravagant things, which everyday were afloat about the great Seminole chief."[54] Some of these stories raised questions about Osceola's training and pedigree; he was reputed to have studied at West Point and be perhaps three-quarters white. But the most extravagant praise for Osceola came after his death in 1838. A letter published in *Niles' National Register* recognized "something in his character not unworthy of the respect of the world. From a vagabond child he became the master spirit of a long and desperate war. He made himself—no man owed less to accident."[55] Here Osceola's successful climb from obscurity to battlefield glory was held up as an ideal, a lesson in individualism for the culture that was determined to destroy him. Despite this paradox, Osceola's stature grew at his death and his public identity was appropriated as a symbol of national valor. He was buried with military honors; his epitaph expressed his safe, new identity: "Patriot and Warrior."

One reason that romance, rumor, exaggeration, and anecdote appeared in the antebellum press was the loose definition of news and the absence of conventional news practices. In a era of news exchanges and wide editorial latitude, Indian news could take a variety of forms. Literature, poems, jokes, and the like appeared in the press on a regular basis. While this material is not considered news today, it was a regular part of the news in the antebellum era, especially in the small-town and rural press. As a result, Indian representations were more diverse in this era than they would be later, when the telegraph, more formal news definitions, and professional standards limited the kinds of news that appeared in papers.

Despite this diversity, the violence surrounding the Seminole Wars ensured that antebellum Indians were regularly identified as evil. While the facts of war are almost always sufficient to demonize an enemy, the newspapers contributed to this stream of negative images by their willing acceptance and repetition of negative and inflammatory stereotypes. Newspapers regularly published rumors and exaggerations that made the Seminoles seem more cruel and violence-prone than they were. Moreover, in contrast to whites, violent Indians were offered no explanation for their actions, as if they were innately violent.

In cultural terms, the newspaper representations of Indians served the interests of the majority white population, marginalizing Native American lives, documenting their differences, and affirming their inferiority and barbarity. This positioning was less the product of intentional racial prejudice than of an informal ethnocentric belief system that operated on and through the press, creating and reinforcing racial differences and limiting the formation of fully rounded, alternative Indian identities. In theory at least, Native Americans might have emerged in the antebellum press in stories that highlighted their humanity or revealed the strengths of their cultures. But the ideological forces at work in antebellum journalism—and in society at large—were far too strong to permit a full or balanced representation of Indians to emerge in any popular or sustained way.

Notes

1. *State-Rights' Sentinel,* 8 Sept. 1836, 3.

2. Richard B. Kielbowicz, *News in the Mail: The Press, Post Office, and Public Information, 1700–1860s* (Westport, Conn.: Greenwood Press, 1989), 142.

3. Thomas S. Woodward, *Woodward's Reminiscences of the Creek, or Muscogee Indians, Contained in Letters to Friends in Georgia and Alabama* (1859; rpt., Tuscaloosa: Alabama Book Store, 1939), 3.

4. Ibid.

5. Ibid., 4.

6. Ibid., 19.

7. *Western Weekly Review,* 28 Sept. 1838, 3.

8. *The United States Gazette,* 14 Mar. 1838, 3.

9. Ibid.

10. This thesis is the topic of Brian W. Dippie's *The Vanishing American* (Middletown, Conn.: Wesleyan University Press, 1982).

11. The dependence of American papers on European news can be traced to the earliest American newspapers and the strong economic and cultural ties between England and the colonies. See, for example, the discussion of John Campbell's Boston *News-Letter* in Frank Luther Mott, *American Journalism,* 3d ed. (New York: Macmillan Company, 1962), 11–12.

12. Providence *Gazette,* 5 Feb. 1823, 1; 19 Mar. 1823, 1; 2 Apr. 1823, 1.

13. Ibid., 15 Feb. 1823, 1.

14. Charleston *Mercury,* 17 Aug. 1838, 2. See also 20 Aug. 1838.

15. *State-Rights' Sentinel,* 5 June 1835, 2.

16. Ibid.

17. See Robert F. Berkhofer Jr., *The White Man's Indian* (New York: Vintage Books, 1979), 3–31, and Henry Steele Commager, *The Empire of Reason* (New York: Oxford University Press, 1977), 67–70, 91–95.

18. *Western Weekly Review* (Franklin, Tenn.), 20 June 1834, 1.

19. Washington *Telegraph* story in the *Western Weekly Review,* 16 Feb. 1838, 1.

20. Quoted in Philip Young, "The Mother of Us All: Pocahontas Reconsidered," *Kenyon Review* 24.3 (Summer 1962): 403.

21. *The United States Gazette* (Philadelphia), 18 May 1830, 4.

22. Ibid.

23. *Western Weekly Review,* 6 Oct. 1837, 3.

24. Augusta *State-Rights' Sentinel,* 21 July 1835, 2.

25. *Constitutional Journal,* 28 Apr. 1836, 2.

26. *Western Weekly Review,* 27 May 1836, 3.

27. Rayna Green, "The Indian in Popular American Culture," in William C. Sturtevant, ed., *Handbook of North American Indians,* 17 vols. (Washington, D.C.: Smithsonian Institution Press, 1988), 4:604, 606.

28. For a discussion of the origins of newspaper exchanges, see Richard B. Kielbowicz, "Newsgathering by Printers' Exchanges before the Telegraph," *Journalism History* 9.2 (Summer 1982): 42–48.

29. Albany *Argus,* 12 Aug. 1829, 2.

30. Cincinnati *Whig* story in the *Western Weekly Review,* 4 Aug. 1837, 1.

31. Milledgeville *Journal* story in ibid., 13 May 1836, 1.

32. Milledgeville *Journal* story in ibid.

33. Albany *Argus,* 15 Aug. 1829, 2.

34. Ibid.

35. *Constitutional Journal* (Helena, Ark.), 26 May 1836, 2.

36. Jacksonville *Courier* story in *The United States Gazette,* 23 Jan. 1836, 3.

37. Jacksonville *Courier* story in ibid.

38. Mobile *Chronicle* story in ibid., 27 Jan. 1836, 3.

39. The number is put at 107 by William Hartley and Ellen Hartley, *Osceola: The Unconquered Indian* (New York: Hawthorn Books, 1973), 149. See also Frank Laumer, *Massacre!* (Gainesville: University of Florida Press, 1968).

40. Hartley and Hartley, *Osceola,* 148. See also Laumer, *Massacre!* 150.

41. Harvey Lewis Carter, *The Life and Times of Little Turtle: First Sagamore of the Wabash* (Urbana: University of Illinois Press, 1987), 108.

42. *Funk & Wagnalls New Standard Dictionary of the English Language* (1963), 1522.

43. Accounts of the engagement can be found in Hartley and Hartley, *Osceola,* 141–49, and Laumer, *Massacre!* 128–56.

44. *The United States Gazette,* 30 Jan. 1836, 2.

45. New Orleans *Picayune,* 24 Mar. 1837, 2.

46. Quoted in the *Constitutional Journal* (Helena, Ark.), 21 Sept. 1836, 3.

47. Quoted in ibid.

48. *State-Rights' Sentinel* (Augusta, Ga.), 4 Dec. 1834, 2.

49. Newark *Daily Advertiser* in the New Orleans *Picayune,* 21 Feb. 1837, 3.

50. *Journal of Commerce* story of 20 June 1835, in the *State-Rights' Sentinel,* 26 June 1835, 3.

51. New Orleans *Picayune,* 14 Apr. 1837, 2.

52. Ibid., 17 Mar. 1837, 2.

53. Ibid., 22 Apr. 1837, 2.

54. Myer Cohen, *Notices of Florida and the Campaigns,* quoted in Richard A. Grounds, "Tallahassee and the Name Game" (Ph.D. diss., Princeton Theological Seminary, 1994), 137.

55. *Niles' National Register,* 2 Feb. 1838, quoted in ibid., 136.

T · H · R · E · E

Explaining Indian Removal

T HE public are either altogether uninformed, or misinformed, with regard to the current state of Cherokee affairs," said an observer of the Cherokee removal in 1838. "On the 24th of May the work of capture commenced, and continued, with unfeeling rigor, until the entire rightful and legitimate population of the country were divested of house and home, and reduced to a state of abject poverty." He continued, "The captors sometimes drove the people with whooping and hallowing, like cattle through rivers, allowing them no time even to take off their shoes and stockings."[1]

This private letter, published on the front page of *Niles' National Register,* was one of the most dramatic news accounts of the cruelty and pain that resulted from the policy of Indian removal. Other press reports were less concerned with the Cherokees than with the need for their removal. Another newspaper correspondent summed up removal in these words: "Georgia is, at length, rid of her red population, and this beautiful country will now be prosperous and happy."[2]

Between these two extremes—the cruelty of forcing people from their lands and the political and economic will to remove the Indians—the press of the 1830s attempted to tell the story of the southern Indians and their controversial and complex relationship with the states, the federal government, and the white population. Indian removal was an important political and social issue in the early decades of the nineteenth century. The press covered the story seriously but haphazardly, reflecting many of the racial attitudes and idiosyncrasies of antebellum journalism. These attitudes and practices devalued the achievements and rights of southern Indians and emphasized the need for land and economic growth in the region. As a result, newspaper representations of the southern tribes were shaped by a powerful ideology of native inequality and white land claims, ideas ensuring that Indian identity in the press would be distorted and the tragedy of Indian removal would be obscured.

The removal of the southern tribes has been the subject of many historical investigations, though neither political nor Native American historians have critically examined the removal as it was reported by the newspapers.[3] Grant Foreman, for example, used press accounts to supplement his examination of manuscript material in *Indian Removal*. But Foreman took news accounts at face value, without consideration of the forces that shaped these reports. This chapter, in contrast, analyzes removal news in order to establish the role of the press in representing and interpreting the southern Indians and their place in American life during the 1830s. Specifically, I examine a powerful set of ideological and institutional forces—ideas, policies, economic and political pressures, and news-making practices—that shaped the newspaper Indian in a crucial period of Indian-white relations.

The Politics of Indian Removal

The forced removal of the "Five Civilized Tribes" from the South was one of the most controversial Indian issues of the nineteenth century. The removal involved Choctaws, Creeks, Chickasaws, Cherokees, and Seminoles. These were Native Americans "distinguished by character and intelligence far above the average aboriginal," according to one historian.[4] Despite such judgments and their very real achievements in the South, these tribes were considered major obstacles to southern development and both state and federal governments promoted their "voluntary" removal to the western territories. One by one during the decade, the tribes signed away their southern lands. In return, the U.S. government promised that the five tribes would have the chance to reestablish their cultures in Indian Territory, safe from white interests and interference.

Although the forced removal of the southern tribes took place during the 1830s, the idea of Indian removal had roots as far back as the 1780s. Some Cherokees, in fact, emigrated to Spanish-controlled Louisiana as early as 1785 because they were dissatisfied with terms of the Treaty of Hopewell.[5] Indian removal received an early boost from Thomas Jefferson.

In 1802, the Jefferson administration signed a pact with Georgia by which the government agreed to extinguish Indian land claims within the state in order to settle a dispute over Georgia's claim to western lands.[6] The Louisiana Purchase soon offered the territory needed to make such an idea practical. Jefferson also recognized the value of the West as a home for eastern Indians and went so far as to propose a Constitutional Amendment authorizing this exchange.[7] Although nothing came of the amendment, Congress liked the idea and in 1804 it passed an act that authorized the president "to stipulate with any Indian tribes owning lands on the east side of the Mississippi . . . for an exchange of lands, the property of the United States, on the west side of the Mississippi."[8]

Nevertheless, the policy of Indian removal developed slowly during the first three decades of the nineteenth century. For one thing, the War of 1812 took precedence over Indian matters. In addition, President James Monroe moved cautiously in his dealings with the southern Indians, particularly the Cherokees, who found themselves under increasing pressure from Georgia during the 1820s.[9] Monroe agreed to removal but only after the establishment of "a well digested plan for their government and civilization which should be agreeable to themselves [and which] would not only shield them from impending ruin, but promote their welfare and happiness."[10] Thus Monroe argued against forced removal, promoting removal instead through a positive program designed to win Indian approval. Among other things, Monroe promised the southern tribes a government in the West that would preserve order, prevent intrusion, and stimulate civilization.[11]

The pressure for removal increased dramatically in 1828, when Andrew Jackson was elected president. Jackson, a southerner and a former Indian fighter and treaty negotiator, was sympathetic to the rights of the southern states and he let it be known that the federal government would not use its powers to defend the Five Civilized Tribes from the states.[12] By 1829, the removal debate had become a national issue. The debate reached its climax in 1830, when Congress debated and ultimately passed the Indian Removal Act, legislation designed to move all eastern Indians to the West by providing guarantees to western lands as well as funds to compensate Indians for improvements left behind.[13] In 1831, the Cherokees sought help from the courts. In *Cherokee Nation v. Georgia,* the Cherokees asked for an injunction to forestall the enforcement of Georgia laws over the tribe. United States Chief Justice John Marshall gave moral support to the Cherokees but ultimately sided with Georgia.[14] Yet in another case, *Worcester v.*

Georgia, Marshall gave the Cherokees reason for hope by recognizing the supremacy of federal treaties with the Indians, thus undermining Georgia's attempts to control the native population.[15] This hope soon turned to despair, however, when Jackson refused to enforce the court's opinion. Georgia was free to continue its anti-Cherokee policies.

This was the political climate in which the press operated. Both Georgia and the southern Indians had partisans in Congress and each side used the press to advance its cause. As a result, press coverage of this controversy followed two general trends: partisan politics, in which the papers lined up for or against Jackson according to their party politics, and a type of hands-off neutrality, in which newspapers left it to Indian sympathizers to promote the Indian cause.

The Press and the Ideology of Indian Removal

The formal debate over Indian removal took place in Congress, but it was also a heated topic in the press. This debate turned in part on the nature of the Indian character. Was the savage really noble? Indian sympathizers said yes, citing the advancements of the southern tribes. Anti-Indian writers said no, arguing that the Indians were weak, cruel, and easily corruptible. In the end, the anti-Indian arguments carried the day and the figure of the proud but doomed Noble Savage was used as powerful evidence in the removal debate. Indians were indeed vanishing, the argument went, and the best hope for their preservation was in the West, far from the vices and corruption of civilized life. The idea of the vanishing Indian grew out of a widespread belief that stronger races were meant to dominate weaker ones, just as the mound builders of prehistoric America were displaced by the current tribes of Indians.[16] This belief, articulated and explained in the press, helped justify Indian removal to Congress and the public. By promoting and repeating the idea of the vanishing Indian in print, the papers helped advance a way of thinking about Indians and their flawed character that helped make removal not only possible but absolutely necessary.

A reading of newspapers and magazines of the day confirms the popularity of the vanishing Indian idea. In 1836, for example, an Arkansas weekly reprinted from the *American Monthly Magazine* a mournful tribute to "the brave and unfortunate race," language that positioned the Indian as noble yet doomed by fate. The author promised that his Indian was not the "ferocious brute" of Cotton Mather nor the "brilliant, romantic, half-French, half-Celtic" Indian of Cooper. But like Cooper, this writer predicted the eventual demise of the Indian. The newspaper headline echoed a familiar theme: "The Last of the Iron Hearts."[17]

A small Tennessee newspaper also recalled Cooper's literary native when it published a romantic lament in 1838 called "The Last Indian." The story, unattributed but probably reprinted from a magazine, traced the retreat of the Indians as the whites moved west across the continent. Before the arrival of the whites, the writer noted, the Indian stood tall and proud. "I am the sole undisputed monarch of this Western world," the Indian said. But now, the story continued, "His form was emaciated, his countenance pale and downcast, his look wild and raving." Broken by the fate of his doomed race, the Indian at last realized the desperation of his situation and responded by casting himself into the Pacific, the sooner to meet his people in the land of the spirits. Again, the Indian's demise was inevitable and assumed. Despite this fate, the story justified itself with this optimistic conclusion: the Indian "will live on in song and story until the sun forgets to shine."[18]

The vanishing Indian was also prominent in more critical assessments of Indian society. An 1837 article in the *North American Review* praised the author of an Indian history for preserving "the scattered memorials of a people that so soon must cease to exist." The reviewer added, "There is something almost holy in the task of thus tracing out the few and faint vestiges that remain of an ill-fated race."[19] The same comment surfaced a year later when the magazine published a review of an Indian history coauthored by Thomas McKenney, the former head of the Office of Indian Affairs. The writer praised McKenney's plan "of collecting and presenting to the world authentic memorials of this race, in a form to give them perpetuity, while the race itself is fast dwindling away."[20] Such statements show how Native Americans were consciously positioned in the antebellum mind as curious but vanishing historical artifacts, not cultural or social equals. In political terms, such attitudes helped make removal acceptable by imagining Indians as rare and exotic creatures, abandoned by progress and destined to disappear, people unworthy to occupy productive land, people requiring protection and a special habitat for their very survival.

The removal debate also invoked another common belief of the day: that Indians in contact with whites quickly lost their natural virtues and took up white vices. Building on the idea of native deficiencies, this notion helped explain the Indians' fondness for strong drink and what whites saw as uncivilized behavior. Thus the "theory of vices and virtues," as one historian called it, became another justification for removal.[21] If the Indians could be preserved at all, according to this rule, it would be west of the Mississippi, where they could avoid the corrupting influences of white civilization. An 1838 reviewer confirmed this tendency, even while acknowledging the strength of the Indian character: "If [the Indian] has yielded too easily to the vices of his unwelcome neighbors, yet even these have not subdued his indomitable spirit, nor weakened his sense of dignity as a man, nor worn off the deep traces of his original character."[22] Unfortunately for the Indian, however, his "indomitable spirit," his dignity and character, did not count for much in view of the race's assigned fate, an end hastened by contact with whites.

Historian Brian Dippie has documented the vices and virtues idea, citing the popularity of *The Last of the Mohicans* as well as the writings of George Catlin.[23] Catlin, in fact, was praised in the press for his efforts to preserve the Indian race. An Arkansas paper, for example, published a page-one article on Catlin in 1838, praising his "fixed determination to reach every tribe on the continent of North America, and preserve . . . memorials to them, as well as every thing of their manufacture, for the instruction of posterity."[24]

Years earlier, Hezekiah Niles, editor of *Niles' Weekly Register,* complained that white traders encouraged the "worst passions" and "most abominable vices" among the Indians, all "for temporary advantages to be gained in trading with them."[25] When the long-running dispute between Georgia and the Cherokees heated up, the governor of Georgia, George Gilmer, also voiced the vices and virtues argument. In a letter published in the *Register* in 1830, Gilmer wrote, "The Cherokees have lost all that was valuable in their character, have become spiritless, dependent and depraved."[26] Gilmer also invoked the laws of nature in reaching this result: "It was the power of the whites and their children among the Cherokees, that destroyed the ancient laws, customs, and authority of the tribe. . . . From the character of the people and the causes operating upon them, it could not have been otherwise."[27] From political leaders and from early students of Indian culture, the lesson about Indian-white contact was clear: Indians had to be segregated because their preservation demanded it. For its part, the press reinforced the vices and virtues idea by repeating it often and without objection, an action that further confirmed the "truth" of the theory. The vices and virtues theory was used in the press to justify Indian removal; it was hardly the cruel deed its critics claimed, but rather a humanitarian act designed to save what was left of the Noble American.[28]

Niles' Weekly Register and the Redeemable Native

Another important way of thinking about the Noble Savage centered not on extinction or corruption but on salvation. Indians might be pagan savages, but a minority of Americans believed that Indians could be saved from extinction and properly civilized. This idea was especially popular with Christian missionary societies, such as the American Board of Commissioners for Foreign Missions, who believed their work in America was to civilize Indians by bringing them the Gospel and educating them in the work habits and personal virtues of nineteenth-century Protestantism.[29]

Within the press, *Niles' Register* was a long-standing advocate of Indian civilization. Founded in 1811 by Hezekiah Niles, the *Weekly Register* was a forerunner of the weekly news magazine and its contents included government reports, important correspondence, and political speeches on a variety of national issues. Niles's editorial energy and fairness distinguished his publication. Journalism historians Michael and Edwin Emery, for example, credit Niles for his "common sense, integrity, and . . . flair for concise reporting on current trends."[30] In addition, Niles tried to provide serious, balanced coverage of controversial issues, thus becoming an early practitioner of "objective" journalism. This policy, along with his personal honesty, allowed Niles to recognize native achievements when he saw them and to express his findings in print. Thus Niles praised the conduct of a group of Cherokee chiefs when they visited Washington in 1819: "These chiefs, by their manners and deportment, exhibit a practical proof, to those who may have had doubts on that head, that the natives of this country only want the means of improvement to place them on an equality with the intelligent part of our citizens."[31] The *Register* also urged support for southern missionaries, lending support to the notion that Indians could be Christianized and educated in the ways of white civilization.[32] In addition, Niles supported an idea, attributed to Jefferson, that the Indians could be civilized by a commitment to agriculture. Therefore, he editorialized against traders who "would have them to rely on the chase, to obtain skins, and keep them in the most abject want and depravity, to compel them to dispose of their spoils at reduced prices—especially in exchange for ardent liquors, which the natives are unhappily too fond of."[33] In short, *Niles' Weekly Register* reflected another familiar belief of the time: the Indians could be civilized—if they pursued farming instead of hunting and if they received Christian instruction from the church as well as protection from unscrupulous whites.

But this attitude—paternalism—again put the Indians in an inferior position. If Indians could be saved, it was because Indians needed to be saved—from extinction, from corruption, and from savagery. While this was true enough—white economics and culture had already disrupted existing Indian ways[34]—paternalism did not permit a full consideration of the "Indian problem" from the Indian point of view. Thus even the well-meaning concern for Indians in *Niles' Weekly Register* positioned them as "poor Indians" and promoted the idea that they were unable to take care of themselves and needed the support and protection of whites, whose self-appointed duty it was to decide what was best for Indians.[35]

Although *Niles' Weekly Register* and other publications honestly tried to support the southern tribes, their paternalism often worked against the best interests of the natives. The press, like most of its readers, assumed that Indians needed help and that their physical and spiritual salvation required major changes in their character and beliefs. Following the logic of the vanishing Indian, these changes could be practiced best across the Mississippi, away from the corrupting influence of a growing population and the expanding plantation economy of the South. The sympathetic press, like the anti-Indian papers, helped clear the way for Indian removal by corroborating the idea of the vanishing Indian and advocating a paternalistic attitude toward Indian life. In short, the ideas popularized both by the pro- and anti-Indian press served the same general end: to separate the Indian from the white majority by emphasizing the predetermined characteristics of the race—especially its unhappy fate and its host of perceived weaknesses and faults. In this way the southern tribes were defined in the press by a set of characteristics that made it impossible, in political terms, for the Indians to receive fair and equal treatment in the South.

Indians as Political Weapons

With an issue as controversial and complex as Indian removal, it is hardly surprising that politics soon became a significant force in news coverage of the issue. In fact, removal became a highly partisan issue during the 1829 Congressional debate over the Indian Removal Bill. The Democrats, of course, were solidly behind the bill, following the president. The Democratic position held, among other things, that the southern Indians were primarily hunters, unable to become farmers and industrious citizens.[36] The National Republicans or Whigs, on the other hand, sought to embarrass Jackson over the Indian issue and thereby gain support for their leader,

Henry Clay. They and their missionary allies argued that the Indians could be converted into farmers and businessmen, a position bolstered by the success of tribal elites, leaders who had already built impressive homes, farms, and businesses in the South.[37] In any event, the party press split along predictable lines, with each side attempting to explain its ideas about Indians and removal in the most favorable light.[38]

More interesting, however, was the political use of removal in the South, where anti-Indian feeling was strong. An illustration of the power of politics in the southern press comes from the Milledgeville [Ga.] *Recorder.* Given its location—Milledgeville was then the state capitol—the newspaper usually supported Jackson, who was Georgia's strongest ally in Cherokee removal. But even Jackson did not move fast enough for the Georgians. Thus an 1835 editorial about a new Cherokee treaty defended John Ross, the Cherokee chief involved, and went on to point out the real culprit: "Why did General Jackson thus hastily and petulantly break up the only feasible arrangement by which Georgia can obtain her rights?"[39] The point of the editorial was not to defend Ross but to prick Jackson and thus assert Georgia's right to evict the Cherokees.

The Augusta [Ga.] *State-Rights' Sentinel* also reflected this political use of Indians. In August 1835, it reprinted the speech of Col. David Crockett, an outspoken critic of his fellow Tennessean, Andrew Jackson, and a Whig candidate for Congress. In this speech, Crockett accused the president of misunderstanding the Constitution, especially in regard to the Removal Act of 1830. "By this bill a handful of Indians were smashed up. Are we justified in this because we are a great and mighty people? In the name of God, if we are great, let us be gracious."[40] This statement expressed real concern for the southern Indians. Yet in the context of a political campaign, it is also clear that the Indians were being used as political ammunition against the Jackson administration.

Back in Washington, the political uses of the Indians served both pro- and anti-Indian forces. In June 1836, the Washington *Globe,* an organ of the Jackson administration, attacked those in Congress who supported the southern Indians against removal. But the same article went on to reprint charges from the *Journal of Commerce* that the government itself caused the Seminole War by making unfair claims to slaves held by the Indians. Wrote an anonymous correspondent: "The Government recognized the claim, and sent agents into Seminole country to kidnap the children of the Seminoles thus claimed as slaves. Our Secretary of War ordered the movement. The Government was advised that this measure would lead to hostilities, but it was persisted in." The writer concluded his argument with a sweeping indictment of administration policies: "When the document and developments to which I allude shall be published, this Government will stand before the nations of the earth, as the most faithless and contemptible that ever held a control over destinies of man."

In such partisan attacks, the southern Indians were almost irrelevant, since the purpose of these stories was less to defend the Indians than to attack the administration. These stories might have helped the southern tribes indirectly by keeping their problems before the reading public. But it seems equally clear that the effect of partisan politics on Indian removal was to reduce the powerful moral issues involved in the treatment of Indians to less compelling political issues in which the southern Indians were only of passing interest.

The case of the "William Penn" essays represents another aspect of the press's political role in the removal debate. This series of twenty-four essays was a thorough and eloquent defense of Cherokee rights. It was published in Washington's *National Intelligencer* between 5 August and 19 December 1829, and reprinted in a number of other newspapers.[41] The essays, signed by "William Penn," were the work of Jeremiah Evarts, an 1802 Yale graduate and devoted friend of the Indians. Evarts was a Christian activist and became acquainted with Indian issues through the American Board of Commissioners for Foreign Missions. He was also a religious journalist, editing a religious monthly called the *Panoplist*. Later, this journal became the *Missionary Herald,* the organ of the American Board.[42]

Despite his editorial work in religious publications, Evarts sought a wider audience for his anti-removal message and he promoted his message in terms that would appeal to all newspapers, even those aligned with Jackson. Thus Evarts stressed the news value of his essays, the *"pending and ripening controversy* between the United States and the Indians."[43] Evarts then made eight points designed to induce the *Intelligencer* and other papers to publish his articles. He began by pointing out the news values of the upcoming debate: "1. This is a subject which must be abundantly discussed in our country. 2. It will be among the most important, and probably the most contested, business of the 21st Congress."[44] In an effort to make his message more palatable to pro-Jackson editors or others who might take offense at his anti-administration message, Evarts assured the editors that his discussions would not "assume a party character at all." Those in power would be discussed "in a respectful manner," he noted. In regard to Jackson, Evarts wrote: "Though I think the President has greatly mistaken his powers and his duty, in regard to the Indians, I have no wish concerning him, but that he may be wise and judicious ruler of our growing republic."[45] Evarts was also mindful of the need for publication of his articles in small, rural papers: "I propose to furnish two numbers a week, that they may be copied into semi-weekly papers, if their editors see fit."[46]

Evarts's campaign on behalf of the Cherokees was a product of his own initiative and tied to his deeply held religious and moral beliefs. To the extent the newspapers published his essays, they aided the cause of the Indians. But many newspapers did not publish Evarts's work and many of those that did were religious newspapers, which reached an audience already predisposed to support the Indian cause.[47] It is significant, too, that the mainstream press did not originate this pro-Indian campaign and there is little evidence that the American press as a whole shared either Evarts's moral convictions or his ideas about removal. For, as we shall see, the press was also willing to publish the views of other writers, many of them less sympathetic to the Indian cause.

There was, however, a continuing show of sympathy for the plight of the Indians in *Niles' Weekly Register.* Most importantly perhaps, the *Register* put Indians on the news agenda, expressing faith both in the race and in their place in the news columns. In 1820, the *Register* declared, "We shall not neglect this subject—for we are deeply interested in the incorporation of this people into our own improved society."[48] This attitude made Hezekiah Niles and the *Register* one of the most consistent voices of Indian sympathy in the early nineteenth century. In 1830, for example, the *Register* found irony in the fact that Georgia sought to count Cherokees for the purpose of taxation and the census but would not recognize them as citizens of the state. In its understated conclusion, the paper said, "There would appear to be a difficulty here, that has not been fully appreciated."[49]

In addition, *Niles' Weekly Register* frequently reprinted editorials from the *Cherokee Phoenix,* thus expanding the audience for the Cherokees' own newspaper voice.[50] When the debate over the Indian Removal Act was heating up in the spring of 1830, the *Register* published a memorial from the *Phoenix* that protested the extension of Georgia laws over the tribe and asked for the right to self-rule under federal treaties.[51] The paper followed this column with the text of the offending laws. One section of the law made it impossible for the Indians to win a legal dispute with whites since it prohibited any Creek or Cherokee from acting as a "competent witness in any court of this state to which a white person may be a party, except such white person resides within the said [Cherokee] nation."[52] By publishing such documents, the *Register* revealed the unfairness of the Georgia legislature and made the Cherokee grievances against Georgia more understandable and dramatic.

Despite this sympathetic treatment, *Niles' Weekly Register* was not one-sided in its treatment of Native Americans. With the Cherokees, as with other subjects, the magazine was interested in presenting both sides of the issue.[53] Indeed, the *Register* did not take a strong editorial position on removal, despite Niles's personal opposition to the policy. The Georgia side of the controversy received prominent play in the press, including the *Register*. In September 1830, for example, the *Register* reprinted, without comment, a letter from the *Georgia Journal* supporting the state and attacking the federal government for its lack of resolve. The writer, who identified himself only as "Hancock," was tired of waiting for a resolution to the problem: "The abortive attempt recently made by gen. Jackson to remove the Indians from our territory, throws us back upon our own resources; and their insolent reply that they would never cede another foot of land for the use of Georgia, demands the united efforts of our people in vindication of their rights."[54] Hancock was clear in his resolve: "As one citizen of Georgia, I am not prepared to give it up—I should go for the territory, the whole territory, and nothing but the territory."[55]

The same issue of the *Register* also contained correspondence between Baltimore lawyer William Wirt, a former United States attorney general and an advocate for the Cherokees, and George Gilmer, governor of Georgia, also taken from the *Georgia Journal*. In its editorial note published over the letters, the *Journal* ridiculed the legal claims of the Cherokees:

> Has it come to this, that a sovereign and independent state is to be insulted, by being asked to become a party, before the supreme court, with a few savages, residing on her own territory!!!—Unparalleled impudence.
>
> As we suggest in another part of this paper, we verily expect that the next movement will be an attempt on the part of the Cherokee nation to extend the Indian laws over the people of Georgia.[56]

Wirt's letter to Gilmer was polite and restrained but Gilmer's reply was hostile both to the lawyer and the Cherokees. For instance, Gilmer disputed Wirt's contention that the Cherokee leaders were gentlemen. Gilmer said, "They are not Indians however, but the children of white men,"[57] a charge directed against Chief John Ross, who was one-eighth Cherokee, and a number of other tribal leaders. The real Indians, Gilmer claimed, were corrupted by the unscrupulous whites. The solution, according to Gilmer, was for the Indians to concede to the rule of the state, which would grant citizenship to those "capable of performing its duties" and remove those who were "ignorant and idle" to a situation "where the inducements to action will be more in accordance with the character of the Cherokee people."[58]

The exchange between Wirt and Gilmer was published not only in the *Georgia Journal* but also in the Baltimore *Gazette* and the Philadelphia *American*.[59] The letters provided both sides of the dispute, a hallmark of "objective" journalism. But by publishing these letters without editorial comment, Niles sidestepped an issue that he obviously cared about, and steered *Niles' Weekly Register* toward a safer, more neutral position, less likely to offend the paper's more partisan readers and advertisers.

Even in 1838, just a few months before the final round-up of the eastern Cherokees, the *Register* presented two sides of the removal debate. When several Cherokee memorials against removal were presented in the Senate on 15 May, the *Register* included a detailed summary of the objections made by Senator Wilson Lumpkin of Georgia. Citing a letter from John Ridge, a Cherokee leader who had already emigrated, Lumpkin emphasized the "happy and contented" condition of the western Cherokees and criticized John Ross, chief of the eastern nation. Senator Davis of Massachusetts answered that the memorialists did not question "the richness and pleasantness of the [western] country," but objected to the enforcement of a removal treaty that did not represent the majority of the tribe and that forced them to emigrate against their will.[60]

As before, both sides got ample space in *Niles' Weekly Register*. This early effort at "objectivity" probably helped the native cause. Specifically, it offered Niles a way to publish the Indian side of the controversy without opening himself to charges of unfairness to his anti-Indian readers. After all, they also got their say in the *Register*. Nevertheless, Niles was limited by his balanced approach, unable to fully commit his paper to the Indian cause. To do so—to campaign vigorously on behalf of the Indians—would surely have risked his self-appointed position as a neutral recorder of national events, the core editorial purpose of his publication. For this reason, the *Register*, a publication generally sympathetic to Native Americans, was less effective than it might have been in revealing the problems of Indian removal and forestalling the ultimate tragedy of the Trail of Tears.

The Sympathetic Impulse

Despite politics and the tendency of the press to ignore Indian problems altogether, some concerned reporting on the southern tribes appeared in the antebellum press. Many reports came from northern visitors to the South, especially from churchmen and missionaries interested in "civilizing" the southern tribes. Such reporting was often paternalistic. Yet this unofficial and informal news-gathering process offered something the "official" political bickering did not—graphic and detailed reports on Indian removal and its consequences.

In 1830, *Niles' Weekly Register* reprinted a story on Colonel Gold of Connecticut, whose daughter had married Elias Boudinot, editor of the *Cherokee Phoenix* and a graduate of the Foreign Mission School in Cornwall, Connecticut. Gold was enthusiastic about life in the Cherokee Nation and reported that most Cherokees "live in comfort, and many of them in affluence and splendor."[61] Gold also noted the industry of the people, their improvements to the land, the Christian education of their children, and even the quality of their roads. "He also attended the meeting of their general council and was astonished at the order and regularity of their business, and the talent displayed by their members." That Gold was surprised by the affluence and industry of the Cherokee people—and was even "astonished" by their business meeting—reveals his lack of faith in the Cherokee character before he arrived in the South. Nevertheless, Gold's report to the paper concluded on an optimistic note: "Every thing detailed to us, relative to the Cherokees, affords strong evidence that the wandering Indian has been converted into the industrious husbandman; and the tomahawk and rifle are exchanging for the plough, the hoe, the wheel, and the loom, and that they are rapidly acquiring domestic habits, and attaining a degree of civilization that was entirely unexpected, from the natural disposition of these children of the forest."[62] Although thoroughly paternalistic, this report is representative of the most positive news accounts about Cherokees in the 1830s and it probably reflected the attitudes of many Indian sympathizers.

Yet positive attitudes were far from universal, even among northern whites. Colonel Gold, for example, so impressed with Cherokee life in 1830, was unimpressed with the prospect of a Cherokee son-in-law in 1824 and he initially refused permission for his daughter's marriage to Boudinot. More dramatically, the citizens of Cornwall rallied on the village green and burned the couple in effigy. The same response greeted Boudinot's cousin,

John Ridge, when he married a white woman from Cornwall earlier the same year. That marriage prompted the editor of the Litchfield *American Eagle* to reflect on the "affliction, mortification, and disgrace of the relatives of the young woman . . . who has thus made herself a *squaw,* and connected her race to a race of Indians."[63] True to form, *Niles' Weekly Register* defended the Gold-Boudinot marriage. Nevertheless, the uproar in Cornwall undermined local support for the Foreign Mission School and it closed just a few months after the ceremony.[64] In short, racism was not confined to the southern states, a fact that helps explain the paternalism and occasional hostility expressed in the northern newspapers.

Despite such attitudes, a good deal of the press sympathy for the Cherokees came from northern newspapers, especially religious papers that had a long interest in the mission work in the South. Thus the New York *Observer,* a Presbyterian journal, followed with particular interest the legal battle between Georgia and two missionaries, S. A. Worcester and Elizur Butler, a case that eventually went to the Supreme Court.[65] In addition, the writings of Cherokee leader Elias Boudinot were published in *The Missionary Herald,* whose editor, Jeremiah Evarts, wrote the "William Penn" essays. At various times during the 1820s and 1830s, Boudinot was also published in the Boston *Recorder,* a Congregationalist newspaper, and the *Religious Remembrancer,* a Presbyterian weekly in Philadelphia, and several other journals.[66] Such publicity helped boost support for the Cherokees—if not the other southern tribes—among a group of Christian activists in the North. But Boudinot himself was skeptical that these activists could carry the day for the Indians. In an 1829 letter, he confessed: "There is not, in my opinion, a sufficient degree of interest for the welfare of the Aborigines in the United States, even in the Christian Community, to save them from oppression."[67]

The case of the Cherokees also generated some significant sympathy in the southern papers, even in Georgia, where anti-Cherokee feeling was strong. In 1835, the Augusta paper ran a long letter from "a gentleman of New York, now traveling in the up country of Georgia."[68] This writer, who was not identified, was concerned both about abolition and the rights of the Cherokees. Concerning the Indians, he wrote: "Nothing has been spared to dislodge them from their country, and the miserable pittance of land left them for a temporary abiding place has been taken from them by the most arbitrary an[d] unjust means."[69] Significantly, the writer believed the power of publicity might bring relief to the Indians: "I do not believe that the good people of Georgia are acquainted with the proceedings that are carrying on among these poor injured and destitute people."[70] In short, this writer called on Georgians to help the Cherokees, people he described as "defenceless creatures . . . set adrift upon a friendless community to exist as they can." He added, "It is enough to draw tears from stones to listen to the wrongs of this once brave and now persecuted people."[71]

More pointedly, this writer identified Bishop, an Indian agent, as one of the causes of the Cherokee trouble. Bishop acted as a European monarch, the writer claimed. "He has lately seized some half dozen of the most respectable heads of the Cherokee nation, and pinioned their arms behind them . . . for no other crime but that of inspecting their lands with a view to assess a value on them preparatory to the holding of a treaty with the government."[72] This article, and a handful of others like it, were outspoken in their defense of the Indians. But like the William Penn essays, these articles came from outside, unofficial correspondents, usually missionaries or travelers who had a personal interest in Indian improvement.[73] The newspapers themselves demonstrated concern for the cause of the Indians by publishing such letters but southern editors did not usually go on to write their own editorials supporting the Indian cause.

As the debate progressed, the press interest in the removal controversy shifted. Although the Cherokees continued to resist in the courts and the Seminoles continued to fight removal from the Florida swamps, much of the press was less concerned with the morality of removal policy than with news of the removal itself. By the late 1830s, the Indian removal story was shaped not so much by moral arguments or politics as by an evolving system of news values and the news-gathering practices of the papers.

News Values and Indian Removal

By the mid-1830s, American newspaper editors were familiar with the concept of Indian removal. Indian emigration, after all, had become increasingly controversial as the decade progressed because it was forced upon unwilling tribal leaders, men who had little choice but to sign away the tribal lands and hope for the best in Indian Territory. In the case of the Cherokees, the removal took on added interest because of the stature of the tribe and their long legal battle with Georgia and the United States government. Thus, the final stages of Indian removal held great news potential and could have been reported in a detailed emotional, even sensational, fashion.

Despite this dramatic potential, Indian removal was not treated as a sensational or even a particularly important news story by most of the press. Instead, the papers frequently treated Indian removal as a simple transportation story, emphasizing such details as the name of the steamboat and its time of arrival at a particular place. There were exceptions, of course, but most of the news about the climactic events of Indian removal was in the form of brief, routine reports that overlooked the dramatic aspects of forced removal, robbed the story of its tragic elements, and, in effect, closed off the debate over the morality of the removal policy.

News concerning the removal of the southern Indians appeared and disappeared frequently throughout the 1830s according to a variety of factors. Although *Niles' Weekly Register* reported on Indian issues frequently, stories of Indian violence were more common in most other newspapers and such stories helped shut out less dramatic reports on the southern tribes and their removal. Grant Foreman noted this imbalance in Indian news when he chronicled the last stages of the Chickasaw removal. This removal was, Foreman concluded, a "comparatively tranquil affair, and there is little to be found about it in the contemporary press, which gave much space to the Seminole war then raging."[74] Even in the 1830s, violence, not tranquillity, was the stuff of news.

This pattern was widely followed in the press. In Annapolis, for example, the weekly Maryland *Gazette* had no apparent interest in Indians and the paper did not publish the William Penn essays in 1829. But when the Seminole War heated up in 1837, the Annapolis paper reprinted reports of Indian violence from the Norfolk and Savannah newspapers.[75] In 1838, however, news of the Cherokee removal was mentioned only through the publication of Gen. Winfield Scott's address to the Cherokees, an official document that reflected Scott's concerns, not the plight of the Indians.[76]

The *United States Gazette,* a Philadelphia newspaper, revealed the Indian news agenda during the 1830s more dramatically. In early 1836, the newspaper began a series of Indian stories reprinted from southern and eastern newspapers. "We regret to learn that the Territory of Florida has become the theater of a petty war, in which already the blood of Indians and whites has been shed," the paper announced on 5 January 1836.[77] Later that month, the newspaper reported details of the growing controversy from two other papers, the Baltimore *American* and the Charleston *Courier.*[78] By the end of January, the *Gazette* was reporting the war in the inflammatory words of the Jacksonville *Courier:* "The whole of East Florida is in danger."[79] This story soon became a first-person narrative designed to arouse support from whites in other states: "It is the general opinion, that unless adequate aid is immediately extended to us, the whole of

Florida, east of the Sawanees River, will be inevitably ruined. We must not only abandon our property to destruction, but, stripped of all our hard earnings, must fight for our lives, our women and our children."[80] This was a dramatic appeal, of course, and it probably represented white attitudes in East Florida concerning the Seminole War. But what of the Seminoles? In the pages of the *Gazette,* they too were viewed—when they were viewed at all—from the perspective of the Florida settlers. Thus the January 1836 issues of the *Gazette* included reports of Indian savagery. One story noted that Charles, a head chief, had agreed to abide by an 1832 removal treaty but that nine Seminole warriors—men "determined to die, arms in hand, on the soil of their forefathers"—entered the council and "discharged nine bullets in the heart of Charles."[81] In another story, the writer focused on the barbarity of an Indian attack: "Through Gen. Thompson were shot fifteen bullets, and sixteen through Rogers. The Indians scalped all, taking off the scalp clear around the head as far as the hair extended, and then beating in their skulls. The heads of Rogers and Suggs were shockingly mangled."[82] With news of this type coming out of the war, it is not surprising that the Seminoles received bad press in 1836. What is more significant is the fact that such news dominated the news coverage of southern Indians in the mid-1830s. That is, violence and barbarity were the themes of most news stories concerning Indians. Stories about peaceful Indians or stories expressing concern for Indians facing removal were, by contrast, much less common.

In the *Gazette,* Gen. Winfield Scott's gathering the Cherokees in the late spring of 1838 was not big news. A removal story published in June 1838 summed up the controversy in one sentence: "The Milledgeville [Ga.] papers say that General Scott has received orders not to enforce the treaty with the Cherokees." Despite the alarming implications of this statement, the paper made no comment about the report.[83] In July 1838 the *Gazette* published General Scott's 10 May address to the Cherokees, again without comment.[84] By the end of July, when the Cherokees had been subdued and collected, the *Gazette* noted this fact in a typical report from Tennessee that focused on the movement of the Indians but failed to consider their conditions: "The Athens (Tenn.) Journal of the 4th inst. says, 'several detachments of Cherokees have passed through this place within the last two weeks. . . . This last detachment, we understand, pretty nearly completes the emigration from North Carolina. The great body of the Cherokees are now collected and will be ready on the first of September to set out for their new homes West of the Mississippi.' "[85] As before, the *Gazette* published this story without editorial comment. Thus the final round-up of the Cherokee people—a story with built-in drama and great news value—was limited to short dispatches and an official Army message about the removal. Such coverage minimized Cherokee evictions and suffering during the summer of 1838. Moreover, the underemphasis of removal news was all the more distorted when compared against the frequent and alarming reports of Indian violence earlier in the decade. Indian news was defined largely in terms of Indian violence against whites; the problems and suffering of the southern tribes were not seen as particularly newsworthy. In this way, the antebellum press further distorted the identity of the southern Indians.

News Routines and Indian Cargo

By 1834, four years before the last of the Cherokees traveled west, the Arkansas *Gazette* reduced emigration to one sentence: "About 540 emigrating Cherokees, from the old nation, east of the Mississippi, passed up the Arkansas a few days ago, in charge of lieut. Harris, U.S.A., on board the steamboat Thomas Yeatman, on their way to join their brethren west of this territory."[86] This pattern—de-emphasizing the tragic aspects of the move—continued during the removal years.[87] Two years later, for example, the weekly in Helena, Arkansas, reported Creek emigration in nearly identical terms: "Emigrating Creeks.—The Steamboat Daniel Webster, arrived here on Tuesday last, with a small party of Creek Indians, mostly women and children with wagons. They have encamped a short distance from this place, awaiting the arrival of the balance of their party, with horses, to convey them to their destination."[88] Still another story, this one in 1837 in a Tennessee weekly, followed the transportation model of an Arkansas paper: "Migration of Indians.—The Little Rock Times of the 5th inst. states that the steamboat Black Hawk arrived at that place on the Wednesday previous, having on board about 500 Creek Indians, under the charge of Lt. Deas, U.S. Army."[89] These three stories, from different papers at different times, are notable for what they say and what they do not. Each provides the name of the steamer on which the Indians traveled and two give the name of the officer in charge. But not one of the stories provides the name of a single Indian nor do they report on the conditions, health, or attitudes of the emigrants. In addition, the primary theme of all three paragraphs is transportation, a logistical concern that obscured the human tragedies of the removal.

This theme carried over in editorials about removal, many of which were concerned less with the Indians than with the efficiency of their removal. An 1837 story in the Little Rock newspaper the *Weekly Times* reported on three different parties of Indians, all of whom passed through town within a few days. Said the paper, "This is driving the emigration with a proper spirit."[90] There was also an editorial tendency to see Indian emigration as successful and noncontroversial, notwithstanding the hardships endured by the Indians. When a group of emigrating Choctaws crossed Arkansas during the winter of 1831–32, Capt. Jacob Brown, their leader, reported: "This unexpected cold weather must produce much human suffering. Our poor emigrants, many of them quite naked, and without much shelter, must suffer, it is impossible to do otherwise; and my great fears are that many of them will get frosted."[91] In February 1832, moreover, rains soaked the Arkansas roads and they became impassable, further prolonging Choctaw suffering. Yet this was not the story told in the Arkansas *Gazette*. "Surprisingly, in complete contradiction of the facts," historian Arthur DeRosier noted, "the Arkansas *Gazette* reported to its readers at this time that the Choctaws appeared to be cheerful, content, and well supplied with food and clothing."[92]

By such means, Indian removal was handled in the press as a routine occurrence, not especially newsworthy in and of itself. Indians became, in effect, mere cargo in transit from east to west. With few correspondents or missionaries along to tell the human story, the typical story generated by Indian removal centered on the logistics of emigration and lacked any hint of moral or political debate. Perhaps this was a natural conclusion, given the long public debate over removal that had already occurred. But whatever the reason, the "transportation model" of Indian removal was common in papers that covered the story.

Press accounts of Indian removal were also notable for their de-emphasis of Indian leaders. Given the ethnocentrism of the press, it is not unusual that individual Indians rarely made news in the 1830s. But some Indians were household words at the time, known mostly for their hostility. Thus the Seminole chief Osceola gained widespread newspaper coverage at his death in 1837. The Milledgeville *Federal Union* described the chief as a "savage, treacherous, murderer."[93] A similar obituary, this one in the Charleston (S.C.) *Mercury,* praised Osceola's abilities, even those that were turned against white settlers in Florida. "From a vagabond child he became the master spirit of a long and desperate war," the paper said. It also described Osceola as "bold and decisive in action, deadly but consistent in hatred, dark in revenge, cool, subtle, sagacious in council."[94] In contrast to Osceola, thousands of less violent Indians moving across the South were assigned only a tribal identity and rarely singled out by name.

An atypical report published in an Arkansas paper in 1838 noted the passage of seven hundred Seminoles up the Arkansas River a few miles below Little Rock. The report identified the two officers in charge of the expedition as well as three Seminole chiefs: Micanopy, Cloud, and Nocoseola, though no details about the chiefs were included.[95] More typical was a story from the same paper the following week that reported the passage of another group of Indians without a single name: "117 Seminoles from Florida, passed up the Arkansas River last week."[96]

Even the eminence John Ross, the respected Cherokee chief who had made much news in his long fight against Georgia, did not generate a full discussion of removal. When Ross and a final party of Cherokees crossed Kentucky on the now-infamous Trail of Tears, a news report provided only minimum coverage: "The Last of the Cherokees.—The Princeton (Ky.) Examiner, of the 15th inst., states that the last detachment of the Cherokees, 1800 in number, had encamped within two miles of that village. Mr. John Ross, their principal chief, was with the detachment.—Thirteen thousand, in all, had passed through that place."[97] This group of Cherokees was especially newsworthy. Ross was one of the most famous of the Cherokees and his transit west represented the final chapter in a decade of controversy surrounding Indian removal. Despite such details—as well as the hardships of an overland journey in winter—this news report included no background about Ross, his party, or their conditions.

If Ross could not get news coverage alive, another emigrating Indian produced news in death. White Path, described in the press as "a distinguished chief of the Cherokee Tribe," died near Hopkinsville, Kentucky, in late 1838. The Hopkinsville *Gazette* described his burial in detail. The paper was especially interested in his monument, "a tall pole with a flag of white linen attached to it," and the paper could not resist a romantic conclusion to his story:

White Path will no more mingle in the councils of his nation, or hear the battle cry.

"The warrior's cold and lowly laid,
His foeman's dread, his people's aid."[98]

Names make news—an old journalistic practice—was true even in 1838.

But in the case of the southern Indians, the rule applied more to the dead—who could be safely romanticized like White Path or berated like Osceola—than to the living, who were still suffering at the hands of the whites. With news defined in this way, individual Indians as well as Indian leaders involved in the western emigration were reduced in stature or ignored by the news-making process of the 1830s.

Sources of Removal News

News of Indian removal came to the press from several sources. Some of the most interesting reports, as noted above, were in the form of private letters from visitors to the South, letters that described the human tragedy faced by the southern tribes. But the day-to-day removal news came in the form of official correspondence and these reports offered a different view of the emigration process. As one would expect, official reports focused attention on the administrative details of removal and usually minimized the human aspects of the story.

The reliance on official sources was widespread throughout the removal years. In fact, news based on official correspondence and speeches was a mainstay in American journalism in the early decades of the century. Since the modern idea of the government reporter had not yet fully evolved, newspapers relied on Congressional debates, presidential addresses, and similar official reports to inform the public about executive and legislative decisions, diplomacy, and other government actions. These documents were frequently published verbatim on the front pages, often without editorial comment. In the case of Indian removal, political and military leaders had easy—often automatic—access to the news columns and were in the position of dominating the news agenda simply by making their speeches or letters available to the newspapers.

In this era, the speeches of the president were often published in full in the newspapers, even on the frontier. When Jackson's successor, Martin Van Buren, addressed the nation in late 1837, the speech was a major story in the Helena (Ark.) *Constitutional Journal.* Van Buren used the speech to tout the success of Indian removal. "These [removal] measures have been attended thus far with the happiest results," the president noted. He also described the success of the Choctaws and the western Cherokees: "The improvements in their condition has [*sic*] been rapid."[99] In particular, Van Buren recognized that removal had helped preserve the Indians because it had protected them "from those associations and evil practices which exert so pernicious and destructive an influence over their destinies." Not only that, but removal helped foster a more civilized existence: "They can be induced to labor, and to acquire property, and its acquisition will inspire them with a feeling of independence.—Their minds can be cultivated, and they can be taught the value of uniform laws, be made sensible of the blessings of free Government, and capable of enjoying its advantages."[100] The wide publication of such ideas and their easy acceptance in the press reinforced the legitimacy of Indian removal and reassured readers that the policy's aims were humane.

During the summer of 1838, when General Scott was rounding up the last of the Cherokees, much of the news about this event originated from the War Department or from Scott himself. General Scott's address to the Cherokees, for instance, was probably the most widely published report on Cherokee removal, appearing in newspapers that published almost no other news of Cherokee removal in 1838.[101] In middle Tennessee, where the Cherokees were of great public interest, official correspondence and government reports on removal were common in the pages of the *Cumberland Presbyterian*[102] in Nashville and the *Western Weekly Review* in Franklin. As the Cherokees sought to stop military action against them in the spring of 1838, the *Review* published the War Department's "Call for Volunteers" addressed to Governor Cannon as well as Cannon's acknowledgment of the order and his promise "that such force as may be required by General Scott, will be furnished promptly."[103] A few weeks later, the paper followed up the progress of the Tennessee volunteers by publishing another Scott letter to the governor. Said the *Review*: "We have been permitted to copy the following letter from Major General Scott, to his Excellency, Gov'r Cannon. It conveys the gratifying intelligence that the Tennessee Volunteers are about to be discharged, and may soon be looked for at home."[104] By publishing official correspondence, the *Review* and other papers helped their readers understand the actions of government officials. But the heavy use of such sources also tended to distort the full picture of Indian removal by focusing attention on government actions rather than the people affected by those actions.

But not all documents were unfavorable to the Indians. Indeed, the Indians and their supporters also gave speeches and produced correspondence that generated wide news coverage. Thus the same issue of the *Review* that included the government's "Call for Volunteers" also included, on page one, the latest Cherokee memorial to Congress, an official tribal document that presented the Cherokee side of the issue.[105] As with most other documents, the memorial was published without editorial comment. Nevertheless, the prominent display of this memorial is evidence that the *Review* was open to the Cherokee cause, at least when it arrived in an official form.

The Human Story

If much of the removal news was routine and underplayed, there were still some reports that told the story of removal in more gripping detail. Though Indian removal produced relatively few such stories, scattered reports did find their way into print. Many of these reports were private letters from individuals who were outraged at the removal activities that they witnessed in the south. Other reports were more routine. But in both cases, the full story of the removal emerged only in bits and pieces, a form that undermined its power among the reading public as well as its political consequences.

The tragedy of removal came through in this July 1836 report from the Montgomery *Advertiser.* It started with the familiar transportation details: "About 3 thousand Indians left our wharves on Thursday last, on board the steamboats Lewis Cass and Meridan, for their destined home across the Mississippi, under charge of Lieutenant Barry, of the United States Army." But this story went on to comment on the prospects for the emigrating Indians: "From the inauspicious season of the year, and the crowded state of the boats, it is but reasonable to expect that the Indians will, on route, suffer from disease. We look forward to such result, but hope for a different one."[106]

Other stories did more than hope. On some occasions, the official version of Indian removal was undermined by reports of tragedy or mismanagement during the removal process. The New Orleans *True American* raised such issues when it questioned the motives of the removal contractors in an 1837 report on the collision of two steam ships. According to the paper, three hundred of the six hundred Creeks aboard the steamer *Monmouth* drowned in the accident. The newspaper blamed greedy contractors: "The avaricious disposition to increase the profits on the speculation, first induced the chartering of rotten, old and unseaworthy boats, because they were of a class to be procured cheaply; and then to make those increased profits still larger, the Indians were packed upon these crazy vessels in such crowds that not the slightest regard seems to have been paid to their safety, comfort, or even decency."[107] The paper went on to ask,

"Why is such a thing permitted?" The *True American* thought the answer was obvious: "The only reason we can assign for conduct such as this, is, that avarice had so blinded all parties concerned, the *mere Indians* were not considered passengers, but were stowed away as cargo, or thought of only as ballast for the boat."[108] Other papers too raised questions about the conduct of the removal, with most criticism directed at the contractors.

The most alarming news about removal came out of the final round-up of Cherokees during the summer of 1838. More than the other southern tribes, the Cherokees were highly regarded for their rapid advancement and their removal, despite such progress, struck some Americans as unfair. In addition, their long legal battle with Georgia—and their continuing mistreatment by the state—had won the tribe many friends and sympathizers, especially among Whig papers in the North. In Albany, New York, for example, the Cherokees found a consistent support in the pages of a short-lived political journal called *The Jeffersonian*. This paper was launched by Thurlow Weed as a Whig campaign paper in support of William Seward, a candidate for governor. As editor, Weed recruited the young Horace Greeley, whose Whig editorials had been published in the *New-Yorker*.[109] *The Jeffersonian* was concerned mostly with state politics, but it also printed a series of reports on the plight of the Cherokees. One of the most emotional accounts came in a letter from a witness to the final Cherokee round-up. "I have never before taken my seat as a correspondent with feelings similar to those of the present moment," the writer began.[110] His purpose, he added, was to tell of the wrongs done to the Cherokees as well as "to arouse sympathy and indignation of the American people in their favor." The writer was particularly incensed over the way the Cherokees were cheated out of their property by "hungry, grasping whites, who are pushing into the nation from every quarter." To illustrate the chicanery of the whites, the correspondent told of an Indian who had refused to sell his farm because the price offered was too low. But the white men had a plan "and it was so arranged that a number of men stationed themselves near and fired in the direction of the house. The consequence was great alarm, and during the confusion the purchaser appears, informing the Indian that the soldiers were coming, and the unsuspecting man sold at the price of the purchaser."[111] A month later, Greeley published another letter from the South, this one equally emotional and grim. Although the letter was unsigned, it was probably written by a Lewis Ross,[112] brother of John Ross and someone for whom removal was a personal tragedy: "I cannot find language to paint all that has taken place to increase the miseries of our people."[113] Like the earlier writer, Ross described how the whites took advantage of the Cherokees as they surrendered their land and possessions. He also reported that General Scott had agreed to suspend emigration due to the heat, if the Cherokees would meet certain conditions, which they agreed to do. Finally, Ross noted that the will of the Cherokees had been broken: "All quietly submit to their fate and are driven off like so many sheep to the slaughter-house."[114] The publication of this letter, and a number of others like it, helped make Cherokee removal more than a series of routine and official reports. But such reports were too few—and too late—to have any effect on policy. Despite a final wave of publicity designed to arouse the sympathy of the public, Indian removal never achieved sufficient status in the press to make an impact either in Washington or in the lives of the Cherokees.

In *Niles' National Register,* the first report of trouble during the round-up was an official denial, from General Scott, that sickness was a problem among the Cherokees. On 23 July, the general wrote: "It is, I learn, reported throughout this country, that the Indians collected in camps for emigration are sickly and dying in great numbers. I mention this report to contradict it. The Indians are, very generally, in excellent health, and so are the troops." To make sure that his message had its intended public relations effect, Scott added this final request to his report: "Please cause this to be officially announced."[115]

But in the *Register,* the denial was followed by letter a week later that raised questions about the general's report. Although the letter did not comment on the health of the Indians, the writer described acts of cruelty and mistreatment inflicted upon the Indians by their captors. The paper introduced the letter by noting that "the praiseworthy and humane injunctions of gen. Scott, have been disregarded in the preparations for removal."[116]

The letter itself was written 24 July—only a day after Scott's report—and was originally published in the New York *Journal of Commerce.* The letter was dated from "Prisoner's Camp, Cherokee Nation" and the writer, who was not identified, was in complete sympathy with the Cherokees. At Ross's Landing, the scenes of distress "defy all description," the writer said. The captors demanded the Indians' horses for immediate sale. "The owners refusing to give them up,—men, women, children *and horses* were driven promiscuously into one large pen, and the horses taken out by force, and cried off to the highest bidder, *and sold for almost nothing.*" Finally, the writer described the way the soldiers forced the unwilling Cherokees onto boats, "regardless of the cries and agonies of the poor helpless sufferers." He concluded, "In this cruel work, the most painful separations of families occurred—Children were sent off and parents left, and so of other relations."[117]

In October 1838, when a group of Cherokees crossed middle Tennessee, the partisan Nashville *Whig* reported the story sympathetically. Although the editor was hard-hearted—he noted that he had not had a chance to see "this miserable remnant of a warlike race"—one of his subscribers did visit the Cherokee camp and was moved by what he saw: "Barefooted and barely clad, they cannot all hope to withstand the fateigues [*sic*] of travel and inclemency of the season. Disease and perhaps death must be the portion of scores of their number before they reach the Western frontier. Indeed four or five were buried near town, and not less than 50 were on the sick list when they passed through Monday."[118] The correspondent was so distressed by the Cherokees' lack of clothing that he urged Nashville citizens to gather clothing for the emigrants. The editor, again, was less kind: "The time is too short and the objects of charity nearer home, too numerous, to bear out such an undertaking." Despite the editor's attitude, the *Whig* story went further than most in portraying the suffering of the Cherokees as they walked to Indian Territory.

This report—and others like it[119]—helped fill in the missing parts of the Indian removal story. Unfortunately, many of these stories were based on the final round-up of the Cherokees and published only after removal was well under way. As a result, the stories had no effect on removal, although they did serve as reminders of the pain that accompanied that policy. It is also clear that most of the sympathetic news coverage about removal was concerned with the Cherokees, the most assimilated of the southern tribes and, arguably, the tribe most damaged by removal. Their removal won them many friends and political allies. More importantly, it helped them generate a good number of sympathetic news stories, especially in religious newspapers and those published by political opponents of the Jackson and Van Buren administrations.

Nevertheless, the published record of injustice and misery caused by removal was only a small part of the news in the 1830s. In contrast to the Cherokees, the other four southern tribes—Choctaws, Chickasaws, Creeks, and Seminoles—never received consistent, sympathetic news coverage of their removal. More often, Indian removal was a small story, published on an irregular basis and without commentary in the press. Examined in its full context, coverage of Indian removal was minor news, haphazardly reported, dominated by official views, and rarely offering a detailed or moving report of the pain of this policy.

It is clear that the southern Indians were unfavorably represented during the removal era. The racism and misunderstanding between whites and Native Americans during these years was simply too great for an even-handed identity in the popular press. Nevertheless, the newspapers of the day had an opportunity to explain the issues and problems of white-Indian relationships in ways that could have benefited both races and helped reduce the disruption and suffering caused by Indian removal.

But the press of the 1830s was bound by a set of dominant ideas about Indians and Indian life. Indians were an inferior race, most Americans believed, destined to disappear before the inevitable advance of white civilization. Besides, the argument went, Indians were easily corrupted by white contact, making their removal to Indian Territory all the more necessary and even humane. Editors and their readers alike had little reason to believe that even "civilized" Indians like the Cherokees should stand in the way of southern progress by holding land that white farmers and speculators found desirable. Finally, the political controversy surrounding Indian removal made removal news useful as a political weapon for and against Jacksonian Democrats, further obscuring the real story of the southern tribes. Although the press did not originate any of these ideas, it accepted them routinely and uncritically, rarely looking beyond familiar stereotypes about Indians or the consequences of removal policy.

In addition, news-making practices of the 1830s defined Indian news in an "us vs. them" fashion, emphasizing Indian violence against whites at the expense of others types of Indian news. When the papers were concerned about Indians at all—which was rare—it was because Indian sympathizers took up the cause. Moreover, the press often framed the actual removal of the southern Indians as a simple transportation matter. In so doing, the press underplayed the tragic aspects of the removal and cut the story off from its moral dimension.

In short, the definition of news as it applied to Indians in the 1830s reduced the natives to stereotypes. The removal of the southern tribes—for all its infamy today—was underplayed in the 1830s because the Indians themselves were not big news, at least not when they were peaceful or subdued. Yet some serious and concerned reporting about Indian removal did appear in newspapers during the 1830s, even in southern newspapers that had little use for the Five Civilized Tribes. These stories came not from government or other "official" sources but from missionaries and northern travelers who took up the Indian cause and thereby undermined the existing news frame. At their best, these stories provided a clear sense of the human pain that lay behind removal policy. Unfortunately, such reports were working against the ideology of the vanishing Indian as well as established definitions of Indian news and, as a result, were exceptions to the general rule. As a result, the newspapers of the 1830s were unable to tell the Indian removal story fully and dramatically, in ways that would have alerted American newspaper readers to the consequences of government policy and might have saved thousands of Native Americans from needless suffering and death.

Notes

1. *Niles' National Register,* 18 Aug. 1838, 385.
2. *Savannah Georgian* quoted in ibid., 21 July 1838, 324.
3. The standard account is Grant Foreman, *Indian Removal* (Norman: University of Oklahoma Press, 1932). See also Francis Paul Prucha, *The Great Father: The United States Government and the American Indians,* 2 vols. (Lincoln: University of Nebraska Press, 1984), vol. 1, chaps. 7–8; Bernard W. Sheehan, *Seeds of Extinction* (Chapel Hill: University of North Carolina Press, 1973); Ronald N. Satz, *American Indian Policy in the Jacksonian Era* (Lincoln: University of Nebraska Press, 1975), chaps. 2–4. The Choctaw removal is told in Arthur DeRosier Jr., *The Removal of the Choctaw Indians* (Knoxville: University of Tennessee Press, 1970). The Cherokee removal is recounted in Samuel Carter III, *Cherokee Sunset: A Nation Betrayed* (Garden City, N.Y.: Doubleday and Co., 1976); Kenneth Penn Davis, "The Cherokee Removal, 1835–1838," *Tennessee Historical Quarterly* 32.4 (Winter 1973): 311–31; William G. McGloughlin, *Cherokee Renascence in the New Republic* (Princeton: Princeton University Press, 1986); Thurman Wilkins, *Cherokee Tragedy* (New York: Macmillan, 1970); Grace Steele Woodward, *The Cherokees* (Norman: University of Oklahoma Press, 1963). An openly sympathetic account is in Helen Hunt Jackson, *A Century of Dishonor* (1881; rpt., New York: Harper Torchbooks, 1965).
4. Grant Foreman, *The Five Civilized Tribes* (Norman: University of Oklahoma Press, 1934), vii.
5. Grant Foreman, *Indians and Pioneers* (Norman: University of Oklahoma Press, 1936), 26.
6. Ibid., 10–11. Also Francis Paul Prucha, *American Indian Policy in the Formative Years* (Lincoln: University of Nebraska, 1962), 227.
7. Foreman, *Indians and Pioneers,* 11.
8. Ibid., 12.
9. Prucha, *American Indian Policy,* 228.
10. Monroe message to Congress, 25 Jan. 1825, quoted in Edward H. Spicer, *A Short History of the Indians of the United States* (New York: D. Van Nostrand, 1969), 229.

11. Prucha, *American Indian Policy,* 229.

12. Ibid., 233–40; see also Michael Paul Rogin, *Fathers and Sons: Andrew Jackson and the Subjugation of the American Indian* (New York: Alfred A. Knopf, 1975), 212–13.

13. Donald Grinde, "Cherokee Removal and American Politics," *The Indian Historian* 8.3 (Summer 1975): 39–40.

14. *Cherokee Nation v. Georgia,* 1831, U.S. Supreme Court *Reports,* 5 Peters, 15–18.

15. *Worcester v. Georgia,* 1832, U.S. Supreme Court *Reports,* 6 Peters, 559–61.

16. Brian W. Dippie, *The Vanishing American: White Attitudes and U.S. Indian Policy* (Middletown, Conn.: Wesleyan University Press, 1982), 17.

17. *The Constitutional Journal* (Helena, Ark.), 23 June 1836, 4.

18. *Western Weekly Review* (Franklin, Tenn.), 29 June 1838, 4.

19. *North American Review* 44.95 (April 1837): 39.

20. Ibid., 47.100 (July 1838): 136.

21. See Dippie, *Vanishing American,* 25. See also Prucha, *American Indian Policy,* 224–27.

22. *North American Review* 47.100 (July 1838): 136.

23. Dippie, *Vanishing American,* 25–28.

24. *Constitutional Journal* (Helena, Ark.), 2 July 1838, 1.

25. *Niles' Weekly Register,* 14 Aug. 1819, 405.

26. Ibid., 18 Sept. 1830, 71.

27. Ibid.

28. Removal as a humanitarian act was the official position taken by Thomas McKenney, head of Jackson's Office of Indian Affairs. See Satz, *American Indian Policy,* 14–15.

29. Robert F. Berkhofer Jr., *The White Man's Indian: Images of the American Indian from Columbus to the Present* (New York: Vintage Books, 1979), 149–51.

30. Michael Emery and Edwin Emery, *The Press and America,* 6th ed. (Englewood Cliffs, N.J.: Prentice Hall, 1988), 103. See also Frank Luther Mott, *A History of American Magazines,* vol. 1: 1741–1850 (Cambridge: Harvard University Press, 1938), 269.

31. *Niles' Weekly Register,* 13 Mar. 1819, 56.

32. Ibid., 7 Aug. 1819, 399; see also 20 Nov. 1819, 192.

33. Ibid., 29 Apr. 1820, 154.

34. See Francis Paul Prucha, *The Indians in American Society* (Berkeley: University of California Press, 1985), chap. 2, esp. 34–36.

35. Ibid., chap. 1. See also Rogin, *Fathers and Sons,* chap. 7.

36. Richard Slotkin, *The Fatal Environment* (New York: HarperPerennial, 1985), 171.

37. Alvin M. Josephy Jr., *500 Nations* (New York: Alfred A. Knopf, 1994), 322–23.

38. For an overview of the politics surrounding the Indian Removal Bill, including some press reactions, see Satz, *American Indian Policy,* chaps. 1–2.

39. Republished from the Milledgeville [Ga.] *Recorder* in the Augusta *States'-Rights Sentinel,* 19 June 1835, 3.

40. Ibid., 7 Aug. 1835, 2.

41. Jeremiah Evarts, *Cherokee Removal: The "William Penn" Essays and Other Writings,* ed. Francis Paul Prucha (Knoxville: University of Tennessee Press, 1981).

42. Ibid., 5–6.

43. Ibid., 46.

44. Ibid.

45. Ibid.

46. Ibid.

47. Ibid., 11. Prucha states that the essays were widely circulated, especially in the religious press, but his evidence on this point is secondhand and it is unclear how many newspapers published the essays. One of Prucha's sources believes the essays were in forty newspapers but another suggests more than one hundred. In any event, many papers probably did not publish the essays due to a lack of space. In addition, Evarts and other Indian supporters carried on a vigorous pamphlet campaign in support of their cause, a fact that suggests that their message was not universally published.

48. *Niles' Weekly Register,* 29 Apr. 1820, 155.

49. Ibid., 8 May 1830, 204.

50. As many as twenty *Cherokee Phoenix* columns by Elias Boudinot were reprinted by the *Register.* See Barbara F. Luebke, "Elias Boudinot, Indian Editor," *Journalism History* 6.2 (Summer 1979): 53.

51. *Niles' Weekly Register,* 13 Mar. 1830, 53–54.

52. Ibid., 55.

53. Frank Luther Mott reached the same opinion regarding *Niles' Weekly Register.* "Whatever the editor's opinions, however, the *Register* printed the documents and speeches on both sides." See Mott, *History of American Magazines* 1:269.

54. *Niles' Weekly Register,* 18 Sept. 1830, 69.

55. Ibid.

56. Ibid.

57. Ibid., 70.

58. Ibid., 71.

59. Referred to in Wirt's letter to the editor of the *Baltimore Gazette,* reprinted in ibid.

60. *Niles' National Register,* 26 May 1838, 194.

61. Ibid., 24 July 1938, 394.

62. Ibid., 395.

63. Litchfield *American Eagle* quoted in Theda Perdue, *Cherokee Editor: The Writings of Elias Boudinot* (Knoxville: University of Tennessee Press, 1983), 9. See also Wilkins, *Cherokee Tragedy,* 146–53.

64. Wilkins, *Cherokee Tragedy,* 146–53.

65. New York *Observer,* 26 Jan. 1833, 14; 9 Mar. 1833, 37. The Supreme Court case is *Worcester v. Georgia.*

66. Perdue, *Cherokee Editor,* 8, 45–48.

67. Quoted in ibid., 48.

68. Augusta *States'-Rights Sentinel,* 1 Sept. 1835, 2.

69. Ibid.

70. Ibid.

71. Ibid.

72. Ibid.

73. Another outside correspondent who generated favorable publicity for the Cherokees was John Howard Payne, an actor and playwright. He and John Ross were arrested in Tennessee by the Georgia guard on 7 November 1835 after Payne dared the guard to do just that in an anonymous letter published in the Knoxville [Tenn.] *Register.* Payne's account of the arrest and imprisonment was also published in the *Register,* the Augusta *Constitutionalist,* and other newspapers. See Clemens de Baillou, ed., *John Howard Payne to His Countrymen* (Athens: University of Georgia Press, 1961), as well as Carter, *Cherokee Sunset,* 181–88, and Wilkins, *Cherokee Tragedy,* 281–84.

74. Foreman, *Indian Removal,* 226.

75. See, for example, the Maryland *Gazette,* 13 Apr. 1837; 30 Nov. 1837, 3.

76. Ibid., 31 May 1838, 2.

77. *United States Gazette,* 5 Jan. 1836, 2.

78. Ibid., 16 Jan. 1836, 3; 20 Jan. 1836, 1.

79. Ibid., 23 Jan. 1836, 3.

80. Ibid.

81. Ibid., 16 Jan. 1836, 3.

82. Ibid., 23 Jan. 1836, 3.

83. Ibid., 9 June 1838, 4.

84. Ibid., 21 July 1838, 2.

85. Ibid., 25 July 1838, 2.

86. Quoted in *Niles' Weekly Register,* 10 May 1834, 174.

87. Stories emphasizing tragedy and human misery were common in early American journalism and they gained even wider acceptance with the rise of the penny press in the 1830s and 1840s. See David Copeland, "Graphic, Shocking, and Violent: Sensational News in Colonial America," a paper delivered to the annual convention of the Association for Education in Journalism and Mass Communication, Washington, D.C., August 1995.

88. *Constitutional Journal,* 24 Nov. 1836, 2

89. *Western Weekly Review,* 14 July 1837, 1.

90. Arkansas *Weekly Times,* 4 Dec. 1837, 2.

91. Quoted in DeRosier, *Removal of the Choctaw Indians,* 145.

92. Ibid., 146.

93. Quoted in the *Constitutional Journal,* 14 Apr. 1837, 2.

94. Quoted in *Western Weekly Review,* 16 Feb. 1838, 2.

95. *Constitutional Journal,* 11 June 1838, 3.

96. Ibid., 18 June 1838, 2.

97. *Western Weekly Review,* 4 Jan. 1839, 3.

98. Ibid., 16 Nov. 1838, 2.

99. *Constitutional Journal,* 21 Dec. 1837, 2.

100. Ibid.

101. See, for example, the Maryland *Gazette,* which published Scott's address on

31 May 1838, 2. Scott's speech also appeared in many other newspapers, both in the South and elsewhere.

102. *Cumberland Presbyterian* (Nashville), 1 May 1838, 3; 12 June 1838, 3.

103. *Western Weekly Review,* 27 Apr. 1838, 1.

104. Ibid., 6 July 1838, 2.

105. Ibid., 27 Apr. 1838, 1.

106. Quoted in the *Constitutional Journal,* 25 Aug. 1836, 3.

107. Printed in the *Western Weekly Review,* 10 Nov. 1837, 3.

108. Ibid.

109. Frank Luther Mott, *American Journalism,* 3d ed. (New York: Macmillan, 1962), 267–68.

110. *The Jeffersonian* (Albany, N.Y.), 30 June 1838, 158.

111. Ibid.

112. Both the language and the information in *The Jeffersonian* letter is similar to a letter written by Lewis Ross at the Cherokee Agency on 18 May 1838, a day before the date on the letter in *The Jeffersonian.* The letter is in the Ayer Collection at the Newberry Library, Chicago.

113. *The Jeffersonian,* 28 July 1838, 188.

114. Ibid.

115. *Niles' National Register,* 11 Aug. 1838, 369.

116. Ibid., 18 Aug. 1838, 385.

117. Ibid.

118. Quoted in the *Cumberland Presbyterian,* 30 Oct. 1838, 2.

119. Foreman cites a number of dramatic news stories in his account of Indian removal. One of the most cited on Cherokee removal is "A Native of Maine, Traveling in the Western Country," from the New York *Observer,* 29 Jan. 1839. See Foreman, *Indian Removal,* 305–7.

The Daily Rocky Mountain News *and the Scandal of Sand Creek*

A S his troops prepared for battle, Col. John M. Chivington inspired his men with words of revenge: "Now, boys, I shan't say who you shall kill, but remember our murdered women and children."[1] His men remembered. A few hours later, the bodies of some two hundred Cheyennes and Arapahos littered the banks of Sand Creek. The Cheyenne chief Black Kettle somehow escaped the slaughter, but not before trying desperately to save his people by raising an American flag and a white flag over his lodge. Other Indians approached the soldiers with their hands raised, begging to be spared. They were answered with bullets.[2] The *Daily Rocky Mountain News* called the attack "the most effective expedition against the Indians ever planned and carried out."[3] Later, some of the soldiers would testify to something less glorious: "I think about half the killed were women and children. Nearly all, men, women, and children, were scalped. I saw one woman whose privates had been mutilated."[4]

Chivington disputed such claims. He maintained then and for the rest of his life that the attack was justified because it punished the Indians for their raids against whites during the summer of 1864. "I stand by Sand Creek," Chivington said many years later.[5] The *Daily Rocky Mountain News* stood by Sand Creek too. When word of the victory reached Denver, the *News* said the soldiers had won "for themselves and their commanders, from Colonel down to corporal, the eternal gratitude of dwellers on these plains."[6]

The truth about Sand Creek has long been the subject of debate among western and Native American historians.[7] Was it, as Chivington claimed, a defeat of the hostile savages responsible for terrorizing the white population throughout 1864? Or was it an unprovoked attack on a band of peaceful Cheyennes and Arapahos who had complied with government officials and believed they were under army protection? Whatever the historical verdict, the press played a major role in defining the original debate over Sand Creek. In particular, the *Daily Rocky Mountain News* shaped this story, using the telegraph to control the eastward flow of information. But the *News* was not a neutral party concerning Sand Creek or Colorado politics. In fact, the *News* was closely aligned with Chivington and John Evans, the territorial governor. *News* editor William N. Byers was also an ardent supporter of economic growth in Denver and of Colorado statehood, positions threatened by hostile Indians. Thus the original and "official" Sand Creek story emanating from Denver was a glorious one—heroic soldiers subduing a vicious band of savages. Weeks later, however, the "unofficial" story began to emerge through private letters, leaked by political enemies of Governor Evans, Chivington, and Byers. These reports told a very different and disturbing tale, one in which peaceful Indian men, women, and children were killed and mutilated by undisciplined soldiers. In Denver, the *News* counter-attacked, singling out the "humanitarian" eastern papers as anti-western and far too sympathetic to the Indians at Sand Creek.[8]

The Telegraph, News Making, and the Frontier

By the time of the Civil War, the telegraph had changed both the nation's news-gathering system as well as the very conception of news. Mailed newspaper exchanges and the casual publication of news and letters were no longer sufficient to reach the increasingly news-hungry public. New York's penny press had long ago demonstrated the value of timeliness, and various papers used their "scoops" as a means of beating the competition. Now the telegraph had conquered distance, allowing news to travel across the land at electric speed. The telegraph's news-carrying potential was recognized early on. In May 1844, inventor Samuel Morse in Washington was able to provide the names of Whig nominees from Annapolis one hour and four minutes ahead of the Baltimore and Ohio train, a publicity stunt that caught the public's attention.[9] Within months, eastern editors began using the wires to speed up the delivery of Washington news. In the West and Midwest, editors clamored to have telegraphic service extended to their cities and towns. By 1846, telegraph lines linked Washington, Baltimore, New York, Philadelphia, and Boston. Heading inland, the lines extended to Albany and Buffalo, Pittsburgh, and on toward New Orleans.[10] The nation was rapidly becoming wired, a development that had enormous short- and long-term consequences.

One effect of the telegraph was a subtle change in the sense of news. With short telegraphic bulletins increasingly available to the press, news could be reported in smaller and smaller segments. This allowed the urban papers to build a sense of suspense about continuing stories. Telegraphic news could also be good for the newspaper business. James Gordon Bennett was soon convinced: "The public mind will be stimulated to greater activity by the rapid circulation of news. The swift communication of tidings of great events will awake in the masses of the community still keener interest in public affairs."[11] But the telegraph was an expensive technology and it soon became apparent to many editors that cooperation could produce more news cheaper. A solution was reached as early as May 1845, when John Wills of Baltimore agreed to serve as a news agent for several southern papers. Later that year, a man named Glen Peeples advertised a similar service, offering "regular and special intelligence or private correspondence through the agency of the telegraph." By 1846, the six New York dailies began cooperating on wire news, laying the foundation for the New York Associated Press. These new services promoted a new occupation: the telegraphic reporter. This position helped professionalize journalism because it provided an occupational incentive to gather and disseminate news quickly. It also shaped the content of the news, promoting more facts than opinions, since these reporters were transmitting news to several different newspapers. In short, the dramatic shifts in newsgathering technology and professionalization of the news in the late antebellum years led to a standardization of news content. Anecdotes, poems, tall tales, and other forms of correspondence fell out of favor in the telegraph era. More than ever, the news came to be seen as the "latest intelligence," reports that were timely and factual but also brief and incomplete.

For Indian news, the extensive use of the telegraph meant that news bulletins from the frontier—most involving violence or threats of violence—became a common way of representing western Indians. The headlines over these dispatches usually told a one-dimensional tale: "Indian Troubles," "Indian Treachery," "Indian Murderers," and the like. Many stories ended with an expectation of more violence: "Considerable excitement prevails here over the anticipated trouble."[12] Because these stories usually centered on conflict, they were newsworthy by traditional standards. But these telegraphic bulletins were also stripped of context and, in contrast to private letters or detailed official reports, they rarely offered any explanation for Indian violence or background about native grievances.

An 1874 dispatch from Indian Territory illustrates this news-making process. In a widely published report from Galveston via Austin, eastern readers learned that

> on June 28 the Comanches, Kiowas and Cheyennes attacked the settlement at Doty Wells, and were repulsed, with the loss of sixteen killed and twenty wounded. A large number of horses were also killed. Three surveyors, employed by Hocklush & Armstrong, were killed by Indians near the Antelope Hills.
>
> The friendly Indians are collected around the Wichita Agency. The warriors and young men of the three tribes above named are all on the warpath.
>
> It is reported that a company of United States cavalry were attacked at Otter Creek, and four men and all their horses captured.[13]

The details—and omissions—of this story bear close examination. The story focuses on the facts of three Indian attacks, one at Doty Wells, one near the Antelope Hills, and one at Otter Creek. Nineteen people were killed and four captured. Three tribes were apparently responsible for these attacks, and the situation appeared ominous since, in the words of the dispatch, "all are on the warpath." Although the story recognizes the presence of some (unidentified) friendly Indians, it offers no reason for these Indian attacks. Were the warriors provoked by intrusions into their hunting grounds? Did they feel threatened by the surveyors or the cavalry? The story provides no answers to these questions and no information about the motives or intentions of the Indians. One conclusion seems obvious: the southwestern frontier is a violent place, where Indian attacks are common and, given the evidence, unprovoked.

The brevity of such telegraphic reports, combined with frequent violent clashes between whites and Indians in the West, ensured that similar telegraphic bulletins would be the most common kind of Indian news in the last half of the nineteenth century. Such stories became the core of an Indian "news frame," a set of standardized ways of writing about Indians. Following this narrative pattern, telegraph agents and western correspondents began to report Indian violence almost automatically, using the same imagery and language to describe a variety of Indian attacks and encounters. As illustrated above, such stories marked the Indians as hostile and provided details of their misdeeds but offered little or no explanation. In this way, the typical Indian report from the West was almost always incomplete and skewed toward violence, resulting in a narrow range of Indian images and distorting the true nature of Indian-white encounters. This news frame helps explain why Chivington's massacre of Cheyenne and Arapaho people at Sand Creek never became a major news story in the nation's press and why the newspapers both before and after Sand Creek continued to emphasize native violence against whites in the West.

Indians, Gold, and the Booster Press in Colorado

The Cheyennes and Arapahos of Colorado were peaceful during most of the decade leading up to the Sand Creek massacre. Under the terms of the Laramie Treaty of 1851, the two tribes agreed to live and hunt in eastern Colorado between the South Platte and the Arkansas rivers.[14] Few conflicts erupted, probably because there was plenty of land for the Indians and few whites to dispute Indian claims.

Everything changed with the discovery of gold near Pike's Peak. When word of these discoveries reached the east in the late 1850s, it set off a Colorado gold rush not unlike the California gold rush a decade before.[15] With prospectors and settlers streaming into gold territory, whites soon began to infringe on Indian lands.[16] By 1860, the stage was set for confrontation. A peaceful solution was tried first. While the territorial government was being organized, federal officials negotiated a new treaty under which the Arapahos and Cheyennes surrendered most of their land. The chiefs agreed to a smaller reservation and federal agents promised government aid to help the Indians make the transition from hunters to farmers.[17]

Despite its promise, the treaty did not stop Indians from hunting nor white emigrants from traveling through or settling on Indian lands.[18] Moreover, not all warriors agreed to the treaty and they felt free to hunt far from their villages. Some historians also believe the Indians grew bolder because they knew the United States army was preoccupied with the Civil War and unable to respond to Indian provocations.[19] In any case, tensions between Indians and whites gradually increased in the early 1860s. Raiding parties stole horses, burned ranches, and interfered with stages and supply wagons from the east. In Denver, food supplies grew scarce and prices shot up. In mid-1864, territorial anxiety had reached the breaking point.

Fear was especially evident in Denver, now a supply and trading center for the nearby mining regions. Denver could boast of several banks, a mint, a daily newspaper, and nearly five thousand hearty residents.[20] So when hostile Indians threatened the city's supply lines, Denver leaders and merchants—and indeed the entire population—reacted with understandable anger and hostility.

The principal newspaper of the Colorado Territory was the *Daily Rocky Mountain News,* founded in 1859. Its editor was an Ohio native named William Newton Byers, a capable and ambitious man who had come to Denver with a plan. "His singularity was evident when he arrived with a printing press and a plan to open a newspaper office," wrote Denver historian Lyle Dorsett.[21] Byers soon became one of the territory's most ardent boosters. "Once he had decided to relocate, the sanguine newspaper editor was determined to build a city. This enterprise became an obsession for Byers," Dorsett wrote.[22] Indeed, Byers used the inaugural issue of the *News* to outline his vision of the prospective state. The "hum of busy men" was rising from the Rockies, Byers said, and the "poor Indian, heretofore quietly displaced by treaty, is now pushed rudely on by the resistless rush of Yankee enterprise."[23] Significantly, this vision did not blame the Colorado emigrants (or anyone else) for dispossessing the Indians—it was simply destiny that a superior race of "busy men" would triumph over an inferior race of "poor Indians" in the development of Colorado.[24] That same year, Horace Greeley himself helped boost Colorado's development, confirming the authenticity of gold strikes near Denver. By 1864, Byers was satisfied that his vision was near success: "If the past four years have been encouraging, what may we not expect in the next four? Confidence is but now established; Colorado is just starting in her glorious career."[25]

As these lines demonstrate, Byers used the pages of the *News* to advocate emigration and economic growth in the territory. In early 1864, for example, Byers wrote a *News* editorial called "Fortunes For The Taking." The editorial began, "No country in the world offers greater inducements for the influx of immigration than does Colorado to-day."[26] But Byers also knew that progress in the territory was not possible without security along the wagon routes and protection for the new emigrants. Not surprisingly, the Indian threat was a frequent theme on the editorial page of the *News.*

Byers had good reason to be ambivalent about Indians. After all, their land claims and potential for violence were very real obstacles to his vision of Colorado progress. But Byers was not an Indian hater, at least not in the beginning. As David Svaldi has documented, the *Daily Rocky Mountain News* was altruistic toward Indians in 1860, admitting "white injustices" against them and debunking exaggerated claims of Indian violence.

In 1861, Svaldi found, Byers was making clear distinctions between hostile and friendly Indians in the *News*.[27] But Byers's attitude grew considerably darker as the perceived Indian threat increased. By 1863, the *News* was publishing regular stories favoring extermination and offering increasingly graphic—and often exaggerated—accounts of Indian "depredations" against travelers and settlers.[28] Byers also used incidents involving non-Colorado Indians to keep the Indian threat alive and discourage movement west from Denver. That same year, Svaldi discovered, Colorado Indians were at relative peace, yet the *News* recirculated old Indian "outrages" and helped reinforce the idea that all area Indians were hostile.[29] In 1864, when the mutilated bodies of the Hungate family were displayed in Denver, the savagery of the natives and the need for their extermination were familiar arguments to readers of the *Daily Rocky Mountain News*.

Byers was no outsider in early Denver. By virtue of his newspaper success and his political savvy, he quickly became one of the most powerful men in Denver.[30] According to Dorsett, Byers and Governor Evans "worked well together. Like Byers, the new governor was a visionary."[31] Moreover, Evans was a prominent Republican, a successful entrepreneur and the wealthiest man in Colorado, all qualities that attracted the aspiring Byers.[32] So close was the relationship between printer and politician that for a time in 1864 the *News* billed itself as "The Official Paper of the Territory."[33] Byers and Evans were also financially linked. When Cherry Creek flooded Denver in May 1864 and washed away the building that housed the *News*, Evans helped Byers purchase the Denver *Commonwealth* so that he could re-establish his newspaper.[34]

Another member of the Denver elite was John M. Chivington, a Methodist elder who had sought a military commission and distinguished himself against Confederate forces in 1862. Chivington emerged as a hero after a battle at La Glorieta, New Mexico, where he aggressively led his men and displayed great bravery.[35] Chivington was also a special friend to William Byers. During the Cherry Creek flood—the same one that destroyed the *Daily Rocky Mountain News*—Chivington led a rescue party to save the Byers family. Temporarily homeless, Byers and his family spent several weeks as guests of Governor Evans.[36] It was common, therefore, to find complimentary words about Evans and Chivington in the pages of the *News*. The paper consistently supported Evans in territorial politics and endorsed Chivington as a candidate for the post of territorial representative to Congress in the statehood election of September 1864.[37]

Indian News East and West

When Indian hostilities intensified in August 1864, the *News* operated as a virtual house organ for Governor Evans, printing his proclamations verbatim and supporting him against local and outside critics. On 10 August, for example, the *News* published the governor's "Appeal to the People," a call for Colorado citizens to "organize for the defense of their homes and families against the merciless savages."[38] The governor said that self-protection was necessary because the military could not be depended upon. Evans sweetened the offer by pointing out that citizens would be "entitled to all the property belonging to hostile Indians that they capture." Evans added an important distinction, one the press sometimes failed to make: "Any man who kills a hostile Indian is a patriot; but there are Indians who are friendly, and to kill one of these will involve us in a greater difficulty. It is important therefore to fight only the hostile, and no one has been or will be restrained from this."[39] In an adjoining editorial, Byers was more alarming and less precise, advocating strong military action against *all* natives. "The Indian uprising is general. It extends from New Mexico to British America; from Missouri and Iowa to California and Oregon."[40] Byers endorsed Evans's call for a militia to fight the Indians and also took a swipe at outside critics who were blind to the native threat: "Eastern humanitarians who believe in the superiority of the Indian race will raise a terrible howl over this policy, but it is no time to split hairs nor stand upon delicate computations of conscience. Self preservation demands decisive action, and the only way to secure it is to fight them in their own way. A few months of active extermination against the red devils will bring quiet, and nothing else will."[41]

Byers had little to fear from the eastern press. In fact, most Indian news in the eastern papers during the Civil War years came from telegraphic reports from the western papers themselves and these stories were often anti-Indian. Both the New York *Times* and the Philadelphia *Inquirer,* for instance, published a 4 August Leavenworth *Conservative* story concerning the "savage infidelity, and the barbaric conduct of the Indians both west of this and further north, in the direction of Denver and Fort Laramie."[42] The following day the *Inquirer* ran a short page-one story from Omaha that began, "The Indians are hourly committing new depredations, stealing stock, burning trains and killing indiscriminately."[43] Governor Evans's call for a militia appeared in Washington's *National Intelligencer* in August 1864 in alarming, anti-Indian language. The paper printed Evans's assertion that war was imminent and "that it will be the largest Indian war this country ever had." The article ended with Evans's warning that "unless authority is given [for the militia], the whites will be destroyed."[44]

Preoccupied by Civil War news and without their own correspondents on the scene, eastern newspapers were unable to develop their own views about Indians or resolve the inconsistencies in western dispatches. On 12 August, for example, the *Times* printed a page-one message from Alvin Saunders, territorial governor of Nebraska. "The news from our Western border is alarming," Saunders wrote. He went on: "No less than four different points on the route between our Territory and Denver were attacked in one day. The Indians are known to be infesting these roads for a distance of several hundred miles."[45]

But an adjoining item on the same page offered a less alarming assessment. Datelined Denver, the report was published under a reassuring headline: "Safety of Travel on the Overland Route." It began: "To correct probable misapprehension in regard to the safety of travel on the overland route, it is proper to say that although the Indians have been very troublesome of late in attacking unarmed trains and murdering emigrants unable to defend themselves, there has, as yet, been no attack by the Indians, as far as known, upon mail coaches, which run regularly both ways."[46] A similar report from Denver appeared in the *Inquirer*, although the headline in that paper was merely "Indian Troubles in the Northwest" and its story did not refer to any "probable misapprehension."[47] In any case, it is clear that both papers were heavily dependent on telegraph dispatches for timely Indian news. It also seems clear that the eastern press lacked the firsthand knowledge required to make sound editorial judgments about Indian life or the safety of western travel.

In sum, the eastern press was not advocating the "superiority of the Indian race," as Byers had claimed. But the eastern papers did take issue with western dispatches on occasion. Specifically, some eastern papers drew attention to frequent discrepancies between exaggerated western news and official Washington reports. On 17 August, for example, the *Inquirer* published a Washington story disputing western assessments of the Indian situation: "It is not thought at the Indian Bureau that the outbreak of Indians on the plains is general . . . but there is information to induce belief that a few bands only have resorted to pillage and massacre to redress individual wrongs committed against them or their families."[48] Such reports—which in this case included a motive for Indian violence—did not sit well in Denver and these East-West disputes also found their way into the press. In late August, the Philadelphia *Inquirer* published a page-one letter from George H. Lane, the superintendent of the Denver mint. Lane found the reports of the Indian Bureau "an outrage on the memory of men, and unoffending women and children, who have been killed and scalped by those treacherous devils. Every band of Indians of any size on the plains is united for the purpose of exterminating and driving all the white men from these mountains and plains."[49]

Lane echoed the pro-growth, anti-Indian ideology common in Denver. He called the Indians "natural enemies to progress and improvement" and he issued a challenge to Washington: "If Colorado has any friends in the States, let them prove it now. Those who sympathize with the wronged Indian, had better cut their hair short before passing the Missouri river, as they are no respecter of persons or sex."[50]

A more western-oriented paper, the Cincinnati *Gazette,* also ran Lane's letter. But the *Gazette* did not need new outrages to take a hard line against the Indians. This commentary was published a few days before Lane's letter: "Lo, the poor Indians! This term will soon cease to have any force, and the red faces will be more likely to be cursed and exterminated than reverenced and protected. The news continues to come in of extensive depredations, and a general war with the savages seems inevitable. These proceedings take all the romance out of the Indian character, and make bare the brutal nature of the race."[51]

This Cincinnati editorial, based on western news reports and thoroughly hostile to the Indian cause, was typical of much national news of the West during August 1864. Although Byers found it convenient to attack "eastern humanitarians," such sentiments were not especially common in the eastern or western press. Most often, eastern news about the West represented the western point of view. Telegraph dispatches and letters from Denver, Leavenworth, St. Louis, and other western locations were a staple of eastern news columns. It is clear, too, that occasional contradictions would appear in the eastern press, usually from Washington or through private letters from Colorado. Nevertheless, the picture of the frontier in general and of the Indians in particular was the westerner's own view and it was highly unfavorable to the Native Americans and their way of life.

Justifying a Massacre

In August 1864, editor Byers was increasingly alarmed about the imminent Indian threat to Colorado Territory. With supply lines frequently interrupted, the *News* could not obtain newsprint and was forced to print "Extra" editions on slips of wrapping paper.[52] In an "Extra" of 17 August, the *News* quoted Indian sources who said that hostile Indians had planned a simultaneous attack on several frontier posts. The next day, the *News* reported that Denver military officials were investigating an Indian attack at nearby Cherry Creek. The paper concluded, "There is one thing certain, however, that Running creek, Cherry creek and Plum creek are at the mercy of those thieving, scalping sons of butchery."[53] If there were peaceful Indians in the territory—Black Kettle's Cheyennes, for instance—this was not apparent in the *News*. For Byers, all Indians in Colorado had become "scalping sons of butchery."

The news reaching the East was also alarming. Over a Denver story, an editor at the New York *Times* wrote: "Adoption of Defensive Measures—Further Depredations and Murders." The story pointed out that the 100-day militia "authorized by the War Department three days ago to fight the Indians, is already more than half filled."[54] The Philadelphia *Inquirer* noted the effect of martial law on the city: "At Denver city the stores remain closed, while the citizens are engaged in drilling and erecting fortifications."[55]

By the end of August, Byers found himself short-handed. "We returned home yesterday after a week's absence to find the *News* office looking more like a soldiers' barracks than a printing establishment. . . . Twelve printers, all but one, joined up."[56] Byers used his influence with Chivington to keep the paper going: "The Colonel commanding the district has ordered a detail . . . of printers to do the necessary military printing, and to give the important telegraphic news."[57]

With general alarm throughout the territory and continued shortages in Denver, the *Daily Rocky Mountain News* advocated a military solution. The paper was "opposed to anything which looks like a treaty of peace with the Indians who have been actively engaged in the recent hostilities. The season is near at hand when they can be chastised and it should be done with no gentle hand."[58] Again, the *News* made no distinctions between peaceful and hostile Indians. A few months later, Byers's blanket condemnation of Colorado Indians bore bloody and tragic fruit.

The attack on Black Kettle's camp about forty miles from Fort Lyon in eastern Colorado began at dawn on 29 November 1864, and was over within a few hours. But the news about Sand Creek was slow to reach the press, in part because Chivington did not return immediately to Denver but continued a half-hearted search for Indians. Since no reporters accompanied Chivington's command, the first news of the attack came from military sources and they described the fight from their point of view. The first story in the *Daily Rocky Mountain News* was a short piece, published 7 December under the headline "Big Indian Fight!" It offered few details, however, reporting only that five hundred Indians had been killed and six hundred horses captured. More news was expected soon, the paper said. Byers ended with this comment: "Bully for the Colorado Boys."[59]

The first full account of the battle appeared in the *News* the following day. Five headlines topped the story: "Great Battle with Indians! The Savages Dispersed! 500 INDIANS KILLED, Our Loss 9 killed, 38 wounded, Full Particulars."[60] But the story that followed was not the newspaper's account of the battle. Instead, Byers simply attached an editor's note to an official dispatch from Chivington to General S. R. Curtis at Fort Leavenworth. Chivington, then, was the source of the original information about Sand Creek and his report put a heroic face on what seemed even then to be a lopsided military victory.

Chivington began with the hardship of the march: "In the last ten days my command has marched three hundred miles—one hundred of which the snow was two feet deep."[61] Chivington said the village consisted of "one hundred thirty lodges, from nine hundred to one thousand warriors strong." As for the battle, Chivington wrote: "We killed Chiefs Black Kettle, White Antelope and Little Robe, and between four and five hundred other Indians; captured between four and five hundred ponies and mules. Our loss is nine killed and thirty-eight wounded. All did nobly."[62] Chivington was wrong about Black Kettle; he and some of his band survived, only to be killed four years later when Custer's Seventh Cavalry attacked their camp on the Washita River, another controversial massacre. In any event, Chivington ended the report with evidence that helped justify the attack: "We found a white man's scalp, not more than three days old, in a lodge." In a second letter published on the same page, Chivington mentioned the scalp again, perhaps to fend off rumors about the true nature of Sand Creek: "I will state for the consideration of gentlemen who are opposed to fighting these red scoundrels, that I was shown, by my Chief Surgeon, the scalp of a white man . . . which could not have been more than two or three days taken."[63]

The *News* also published a list of the killed and wounded as well as private letters from several other officers who commanded at Sand Creek. Like Chivington, these accounts portrayed the attack as a major military victory. Colonel George Shoup, for example, wrote to a fellow officer, "I think this the severest chastisement ever given to Indians in battle on the American Continent."[64] Shoup also praised the fighting spirit of his soldiers, making a regional point in the process: "The story that Indians are our equals in warfare is nailed. This story may do to tell to down-easters, but not to Colorado boys." A letter from Major Anthony to his brother praised the Indians' bravery but added a more ominous comment: "We, of course, took no prisoners."[65]

Although Byers published no independent report on the battle, he recognized Sand Creek as an important step toward a more secure territory. In his editorial on the battle, he began, "This noted, needed whipping of the 'red skins,' by our 'First Indian Expedition,'... was the chief subject of comment and glorification through town today."[66] Byers said that the effect of the victory would be to subdue the Indians, who would now see the futility of violence against the whites. He wrote that "our people may rest easy in the belief that outrages by small bands are at an end, on routes where troops are stationed. Having tasted of the 'bitter end,' the news of which will quickly be dispatched among the others, the supremacy of our power will be seriously considered, and a surrender or a sueing for peace be perhaps very soon proclaimed."[67] Unfortunately, Byers was wrong. Instead of surrender, the Colorado Indians were inflamed by the injustice of Sand Creek and began a new series of attacks on whites along the frontier.[68]

Once the news of Sand Creek reached Denver, it began to appear in the nation's press. The New York *Times,* New York *Herald,* Philadelphia *Inquirer,* and Cincinnati *Gazette* published essentially the same short account of the battle on 9 December. The story appeared a day later in the Washington *Intelligencer.* These stories were short and included the same information contained in Chivington's official report in the *Daily Rocky Mountain News.* More telling, however, is the language of the last sentence in these dispatches: "Our loss was nine killed and thirty-eight wounded." Except for a tense change, this is exactly the same wording as the sentence written by Chivington in his official report. Thus the first news about Sand Creek in the East was shaped not simply by a Colorado point of view but by Chivington himself.

Denver histories provide no clue as to who actually composed the first telegraph dispatch about Sand Creek.[69] But it is apparent that the initial Sand Creek story was closely related to Chivington's reports and other accounts in the *Daily Rocky Mountain News.* It seems likely, then, that Byers or another Denver newsman or telegraph operator composed the initial dispatch and that he used Chivington's official military report as the basis of this dispatch.

The publication of the same Sand Creek dispatches in the eastern press demonstrates the gatekeeping process at work on the Sand Creek story. This process was both economic and political. First, it was expensive to send long messages over the wires.[70] Short bulletins—usually a paragraph or two—were the most common type of news transmissions from the West. More importantly, such bulletins were often sympathetic to those in authority. In this case, Governor Evans, Colonel Chivington, and the *Daily Rocky Mountain News* were major political forces in the territory and telegraph reports from Denver in late 1864 reflected their views of Indians.

The power of this gatekeeping process was demonstrated again in late December when the first full reports of Sand Creek appeared in the East. These stories, published in the New York *Tribune* as well as the *National Intelligencer,* were attributed to the *Daily Rocky Mountain News* of 8 December. The time lag—nearly three weeks—suggests that mailed copies of the *News* had arrived back East. These stories included Chivington's full official account of the battle and distilled parts of the letters from other officers. But the story was not big news in the eastern papers, perhaps because some particulars had already been published in the telegraphic bulletins. The *Tribune* published the story on 27 December on page six and the *Intelligencer* ran it on 28 December on page three. Neither report inspired editorial comment; Civil War concerns continued to dominate the editorial columns.

Back in Denver, new articles about Sand Creek appeared several days before the troops returned from the field. In a 13 December column, Byers praised the troops and explained the significance of Sand Creek. Byers noted that Chivington had failed to make a second attack because "the red devils were not disposed to stand for another battle." And Byers summed up the campaign by calling it "short but brilliant."[71]

Four days later, Byers wrote his longest commentary on the battle and he was generous in his judgments toward Chivington and his men. Byers began with the brash observation that the campaign would "stand in history with few rivals and none to exceed it in final results." The article then reviewed the campaign and listed a variety of hardships endured by the troops. Byers reported, with italics for emphasis, that Chivington's men marched "a distance of *two hundred and sixty miles in less than six days.*"[72] And he praised the command's ability to march to Sand Creek undetected by the Indians—omitting the fact that Chivington had ordered guards to kill anyone attempting to leave Fort Lyon to warn the Indians the day before the attack.[73]

According to Byers's account of the attack, the Indians were surprised—but not unprepared: "The Indian camp was well supplied with defensive works. For half a mile along the creek there was an almost continuous chain of rifle pits."[74] The pits, hastily dug along the creek by the fleeing Indians, were cited in the *News* as support for Colonel Chivington's contention that Black Kettle's camp was full of hostiles who had prepared defensive positions. Not surprisingly, this conclusion was disputed by later testimony.[75]

Byers summed up the campaign by praising its success, glossing over any details or moral issues that might have tarnished Chivington's glory: "Whether viewed as a march or as a battle, the exploit has few if any parallels. A march of 260 miles in but a fraction more than five days, with deep snow, scanty forage and no road, is a remarkable feat, whilst the utter surprise of a large Indian village is unprecedented. In no single battle in North America, we believe, have so many Indians been slain."[76]

Byers's last words in the column concerned the heroism of the troops: "All acquitted themselves well, and Colorado soldiers have again covered themselves with glory." Within a few days, however, these words would sound more than a little ironic.

Chivington's command returned to Denver on 22 December. The *News* reported that the troops "were the admired of all observers, on their entry into town this morning."[77] Byers even noted the response of Denver's women, using the opportunity to make clear the threat the women faced from Indians. Byers wrote: "the fair sex took advantage of the opportunity . . . of expressing their admiration for the gallant boys who donned the regimentals for the purpose of protecting the women of the country by ridding it of redskins."

The *News* also published a "Complimentary Order" written by Chivington to thank his troops. He opened with a rhetorical justification of the attack, listing a host of Indian crimes against Colorado. Like Byers and other local promoters, Chivington pointed out that the Indian raids had "most seriously retarded the growth and prosperity of our Territory." And Chivington gave credit to his men for the Sand Creek victory "which is unparalelled [*sic*] in the history of Indian warfare."[78] These words, too, would soon take on a less complimentary meaning.

Politics Makes a Massacre

Sand Creek was being touted as a great victory in the New York *Tribune* as late as 27 December and in a page-one story in the New Orleans *Pica-*

yune on 28 December.[79] But new reports—unofficial and outside the established news-gathering process in the West—soon surfaced, contradicting the original press accounts. The Cincinnati *Gazette,* for example, first raised the question of a massacre on 26 December. The story, a paragraph in a "News of the Day" column, appeared on page two: "The 'brilliant victory' of Col. Chevington [*sic*] over the Indians in Colorado Territory . . . it is now reported was an atrocious massacre of unarmed men, women and children."[80] No source for the report was given. The *Gazette* ended with a single opinion on the matter: "For the credit of humanity we hope that this was not the case."

The same day, James Gordon Bennett's New York *Herald* published an anonymous letter from a person who, the paper said, "occupies a highly responsible position in the Territory."[81] The letter openly challenged the original news reports by claiming that the attack "was one of the most cruel in history." Specifically, the writer charged that "most of the victims were women and children. None were spared." And he added, "If such is military glory, God deliver me from all such."

Datelined Washington, this letter had political overtones, though the Democratic *Herald* did not explain them. Indeed, with the publication of this letter, the *Herald* thrust itself into the middle of an ongoing controversy within the Republican Party over the leadership of the Colorado Territory.[82] The letter, written by Stephen S. Harding, was politically inspired and it took direct aim at the ambitious Chivington. "This man, Col. Chivington, will attempt to make reputation as a military commander out of this massacre, which should cause a shudder of horror through the whole country." Harding, the chief justice of the territory, was a political rival of Governor Evans and Chivington.[83] Although published in New York, the letter came to the *Herald*'s Washington office through its addressee, Jack W. Wright, a friend of Harding's and a former Indian agent in Colorado. In fact, Wright, using information from Harding, seized upon Sand Creek as a way of settling an old score with Governor Evans. In 1863 Wright had antagonized Evans during a bungled survey of Indian lands.[84] Anxious to shift the blame, Wright pushed the Sand Creek story at the *Herald* and he wrote and published a pamphlet that accused Evans of starting the Indian trouble through neglect of duty. Finally, Wright lobbied with key senators in Washington to see that Sand Creek was investigated, all in an effort to undermine the political career of Evans.[85]

Thus the *Herald*'s exposé of the Sand Creek massacre had less to do with journalistic enterprise than with frustrated ambition and political revenge. As for Bennett, he used the Sand Creek story as a means of criticizing the Republican leadership and the *Herald* quickly took credit for instigating the Congressional investigation: "The publication in the Herald on Monday of the letter from Colorado . . . has aroused attention to the treatment of Indians, and is said to be made the subject of Congressional investigation upon the reassembling of Congress."[86]

In Denver, Byers published a Washington dispatch about the investigation on 29 December. But the story raised almost as many questions as it answered: "Washington, Dec. 28—The affair at Fort Lyon, Colorado, in which Colonel Chivington destroyed a large Indian village, and all inhabitants, is to be made the subject of a Congressional investigation. Letters received from high officials in Colorado, say that Indians were killed after surrendering, and that a large proportion of them were women and children."[87] Having acknowledged the investigation, Byers used the *News* columns to mount a strenuous counter-attack on the *Herald*'s "high officials in Colorado." Byers wrote that some of the Colorado soldiers "were very persistent in their inquiries as to who those 'high officials' were, with a mild intimation that they had half a mind to 'go for them.' This talk about 'friendly Indians' and a 'surrendered' village, will do to 'tell the marines,' but to us out here it is bosh."[88] Byers then defended Colorado's aggressiveness by compiling a detailed list of Indian outrages during 1864, including the murder and mutilation of the Hungate family near Denver and a series of attacks along Colorado roadways. The Indians who committed these crimes, Byers wrote, "were 'friendly Indians,' we suppose, in the eyes of these 'high officials.'"[89] Byers also claimed that the large amount of supplies found at Sand Creek—including "underclothes of white women and children stripped from their murdered victims"—was proof that the Sand Creek Indians were far from peaceful.

Byers became more ironic on the subject of scalps: "Probably those scalps of white men, women and children—*one of them fresh—not three days taken*—found drying in their lodges were taken in a friendly, playful manner; or . . . were kept simply as mementos of their owners' high affection for the pale face. At any rate these delicate and tasteful ornaments could not have been taken from the wives, sisters or daughters of these 'high officials.'"[90]

Byers concluded with the suggestion that the origin of the investigation was economic, not humanitarian. Indeed, he noted, an investigation would "let the world know who were making money by keeping the Indians under the sheltering protection of Fort Lyon." The Indians at Sand

Creek were thieves, Byers added, and "it is shrewdly suspected that some-body was all the time making a very good thing out of it."[91]

As before, Byers was highly sensitive to eastern criticism of Colorado affairs. He was especially outraged at two stories in the Auburn, New York, *Advertiser & Union* and he later reprinted these accounts in the *News.*[92] The first story in the *Advertiser* was published on 28 December and it began with a paragraph from another newspaper, the Washington *Star.* This story included the allegation that the battle was not a victory but was instead "a massacre of helpless savages." Like the original massacre story in the *News,* the *Star* story was attributed to a letter from a "gentleman of high posi-tion from Colorado Territory."[93]

The *Advertiser* identified this official as Judge Harding, the same official whose letter exposed the massacre in the New York *Herald.*[94] The *Advertiser* went on to denounce the character and judgment of Colonel Chivington, calling him an "uncultivated Methodist preacher of native western growth . . . who tries to make the public think he is very brave." In fact, Chivington was a native of Ohio and a true hero at La Glorieta. Nevertheless, the *Ad-vertiser* continued, "[Chivington] is low and brutal enough to believe that an Indian has no right to live and ought to be exterminated."[95]

The last paragraph of the *Advertiser* story again reveals the indirect na-ture of information from the West. It begins, "We are told . . ." and ends with these two sentences: "It seems from what we can learn that all this Indian trouble with the weak bands on the plains is wholly unnecessary. We are told that they are harmless."[96] Clearly, the *Advertiser,* like the New York *Herald,* was dependent upon Judge Harding for much of its Colorado infor-mation. It is notable, too, that this kind of information—unofficial, uncom-plimentary to Colorado, and sympathetic to the Indians—came from a let-ter, not a Denver telegraph dispatch. Since the *Daily Rocky Mountain News* and official Denver would not reveal the real nature of Sand Creek, private channels were used to tell the massacre story. The second *Advertiser* article appeared on 29 December and compared Chivington's massacre to an infa-mous murder case in Baltimore involving one Colonel Cræsop. But Cræsop had killed only one family, the paper said, while Chivington had "murdered two hundred families of Cheyennes . . . without provocation."[97]

The *Advertiser* attributed this information to Judge Benjamin F. Hall, an Auburn resident who had served three years as chief justice in Colo-rado. Hall told the paper that his encounters with the Indians had been friendly and they had visited and smoked with him in Denver to show their affection for him. The *Advertiser* continued: "The Judge is highly incensed at this outrage, and has authorized us to cite him as authority for stating that Chivington's murder of those five hundred unoffending Cheyennes is an outrage which has no parallel in history, and that Chivington's Commission should be taken from him instantly by the War Department."[98] Judge Hall had no firsthand knowledge of Sand Creek or other recent events in Colorado. But his successor, Judge Harding, did. According to the *Advertiser,* the judges had conferred recently and "they both agreed that Chivington was getting up this Indian fuss without any adequate cause, merely to keep up Pollock's (his son-in-law's) exorbitant contracts for supplies in that quarter."[99] Here was another economic motive for the Sand Creek massacre—Chivington's desire to help his son-in-law.

The appearance of the massacre story in Auburn was both personal and political. The chief political issue dividing Colorado in 1864 was statehood; Evans, Chivington, and the *News* were supporters while the anti-state forces were led by the Black Hawk *Journal* and some of the territorial judges. The battle was fought almost daily in the pages of the *News* and the *Journal* in the weeks leading up to the September election.[100] Months before Sand Creek, in fact, the *News* identified one of its political enemies by name. He was Judge Benjamin Hall, who appeared in the paper in early September when he spoke as an "Anti" at a Denver meeting. The *News* concluded: "The Judge is a good speaker, but his arguments were very flimsy."[101] So polarized was the statehood debate that Evans withdrew his name as a candidate for the senate in order to help gain additional support for the pro-state forces.[102]

In short, the running argument over Colorado statehood was one of the major forces behind the appearance of the massacre scandal in the eastern press. Even so, the massacre story was not big news there. It made headlines in some, but not all, eastern papers and it seemed to make headlines for particular reasons. It was big news in Auburn, for instance, because Judge Hall lived there. It made news in Washington because it was a convenient tool for Wright in his war against Evans, for anti-state forces to discredit both Evans and Chivington, and for the Democratic New York *Herald* to publicize Republican in-fighting.

This behind-the-scenes maneuvering did not surface in the press. Instead, the newspapers were content to play along in a highly partisan dispute that had already divided Colorado and was now spilling over into Washington. By publishing private letters from judges Hall and Harding, the New York *Herald* and the Auburn *Advertiser* exposed the Sand Creek massacre and drew attention to the deaths of innocent Cheyennes and

Arapahos. Surely this publicity helped the native cause and promoted an investigation of the Sand Creek massacre. But the underlying purpose of the publicity was less to help the Indian than to ruin the political careers of Evans and Chivington. The majority of the eastern papers showed little interest in the death of Indians; they simply responded to the personal and political motives of judges Harding and Hall. In sum, the actions of the eastern papers provide little evidence to support Byers's charge that the "humanitarian press" was responsible for the investigation of Sand Creek.[103]

An examination of other eastern papers also confirms that the press was responding to the investigation story, not leading it. On 4 January 1865 the *National Intelligencer* published its first news of the massacre and attributed the story to the Committee on the Conduct of the War. The committee, the story said, would soon investigate "what seems to have been a wholesale massacre of Indians in Colorado for no just cause, so far as is known at the Indian Bureau."[104] The mention of the Indian Bureau here confirms the bureaucratic origins of the investigation news.[105]

The remainder of the story quoted another letter from Judge Harding. In this letter, Harding mentioned the *Daily Rocky Mountain News* in making his case that the Indians were peaceful in the weeks before Sand Creek. "It is observable that the paper and its correspondents do not speak of any outrages committed by the Indians precedent to the attack upon them."[106]

Despite the seriousness of the charges and the fact that a Congressional committee would be investigating them, the *Intelligencer* made no editorial comment on Sand Creek. But the *Intelligencer* was sympathetic to the investigation in one self-congratulatory instance. The Louisville *Journal* used Judge Harding's charges in the *Intelligencer* as the basis for its own editorial on Sand Creek. The *Intelligencer,* in turn, was so pleased that on 13 January it reprinted the *Journal* editorial on page one.

The Kentucky paper said it understood the "fiendish treatment" of white women and children in the West, but "we can afford to be just and honorable towards their feeble race." Following the popular racial logic of the day, the editorial ennobled the vanishing native: "Not many years hence the Indian race will have been extinguished. They are passing rapidly away before our civilized immigration, and at last they will be known only in the fiction of Cooper and the poetry of Longfellow."[107]

The *Journal* called on the highest instincts of the whites in their treatment of the Indians. The Indians were "poor children of nature" and they deserved "pity from the philanthropic world." Thus the recent attack of

Chivington "should excite for those poor creatures the generous pity of the nation, and we are gratified that it is to be subjected to Congressional investigation."[108] This was one of a handful of newspaper editorials sympathetic (but condescending) to the "poor children of nature." But it is notable that in Louisville, as elsewhere, the editorial came primarily as a response to a Congressional inquiry.

A review of the eastern papers also shows that the Sand Creek story quickly lost favor there and never became a leading subject in either the news or editorial columns. There was little follow-up on the story and even less on the Congressional debate concerning the proposed investigation. The New York *Times,* for example, published nothing about the massacre or the possibility of an investigation during December 1864 or the first several months of 1865. The New York *Tribune* was also silent about the massacre and investigation during this period. Even the *National Intelligencer,* which regularly published extensive Congressional reports, covered the planned investigation in a single, bland paragraph: "Mr. [James] Harlan [of Iowa] offered a resolution instructing the Secretary of War to suspend all pay and allowances of the officers of the command of Col. Chivington, of Colorado, until an investigation of the conduct of Col. Chivington in a late attack on an Indian camp shall take place; and that all articles taken from the Indians shall be returned."[109] The actual Senate debate on this resolution involved ten senators and included a vigorous discussion of Chivington's actions, the nature of the Indian character, and government policies in the West. None of this was major news in the eastern press. The Senate debate also confirmed the private origins of the complaints against Chivington and his men. According to Senator Harlan, evidence that prompted the investigation included letters from an Indian agent, a judge in the territory, and several "private gentlemen." All of these people, Harlan said, corroborated "the same general facts, implying that the massacre was unprovoked, premeditated, and cold-blooded; that it was probably perpetrated for plunder."[110] But none of this information stirred significant editorial outrage in the eastern press. With Civil War news dominating page one as well as the editorial pages, the news about the Colorado militia and a few hundred Cheyenne and Arapaho Indians in the West quickly disappeared from the news.

Yet there was continuing Indian news from the frontier, news that illustrates the power of the Indian news frame. When the Cheyennes attacked a small outpost in northeastern Colorado in early January 1865, the national press relayed the story in brief telegraph reports. The Cincinnati

Gazette, for example, ran a page-one article on the Julesburg attack on 11 January that echoed the themes of the Indian panic in Colorado six months earlier: "A general massacre and destruction of the whites was only prevented by the perseverance and bravery of our troops and an efficient artillery fire." Even the language was familiar: "This is by far the most determined invasion made by the Indians."[111] The *Gazette* followed up this report a few days later with a story reprinted from the Omaha *Republican.* Not surprisingly, this story was composed of official reports from some of the officers who had defended Julesburg.[112] The *Intelligencer,* the *Inquirer,* and other eastern papers also published accounts of the new Indian threats.[113] In the *Daily Rocky Mountain News,* Byers recognized that these attacks were a response to Sand Creek.[114] But the eastern papers did not link these new attacks to Sand Creek, accepting at face value the sketchy and incomplete reports emanating from Omaha and other midwestern and western cities. During the Civil War years at least, the eastern papers had neither the economic means nor the editorial interest to look beyond the telegraph dispatches they received or to challenge the ordinary way that Indians were represented in the news.

The theme and tone of Indian news in January 1865 shows that within a few weeks of the Sand Creek massacre—and at the same time that the Sand Creek investigation was being debated in Congress—the eastern newspapers returned to routine coverage of the Indian frontier, almost all of it involving violence against whites. In other words, the normal flow of Indian news, briefly subverted as a result of Sand Creek, was re-established within weeks of the massacre. Without the death of innocents or some other type of tragedy to stir support for the natives, there was no cause for dissenting views or unofficial news to travel East. Thus the dominant and continuing news story of Indian-white relations from Colorado in 1864 and 1865 was tipped in favor of Evans, Chivington, and Byers, all powerful men in the territory. News critical of the Colorado political establishment and sympathetic to the Indians was all but banished from the routine news-making process.

Yet the Sand Creek story had one final burst of life in the newspapers in 1865. On 19 May the New York *Tribune* provided a preview of the upcoming Congressional report on the Sand Creek affair. The report, the *Tribune* stated, provided evidence that the attack was "a most brutal and unprovoked slaughter of men, women and children, who were living in a quiet manner in a state of entire peace with the whites."[115] When the report was released in mid-July, a number of eastern papers joined in the condemnation of the Colorado militia.[116] Other papers, such as the New York *Times*[117] and the New York *Observer,*[118] ran Senator Wade's report in full but without editorial comment. Further west, the Cincinnati *Gazette* ran part of the Sand Creek report on page one, but it appeared as the shortest and least prominent of the four reports released by the committee.[119] For many eastern and midwestern readers, however, the publication of the Congressional report was the fullest explanation of the Sand Creek massacre to appear in print.

The Sand Creek massacre was a major news story only in the Colorado press and the leading Colorado newspaper, the *Daily Rocky Mountain News,* was highly partisan in its coverage of the incident. Byers had many reasons to slant his paper's reporting about Sand Creek. He had established the *News* as a major organ of development in Colorado and the Cheyennes and Arapahos represented a major obstacle in that effort. In addition, as we've seen, Byers was personally and politically aligned with Governor Evans and Colonel Chivington, both supporters of Colorado statehood and both anxious to advance their political careers. Given these circumstances, it was inevitable that the *News* would forgive Chivington and the excesses of Sand Creek.

The eastern press paid little attention to the massacre. Colorado Territory made news only occasionally in 1864 and when it did, the westerners' strong anti-Indian sentiment dominated these stories. Not coincidentally, the brutal nature of Sand Creek surfaced not in news reports from Denver but in private, highly political letters that surfaced in the East, bypassing the western news-making process. Nevertheless, the sympathy of the eastern press toward the victims of Sand Creek was irregular at best; more often the massacre story was overlooked and under-reported. No eastern newspaper examined here gave the Sand Creek massacre more than minimal news coverage and a modest editorial. Except for the Albany *Advertiser,* no eastern paper sought to vilify Chivington. For all its horrors, the Sand Creek massacre inspired little editorial outrage. A major reason, of course, was the Civil War, the century's biggest news event. With most of its attention on the war, the eastern press demonstrated little sustaining interest in Indian news from the West, even news as dramatic as Chivington's massacre of Indians at Sand Creek. It was left to Congress and the army itself to investigate the massacre in 1865. Although both investigations produced substantial evidence of misconduct and savagery on the part of the Colorado soldiers, this story too was underplayed in the eastern papers, now fixed on the final days of the Confederacy. Thus the only newspaper that covered the Sand Creek investigation thoroughly was the one with the most to lose—the *Daily Rocky Mountain News*—and, with an embittered William Byers as editor, it remained partisan and highly anti-Indian.[120]

As for John Chivington, he never gained the political stature he sought in Colorado. A few months after Sand Creek, he was dismissed from the Methodist Church and moved to California.[121] A few years later, he married the widow of his son, an act that prompted the woman's parents to publish a letter condemning the marriage.[122] Chivington lived for thirty years after Sand Creek and eventually returned to Denver. But he never outlived the controversy surrounding his brutal attack on the Cheyennes and Arapahos in eastern Colorado. When he died, the obituary writers remembered the blood and gore of Sand Creek.[123]

Notes

1. Janet Lecompte, "Sand Creek," *The Colorado Magazine* 41 (Fall 1964): 329.

2. Margaret Coel, *Chief Left Hand* (Norman: University of Oklahoma Press, 1981), 279.

3. *Daily Rocky Mountain News* (hereafter *DRMN*), 13 Dec. 1864, 2.

4. Quoted in Stan Hoig, *The Sand Creek Massacre* (Norman: University of Oklahoma Press, 1961), 176.

5. Ibid.

6. *DRMN,* 8 Dec. 1864, 2.

7. See Lecompte, "Sand Creek," and Hoig, *Sand Creek Massacre.* The most complete studies of the massacre and its symbolism are David Svaldi, *Sand Creek and the Rhetoric of Extermination: A Case Study in Indian-White Relations* (Lanham, Md.: University Press of America, 1989), and Gary L. Roberts, "Sand Creek: Tragedy and Symbol" (Ph.D. diss., University of Oklahoma, 1984). See also Raymond G. Carey, "The Puzzle of Sand Creek," *The Colorado Magazine* 41 (Fall 1964): 279–98; J. D. Dunn Jr., *Massacres of the Mountains* (New York: Archer House, 1958); George Bird Grinnell, *The Fighting Cheyennes* (Norman: University of Oklahoma Press, 1956); George Hyde, *Life of George Bent* (Norman: University of Oklahoma Press, 1968); Harry Kelsey, "Background to Sand Creek," *The Colorado Magazine* 45 (Fall 1968): 279–300; and Lonnie J. White, "From Bloodless to Bloody," *Journal of the West* 6 (Oct. 1967): 535–81. Polemical literature includes, on the Indian side, Helen Hunt Jackson, *A Century of Dishonor* (Boston: Roberts Bros., 1886), and Dee Brown, *Bury My Heart at Wounded Knee* (New York: Bantam Books, 1972); and, on Chivington's side, William R. Dunn, *I Stand by Sand Creek* (Fort Collins, Colo.: Old Army Press, 1985), and Reginald S. Craig, *The Fighting Parson* (Los Angeles: Western Lore Press, 1959).

8. This charge has been repeated by some contemporary historians. See, for example, Lecompte, "Sand Creek," and Robert L. Perkin, *The First Hundred Years:*

An Informal History of Denver and the Rocky Mountain News (Garden City, N.Y.: Doubleday and Co., 1959).

9. Menahem Blondheim, *News over the Wires* (Cambridge: Harvard University Press, 1994), 32–33.

10. Ibid., 55.

11. Quoted in ibid., 38.

12. Washington *Post*, 26 Oct. 1878, 1.

13. New York *Tribune*, 22 July 1874, 1. The same dispatch also appeared the same day in the New York *Herald*, New York *Times*, Chicago *Tribune*, and other papers.

14. Carl Ubbelohde, Maxine Benson, and Duane A. Smith, *A Colorado History* (Boulder, Colo.: Pruett Publishing, 1976), 104.

15. Ibid., 59–96; see also Jerome C. Smiley, *History of Denver* (Denver: Old Americana Publishing, 1978), 236–42.

16. Lyle W. Dorsett, *The Queen City: A History of Denver* (Boulder, Colo.: Pruett Publishing, 1977), 38–39.

17. Ubbelohde et al., *Colorado History*, 106.

18. Dorsett, *Queen City*, 40.

19. Ibid., 40; also Ubbelohde et al., *Colorado History*, 106–7.

20. Ubbelohde et al., *Colorado History*, 77.

21. Dorsett, *Queen City*, 3.

22. Ibid., 4.

23. *DRMN*, 23 Apr. 1859, quoted in Svaldi, *Sand Creek and the Rhetoric of Extermination*, 135.

24. Ibid., 137.

25. *DRMN*, 25 Mar. 1864, 2.

26. Ibid.

27. Svaldi, *Sand Creek and the Rhetoric of Extermination*, 138–41.

28. Ibid., 150–51.

29. Ibid., 155–57.

30. Dorsett, *Queen City*, 14.

31. Ibid., 11.

32. Roberts, "Sand Creek," 319.

33. See, for example, any issue of the *DRMN* in January 1864.

34. Roberts, "Sand Creek," 322.

35. LeRoy R. Hafen, *Colorado: The Story of a Western Commonwealth* (Denver: Peerless Publishing, 1933), 160–62. See also Perkin, *First Hundred Years*, 235–52.

36. Perkin, *First Hundred Years*, 267.

37. See any issue of the *DRMN* in August 1864.

38. *DRMN*, 10 Aug. 1864, 2.

39. Ibid.

40. Ibid.

41. Ibid.

42. New York *Times*, 9 Aug. 1864, 5; Philadelphia *Inquirer*, 10 Aug. 1864, 1.

43. Philadelphia *Inquirer*, 11 Aug. 1864, 1.

44. *National Intelligencer*, in the Cincinnati *Gazette*, 15 Aug. 1864, 1.

45. New York *Times*, 12 Aug. 1864, 1.

46. Ibid.

47. Philadelphia *Inquirer,* 12 Aug. 1864, 4.

48. Ibid., 17 Aug. 1864, 1.

49. Ibid., 23 Aug. 1864, 2. This story also appeared in the Cincinnati *Gazette,* 22 Aug. 1864, 1.

50. Philadelphia *Inquirer,* 23 Aug. 1864, 2.

51. Cincinnati *Gazette,* 18 Aug. 1864, 2.

52. Perkin, *First Hundred Years,* 266.

53. *DRMN,* 18 Aug. 1864, 2.

54. New York *Times,* 20 Aug. 1864, 8.

55. Philadelphia *Inquirer,* 22 Aug. 1864, 4.

56. *DRMN,* 28 Aug. 1864, 1.

57. Ibid.

58. *DRMN,* 27 Sept. 1864, 2.

59. *DRMN,* 7 Dec. 1864, 2.

60. *DRMN,* 8 Dec. 1864, 2.

61. Ibid.

62. Ibid.

63. Ibid.

64. Ibid.

65. Ibid.

66. Ibid.

67. Ibid.

68. Perkin, *First Hundred Years,* 279–80; Grinnell, *Fighting Cheyennes,* 181–203.

69. See Perkin, *First Hundred Years,* 203–7, for a discussion of early telegraph operations in Denver.

70. Ibid.

71. *DRMN,* 13 Dec. 1864, 2.

72. *DRMN,* 17 Dec. 1864, 2.

73. Coel, *Chief Left Hand,* 272.

74. *DRMN,* 17 Dec. 1864, 2.

75. See Hoig, *Sand Creek Massacre,* 151, and Coel, *Chief Left Hand,* 280–81. See also conflicting testimony quoted in Hoig, *Sand Creek Massacre,* 187, 191.

76. *DRMN,* 17 Dec. 1864, 2.

77. *DRMN,* 22 Dec. 1864, 2.

78. Ibid.

79. New York *Tribune,* 27 Dec. 1864, 6.; New Orleans *Daily Picayune,* 28 Dec. 1864, 1.

80. Cincinnati *Gazette,* 26 Dec. 1864, 2.

81. New York *Herald,* 26 Dec. 1864, 5.

82. Kelsey, "Background to Sand Creek," 280.

83. White, "From Bloodless to Bloody," 567.

84. Ibid. See also the discussion in Kelsey, "Background to Sand Creek," 292–93.

85. Kelsey, "Background to Sand Creek," 292–93.

86. New York *Herald,* 29 Dec. 1864, 5.

87. *DRMN,* 29 Dec. 1864, 2. The story also appeared in the Philadelphia *Inquirer* and other papers on this date.

88. *DRMN,* 29 Dec. 1864, 2.

89. Ibid.

90. Ibid.

91. Ibid.

92. *DRMN,* 30 Jan. 1865, 2.

93. Ibid.

94. Roberts, "Sand Creek," 337.

95. Ibid.

96. Ibid.

97. Ibid.

98. Ibid.

99. Ibid.

100. See various issues of the *DRMN,* late August and early September 1864.

101. *DRMN,* 9 Sept. 1864, 2.

102. *DRMN,* 1 Sept. 1864, 2.

103. See, for example, Lecompte, "Sand Creek," 315, and Perkin, *First Hundred Years,* 277.

104. *National Intelligencer,* 4 Jan. 1865, 2.

105. One source for the massacre story was Indian agent Samuel G. Colley, whose letter on Sand Creek appeared in the Missouri *Intelligencer,* 6 Jan. 1865; see Grinnell, *Fighting Cheyennes,* 175. Colley is probably the Indian agent who was referred to in Congressional debate; see the *Congressional Globe,* 38th Cong., 2d Sess., 14 Jan. 1865, 251.

106. *National Intelligencer,* 4 Jan. 1865, 2.

107. Ibid., 13 Jan. 1865, 1.

108. Ibid.

109. Ibid., 4.

110. *The Congressional Globe,* 13 Jan. 1865, 250–56.

111. Cincinnati *Gazette,* 11 Jan. 1865, 1.

112. Ibid., 20 Jan. 1865, 1.

113. *National Intelligencer,* 12 Jan. 1865, 3; Philadelphia *Inquirer,* 11 Jan. 1865; New York *Times,* 27 Jan. 1865, 4.

114. See Dorsett, *Queen City,* 42; Perkin, *First Hundred Years,* 279.

115. New York *Tribune,* 19 May 1865.

116. Roberts, "Sand Creek," 506–7, cites editorials from three papers: the Philadelphia *Public Ledger and Daily Transcript,* the Washington *Chronicle,* and the Boston *Journal.*

117. New York *Times,* 23 July 1865, 2.

118. New York *Observer,* 3 Aug. 1865, 246.

119. Cincinnati *Gazette,* 24 July 1865, 1.

120. See, for example, *DRMN,* 31 Dec. 1864; 31 Jan. 1865; 1 Feb. 1865; 6 Feb. 1865.

121. Dorsett, *Queen City,* 42; Perkin, *First Hundred Years,* 279.

122. New York *Times,* 11 June 1868, 5.

123. Ibid., 13 Oct. 1894, 23.

The ideology of Manifest Destiny was made plain by Frances Flora Bond ("Fanny") Palmer in this 1868 hand-colored lithograph, "Across the Continent. 'Westward the Course of Empire Takes Its Way,'" after Currier and Ives. In Palmer's vision, Native Americans are mere bystanders to the pioneers' civilizing task: people intent on building a town and a school in the wilderness. (© Amon Carter Museum. Courtesy of the Amon Carter Museum, Fort Worth, Texas)

THE ATTACK ON THE STAGE.

This "classic" image of western life appeared in an 1889 Buffalo Bill novel. Despite the fact that most emigrants traveled across the continent peacefully, the excitement and drama of Indian attacks inspired many news stories—some true, some not—and became one of the most popular features of the nineteenth-century western experience. (Author's collection)

HARPER'S YOUNG PEOPLE

AN ILLUSTRATED WEEKLY.

VOL. VI.—NO. 262. PUBLISHED BY HARPER & BROTHERS, NEW YORK. PRICE FIVE CENTS.

TUESDAY, NOVEMBER 4, 1884. Copyright, 1884, by HARPER & BROTHERS. $2.00 PER YEAR, IN ADVANCE.

THE INDIAN CHILD.—SEE POEM ON PAGE 2.

The romantic Indian stereotype was easily attached to Native American children, whose perceived virtues could serve as a useful lesson for white children. "The Indian Child" illustrated a poem by M. E. Sangster, a hymn to the doomed but gentle life of the Indian. The poem concludes: "Better things one day shall be / For thy dusky race and thee, / Indian child, so sad and grave, / Boastful, ignorant, and brave." (From *Harper's Young People,* 4 November 1884, author's collection)

FRANK LESLIE'S ILLUSTRATED NEWSPAPER

No. 761—Vol. XXX.]   NEW YORK APRIL 30, 1870.   [Price 10 Cents

"The Sick Indian Girl—an Incident of the Plains," shows a side of Native American life not commonly revealed in the press. Unfortunately, A. J. Russell, whose photograph was the basis for this illustration, used the occasion to ridicule the woman's vanity. He reported that when he presented the photograph to her, "she was restored, almost instantly, to perfect health!" (From *Frank Leslie's Illustrated Newspaper,* 30 April 1870, author's collection)

AFTER MOTHER COUNTRY'S SCALP.

"To whom do the spoils belong if they do not belong to the victors?"—Senator Vance at Tammany Hall, July 5.

The idea of the savage was a useful device for editorial writers and cartoonists making political points, as in Thomas Nast's "After Mother Country's Scalp." Nast criticized New York's Tammany machine—a name derived from the Delaware chief Tamanend—by creating grotesque warriors dancing around a "Hungry Tammany" pole and taking the scalp from the young "Mother Country." (From *Harper's Weekly*, 17 July 1886, author's collection)

No army witnesses lived to tell of the Fetterman massacre, a fact that did not stop the *Harper's Weekly* artist who drew "The Indian Battle and Massacre Near Fort Philip Kearney, Dacotah Territory." Ten years later, the Custer massacre was represented in similar ways: a mass of men and horses, guns and arrows—all of it speculative. (From *Harper's Weekly,* 23 March 1867, author's collection)

Bismarck *Tribune* editor Clement A. Lounsberry missed the Custer expedition—and immortality—because of a family illness. Like many western journalists, his opinion of the Plains Indians was largely negative. (Sandy Barnard Collection)

FRANK LESLIE'S ILLUSTRATED NEWSPAPER

NEW YORK, SEPTEMBER 18, 1875.

OUR INDIAN POLICY

J. Keppler's "Our Indian Policy," which depicts the controversy over President Grant's "Peace Plan," treats Indians sympathetically while pointing out the corruption of the bureaucrats who supplied them with rifles, rotten beef, and "ventilated" blankets. The caption identifies the man with the tomahawk as "Howling Tadpole," evidence of the status of Indian warriors in the 1870s. (From *Frank Leslie's Illustrated Newspaper,* 18 September 1875, Sandy Barnard Collection)

THE RIGHT WAY TO DISPOSE OF SITTING BULL AND HIS BRAVES.
WHAT THE COUNTRY EXPECTS OF GENERAL SHERIDAN.

The spectacular defeat and death of Custer in June 1876 led to a wave of racial hatred. Weeks after the battle, the *New York Graphic* printed "The Right Way to Dispose of Sitting Bull and His Braves," depicting the Lakota warrior as half-buck and half-man, a creature so violent and hideous that he deserved extermination. (From *New York Graphic,* 15 August 1876, Sandy Barnard Collection)

A New Englander by birth, Helen Hunt Jackson became one of the most energetic Indian reformers from 1879 to her death in 1885. Her polemic *A Century of Dishonor* helped to inspire a generation of activists, but many of the reforms she and others championed were destined to fail. (Courtesy of Special Collections, Tutt Library, Colorado College, Colorado Springs, Colorado)

A preacher turned journalist turned Indian reformer, Thomas H. Tibbles was instrumental in the Ponca publicity campaign. The campaign included a Ponca tour of the East, which won the tribe sympathy and fueled the Indian reform movement. (Courtesy of the Nebraska State Historical Society)

Although she preferred her Christian name, Susette LaFlesche was known to the public as Bright Eyes. She proved to be an attractive and effective speaker for the Ponca cause, even though she was an Omaha. Like the Poncas, she was idealized by the press and public. (Courtesy of the Nebraska State Historical Society)

The Ponca chief Standing Bear was a heroic man who led a group of Poncas from Indian Territory to the tribe's homeland on the northern plains. His court case, *Standing Bear v. Crook,* provided legal support for Indian citizenship but he proved somewhat too "Indian" for many eastern supporters, including some in the press. (Courtesy of the Nebraska State Historical Society)

Like many western editors, William N. Byers of the *Daily Rocky Mountain News* used his paper to promote his town. When Indians seemed to threaten Denver in 1864, Byers urged military action against the "scalping sons of butchery." The result was the notorious Sand Creek massacre. (Courtesy of the Denver Public Library, Western History Collection)

Denver had dirt streets but big dreams in the early 1860s, a fact that moved the *Daily Rocky Mountain News* to view Indians as a threat to the city. When reports of the Sand Creek massacre reached Denver in late 1864, Byers wrote, "Bully for the Colorado Boys." (Courtesy of the Denver Public Library, Western History Collection)

TOO TRUE.

The Appalling Tale of Indian Butchery Officially Confirmed.

A Feeling of the Most Bitter Resentment Awakened in the Country.

General Demand that the Demons Be Pieganized into Harmlessness.

Some History of the Principal Wild Beast Called Sitting Bull.

The Multiplicity of Instances in Which He Has Courted Extermination.

A Sketch of the Life and Military Career of the Gallant Custer.

An Outline of Gen. Sheridan's Plans for the Campaign.

The Sioux and Cheyenne victory over Custer at the Little Bighorn caused a wave of anti-Indian news. The Chicago *Tribune* headline summarized the popular reaction by demonizing the Indians (especially Sitting Bull), expressing sorrow over the loss of Custer, and detailing the army's campaign to punish the victors. (Chicago *Tribune,* 7 July 1876, 1)

BUFFALO BILL!

"He is King of them all."—General E. A. Carr.

ATHLETIC PARK,

COMMENCING TO-MORROW AFTERNOON.

JUNE 22 FOR THREE DAYS ONLY

Two Performances Daily, Afternoon and Evening, Rain or Shine.

Buffalo Bill's WILD WEST

AMERICA'S NATIONAL ENTERTAINMENT

...THE RENOWNED SIOUX CHIEF,

SITTING BULL

And Several of the Celebrated Late Hostile Warriors.

White Eagle and 52 Pawnee and Wichita Braves.

We fulfill every promise.—Cody and Salsbury.

Admission, 50 cents.   **Children, 25 cents.**

Music furnished by the Wild West Cowboy Band.

Gates open 1 and 6 P. M.   Performance commences at 3:30 and 8 P. M.

Street Cars to the Gate.

Grand Street Parade to-morrow at 10 A. M.

Sitting Bull's identity as "Custer's killer" was both exploited and softened when he became part of "America's National Entertainment." Sitting Bull's popular appeal was second only to Buffalo Bill's. (Washington *Post,* 21 June 1885, 8)

SITTING BULL

Killed by the Indian Police.

Fierce Battle at Camp of the Chief.

Wily Savage Resisted Capture.

Followers Rallied to Rescue.

The murder of Sitting Bull in 1890 made page one in Boston and other cities far from the northern plains, testimony to Sitting Bull's fame and a sign that violence was still a popular way of representing Indians. (Boston *Daily Globe,* 16 December 1890, 1)

F · I · V · E

The War in Words:
Reporting the Fetterman Fight

T HE first news of the Fetterman massacre came via telegraph from Fort Laramie almost a week after the fact. The dispatch was only one paragraph, but the story seemed clear enough: Brevet Lt. Col. William J. Fetterman, two other officers, and eighty men stationed at Fort Phil Kearney on the Bozeman Trail "were surrounded by Indians and every officer and man killed."[1] The New Orleans *Picayune*, like many other newspapers, ran the story on page one under a dramatic headline: "Terrible Massacre Near Fort Kearney."[2]

But the "terrible massacre" that appeared in the press was not the same as the one inflicted upon Colonel Fetterman and his command in late 1866. Indeed, the variations between the real tragedy and the one reconstructed by the newspapers started with the initial dispatch and soon grew to encompass a host of published distortions, rumors, and misinterpretations. Not all the fault belongs to the press. Indeed, the annihilation of Fetterman's command soon became the subject of debate within Congress, the War Department, and the Indian Bureau, each with its own view of the tragedy. The eastern humanitarians also had a point of view, as did the outraged frontiersmen. For all these reasons, the Fetterman massacre touched off a new public controversy over Indian policy and the settlement of the West.

As one of the first big Indian stories following the Civil War, the Fetterman massacre also helped define the way newspapers represented and explained Indians during two turbulent decades of western expansion. Indeed, I argue that newspaper coverage of the Fetterman massacre helped establish an explanatory frame for Indian war news in the postwar era and was for this reason influential in the tone and theme of subsequent reports from the Indian wars. This standardized response to Indian violence was reinforced by organizational and technological changes growing out of Civil War reporting. These changes included increased newspaper reliance on the telegraph, the new power of the Associated Press, and the rising status of the war correspondent. Ultimately, these forces helped create and promote a series of formulaic narratives about Indian violence in the West that eventually became more important than the facts themselves in telling the story of the Indian wars.

New Forms of News

The organization that would become the Associated Press began in 1846 as a cooperative arrangement between six New York newspapers. By the time of the Civil War, the New York Associated Press was powerful enough that its goals began to conflict with the editorial needs of western editors, a dispute that revealed the liabilities of a single, powerful news agency. Early in the Civil War, a group of midwestern editors recognized the New York orientation of the NYAP and objected to the incomplete wire reports provided by the agency. In response, they formed a loose association known as the Western Associated Press. By 1865, the Western AP had enough clout to issue four rules for its agent in New York, including a rule that Western AP news "should be selected for its interest to the subscribing papers, not for its importance in New York."[3]

This early dispute over news and its processing foreshadowed a new problem in the larger and more complex news environment that grew out of the Civil War: Who decides the news and whose interests are served by news selection and emphasis? As it turned out, the editors of the Western AP soon settled their differences with the NYAP. But in the case of the warring Plains Indians, the news-making process that defined them—and that distorted and undermined their cultures—was largely closed to them and their representatives. Thus the formation of the AP was an institutional advance that came at the cost of diversity, as individual or dissenting interpretations of news events became subordinate to a routine set of ideas about hostile Indians. The consolidation of news-gathering in a powerful institution as well as the development of an enlarged network for the distribution of news helped to standardize the emphasis and tone of Indian war news in American newspapers. For the Indians of the plains, the result was a limited range of ideas about their lives, their cultures, and their relations with whites in the American West.

Another important source of Indian ideas in the postwar period was the illustrated press. *Frank Leslie's Illustrated Newspaper,* founded in 1855, and *Harper's Weekly* ("A Journal of Civilization") founded two years later, were forerunners of the contemporary news magazine, offering national and international news, commentary, and a variety of other editorial and literary items. But these publications were most well known for their prolific use of illustrations, images that contained considerable power in the era before editorial photography. The strength of these illustrations was their vividness and apparent realism. To produce these images, *Leslie's* and *Harper's* employed a new category of employee, the "special artist." These journalists traveled to various "newsworthy" places, where they gathered firsthand impressions and drew on-the-spot sketches. These sketches were transported to New York, where a group of engravers was deployed to copy them onto wooden blocks. In this way, relatively timely and exciting images of Civil War battlefields and other dramatic scenes became major features of the illustrated press. To ensure a steady supply of images, the illustrated papers also employed army officers and others to produce sketches of distant scenes. On other occasions, engravers turned photographs into illustrations, a fact regularly noted in the papers and one that underscored the apparent fidelity of the images. A typical example can be found in *Harper's* in October 1863. The paper published a full-page illustration of "The Sioux War" in Dacotah Territory, "Sketched By an Officer Engaged."[4] The officer helpfully provided an explanation of the attack (an expedition "to punish the savages for the massacres in Minnesota last year"), proclaimed its success (nearly two hundred killed, more than one hundred fifty captured), and praised its commander, Brigadier Gen. Alfred Sully.[5] These firsthand details added veracity to the image and let the paper claim a competitive edge in both truth and uniqueness, points not lost on the perceptive reader.

But the illustration process was not always so straightforward. The need for dramatic images, especially from the Indian wars, ensured that excitement would be a major feature in these drawings. In addition, many images were quite imaginary, created solely from written reports—a fact not advertised in the press. Even more troubling were those illustrations created in New York by artists and engravers who had little or no firsthand knowledge of the events they were depicting.[6] Again, the illustrated press did not mention this fact. Nevertheless, both *Frank Leslie's* and *Harper's* were enormously popular. *Harper's* achieved a circulation of 120,000 during the Civil War, becoming the nation's largest magazine. *Leslie's* circulation was less than half that in 1865. Together, these papers popularized standard battle images and heaped praise on heroic soldiers. Custer's rise to fame during the Civil War, in fact, was due in part to his flamboyant personal style as illustrated in *Leslie's* and *Harper's,* where he was portrayed in thoroughly romantic images, including one *Harper's* drawing of Custer in a brigand jacket "of black velveteen with swirls of gold braid from wrists to elbows."[7] The need for colorful, reader-pleasing images also affected the imagery of the Indian wars. One "classic" image was drawn for *Harper's* by Theodore R. Davis, a well-known Civil War correspondent and artist. On his first trip west after the Civil War, Davis lived through an Indian attack on a mule-drawn stagecoach on the road to Denver. He made two very similar drawings of this attack, one for *Harper's Monthly* and another for *Harper's Weekly,* and his written account of the incident appeared in the *Daily Rocky Mountain News* and *Harper's Weekly.* L. K. Perrin, a New York *Times* correspondent, also wrote a story of the incident for his paper. Directly or indirectly, this tale and Davis's images of it became representative of Indian-white violence in the romantic Wild West, inspiring reenactments by Buffalo Bill's troupe and in hundreds of western stories, dime novels, movies, and television shows.[8]

In sum, the accuracy of the illustrations in *Leslie's* and *Harper's* was problematic. At their best, such images might capture some sense of reality, at least from the (white) artist's point of view. But the illustrated papers did not want images of the mundane or the dull. Artists and engravers had every incentive to improve reality, to make their images as interesting and exciting as possible. Such images might depart from the literal truth, but they could be justified as emotionally true, capturing that sense of adventure that western journeys were supposed to possess. The myth, after all, was what sold papers. For Indians, however, the popularity of these images and the process that produced them meant that they were regularly and dramatically portrayed as enemies of progress, all too ready to attack white settlers and soldiers all across the West.

The Indian War Correspondent

Another organizational change accelerated by the Civil War was the rise of the reporter. Although the Civil War was not the first war covered by on-the-scene correspondents,[9] the Civil War brought the war correspondent to prominence in American journalism. "Probably no great war has ever been so thoroughly covered by eye-witness correspondents as the American Civil War," wrote journalism historian Frank Luther Mott.[10] With profits as well as prestige hanging in the balance, editors pushed their correspondents harder than ever for news from the front, and competition between correspondents became a significant factor in daily journalism. So when the Indian wars erupted shortly after Appomattox, it was no surprise that a hearty group of staff correspondents accompanied the soldiers.

The increased status of the Civil War reporter affected coverage both of that war and the Indian wars that followed. Some Civil War reporters quickly became journalistic legends, known for their extraordinary efforts to get their stories from the front, through the military censors, and on to their papers. Henry Villard, for example, broke the news of the Union defeat at Fredericksburg for the New York *Tribune* by defying the commanding general, riding miles on bad roads, and sending his story by train because the telegraph was closed to news of the battle.[11] After the Civil War, journalists traveling on the Indian campaigns followed this example, working hard to get dramatic, firsthand reports in print before the competition. Unfortunately, such practices placed audience expectations and speed before honesty and did little to encourage a full understanding of western Indians or the complex issues that brought them into conflict with whites.

The rise of the war correspondent contributed to an evolving myth in American journalism: the journalist as hero. Covering any war was obviously dangerous work and this danger helped elevate the stature of many Civil War correspondents. Similarly, the Indian wars involved great challenges, because battle lines were not well defined and, in any case, Indians did not behave like "civilized" Confederate soldiers. Moreover, correspondents on the Indian frontier had to overcome the hardships of life on the plains as well as the long lines of communication between the battlefield and the nearest telegraph office. All of these obstacles contributed to the growing myth of the tough, hard-riding Indian war correspondent. This heroic stance, in turn, took on a life of its own, eventually affecting the way Indians of the plains were portrayed in the press.

In a variety of ways, then, the experience of the Civil War set the pattern for news coverage of the Indian wars. In both cases, reporters sometimes resorted to inventing sensational or dramatic details in order to improve their copy. Historian J. Cutler Andrews, for instance, discovered many Civil War dispatches that were thorough and accurate. On occasion, reporters wrote highly descriptive stories about the trauma and hardship of war. But on too many occasions, Andrews noted, the press printed rumors and hearsay. Many of its lapses were not intentional, Andrews concluded, but due to the haste and confusion of gathering news on the battlefield. At its worst, however, the press resorted to "sensationalism and exaggeration, outright lies, puffery, slander, faked eyewitness accounts, and conjectures built on pure imagination."[12] Such practices, unfortunately, soon surfaced on the Indian frontier as well.

Competition prompted editors and reporters to favor bigger and more colorful war reports because such reports generated public interest and higher circulation. In short, there was a professional incentive for reporters to make every battle the grandest, most heroic victory and every defeat the bloodiest and most threatening. Andrews, for example, noted that news-hungry readers loved defeat as much as victory: "In fact, the worse a defeat was made to appear, the more eager the public seemed to be to hear about it."[13] Not surprisingly, reporters began to rely on a series of stock expressions to add drama to their stories. On the Indian frontier, for example, hostile Indians were routinely described as "red devils" and "Indian murderers" who were invariably "treacherous." In this way, Indian identity in the postwar era was shaped by competitive reporters who used colorful and dramatic language to write stories that readers wanted to read.

Despite the emphasis on speed and the tendency toward exaggeration, the use of correspondents in the West promised increased accuracy and reliability of frontier news. Oliver Knight, who made the most complete study of Indian war correspondents, concluded that the appearance of on-the-scene reporters in 1867 did improve the quality and accuracy of western reporting.[14] But the Indian war correspondent did not solve all the problems of accuracy or bias. Indeed, newspaper correspondents varied in skill and reliability, factors that complicated the news-making process in the West. More importantly, frontier reporters were influenced by their close identification with the army, their restricted view of the Indian, and, ultimately, by their sense of national destiny.

In *Following the Indian Wars,* Knight traced the editorial need for exciting stories from the frontier, the better to keep editors and readers back east reading about the Indian wars. "Adventure and the hero rated high in reader appeal, and war correspondents contributed their bit through accounts of their own adventures as well as adventures of others," Knight wrote.[15] Newspapers sent their reporters west, Knight concluded, because "the future of the nation was involved in the outcome." But the motives of journalists were not really that idealistic. As Knight pointed out, the Indian wars also "made exciting reading."[16] Thus the press sent reporters into Indian campaigns with a mission not only to chronicle the winning of the West—fulfilling America's rightful destiny—but also to provide exciting stories of heroic soldiers and vanquished savages for the folks back home.

Frontier reporters often defined their success in terms of adventure and excitement. Charles Sanford Diehl, an Indian war reporter for the Chicago *Times* who later became superintendent of the AP, made action and romance main themes of his autobiography. Although he denied that the Indian campaigns were either romantic or heroic,[17] his "Dedication To My Seven Grandchildren" cast his career in terms of "historic happenings, not all of them large, but many of them full of action."[18] Action was also central to Diehl's conception of journalism. "Journalism and the army have a certain relationship," he wrote. "They both represent action."[19] Journalists, Diehl added, "are compelled to see the moving panorama of life in its actuality as cannot be known to the dilettante or to the one who looks out upon his world from his closet window."[20] Diehl also pointed to romantic literature—*The Three Musketeers* and *Ivanhoe,* among others—as models of "real literature."[21]

More pointedly, Diehl stressed the romance of Indian war reporting. Diehl recalled, for example, that he had been rereading the adventurous exploits of Charles Lever's *Charles O'Malley* when he learned that Gen. Nelson Miles had surrounded Chief Joseph and his Nez Perce, bringing an end to their heroic march toward Canada. "I wrote my story, by candlelight, in a cold army tent, and dispatched it by courier to Helena, Montana."[22] Later, in Chicago, Diehl was complimented on his story. "I looked up my printed narrative, and found it interesting," he wrote. Diehl added: "The story was full of action. Going back over the circumstances, I had to ask myself, whether I could have embodied all the swing of battle stir, had I not, that day, been fighting with the valorous O'Malley, in the Spanish Peninsula."[23] Diehl was not with General Miles and was not a witness to the surrender of the Nez Perce. Yet his powers of imagination were fired by the romance of *Charles O'Malley* and he produced an action-filled story that won praise from his colleagues. Success in Indian reporting, as Diehl made clear, was not measured in terms of explanation or analysis but in terms of action and excitement. The job of the Indian reporter was to find excitement, even when it was inspired by fiction.

The Ideology of Indian War Reporting

Although the front-line correspondent could rely on his own observations for his reporting, he was not an independent observer. Indeed, the Indian war reporter was completely dependent upon his army sources not simply for military information and Indian news but for survival. Following their news instincts, reporters usually attached themselves to the staffs of various officers, the better to understand the leadership of the Indian campaigns—and live to write about it. This was a practical decision but it had ideological implications. Even before they saw an Indian or heard a shot fired in anger, Indian war reporters approached the West with a set of ideas about Indians. They certainly did not go West with the idea of "objective" war reporting. Such a notion was both impractical and naive. After all, reporters, like most Americans of that age, approached the plains with the clear sense that Indians had to be subdued and disarmed so that white emigration could proceed in an orderly fashion. To almost all reporters and editors, this was the nation's destiny, and the Indians were an obstacle. In this sense, there was no "Indian side" to the Indian wars—and no need for military censorship—because Indians had no legitimate standing in the public conception of the West.

Evidence for such conclusions can be found in the copy of almost every western war reporter. Most of them felt a kinship with the soldiers and officers whose lives they described. In addition, many of them were respectful of the commanding officers at whose pleasure they worked. Naturally, the closeness of the reporter to the commander precluded most negative reporting about the army. Thus Knight discovered that Joe Wasson, one of the first Indian war reporters, was a consistent supporter of General Crook. Wrote Wasson: "The success of the Command so far, and upon success alone is everything judged in this practical world, implies that Gen. Crook's plan is as good as any; and I believe he has the Indian character a little nearer down to scratch than any man in the regular service."[24] The connections between reporters and the officers under whom they served were not neutral because they boosted the aspirations of the commanding officer whether he was actually successful or not. Even Crook, who had generally favorable publicity during the Indian campaigns, noted that "it was not what a person did, but it was what he got credit for doing that gave him a reputation."[25]

This one-sided process created news in which the Indian was little more than a shadowy yet fearsome creature. Most of all, he was a savage enemy and no reporter could fail to see the horror of Indian raids and torture during these violent years. Left out of the process, however, were the peaceful tribes. Even the Crows and other tribes allied with the army against hostile Indians were barely visible in Indian war stories. In short, the Indian war correspondent saw the conflict almost exactly as the army saw the conflict. The army's position was hardly surprising, but the press was not obliged to follow the army lead. In theory, it could have offered a wider and more differentiated view of the western tribes. Instead, Indian war correspondents offered readers excitement, danger, and a thoroughly simple view of the Indian frontier.

The case of John F. Finerty, one of the most famous Indian war correspondents, illustrates this process. Finerty, who wrote for the Chicago *Times,* claimed in his memoirs that his reporting was a faithful narrative "as far as human fallibility will permit."[26] But Finerty admitted that invention also played a part in the popular image of the Indian: "Stories of Indian warfare, even when not founded entirely upon fact, have ever been popular with people of all nations, and more particularly with the American people, to whom such warfare is rendered familiar both by tradition and experience."[27] This is a remarkably candid statement because it confirms that popular Indian themes and stories—even those not necessarily true—were the basis for at least some Indian war reporting. Finerty himself was accused of inventing facts, though one of his scholarly defenders believed such charges themselves were exaggerated.[28] In any case, Finerty did not have a high opinion of Indians in general and relied on his own stereotypes to describe them: "The average Indian is still unchanged— still the same mysterious, untamable, barbaric, unreasonable, childish, superstitious, treacherous, thievish, murderous creature, with rare exceptions, that he has been since Columbus set eyes upon him at San Salvador."[29] This summary is unfair, of course, in that it lumps all Indians together, even those Indians of the Caribbean islands who were originally described by Columbus in a more favorable light.[30] On the other hand, such oversimplified comments might well be expected from a war correspondent who had been both witness and participant in a number of Indian battles. Above all else, Finerty knew about Indian fighting because he had fought against them many times. Unfortunately, this familiarity did not expand his appreciation for the variety or richness of Indian life. Finerty concluded that all Indians were thieves: "Whether friendly or hostile, the average Indian is a plunderer. He will first steal from his enemy. If he cannot get enough that way, he steals from his friends."[31] Finerty also had a low opinion of Indian women and the division of labor in Indian society. Indian women, he noted, were "squatty, yellow, ugly, and greasy looking." The reasons for this, he added, were the hard work they endured for the sake of "their lazy brutes of sons, husbands, and brothers [who] will do no work."[32]

It is difficult to blame Finerty for such views. As a war correspondent, he was exposed to the most brutal aspects of Indian life. He saw the battered bodies of settlers and soldiers caught in Indian raids and, like all whites, he was shocked by Indian practices of torture and mutilation. Moreover, Finerty was more than a passive observer of Indian warfare; he knew full well that he could be the next Indian victim. With arrows whizzing past his head, it is little wonder that he had a passionate dislike for Indians and their apparently savage life on the plains.

The effect of these circumstances, however, was Finerty's oversimplification of all Indian life. The gap between cultures, already stretched to the breaking point by years of misunderstanding and war, was made wider by such attitudes. It was not Finerty's job, of course, to negotiate peace or to improve race relations. He was sent west to describe war. Thus the role of Finerty and the other western war correspondents was to create enemies so alien and inhuman that their traditions and culture could be destroyed and their very existence threatened. In this manner, war reporting from the Indian frontier reinforced racial stereotypes and hindered the search for peaceful solutions to the "Indian problem."

The Facts about Fetterman

The Fetterman massacre was the most notable incident in the short life of Fort Phil Kearny, or Fort Phil Kearney as it was usually spelled.[33] The story of the disaster was a complex one, involving army politics and mismanagement, personal ambition, Indian tactics, and a host of other forces. But the story that emerged in the press reduced the disaster to a simple case of good versus evil—an evil defined according to a specific set of cultural values.

Fort Phil Kearney was established in the summer of 1866 in present-day Wyoming by Col. Henry B. Carrington, a Yale Law School graduate and former Republican leader in Ohio. Although Carrington was a Civil War veteran, his military appointment was political and he spent most of the war as an aide to the governor of Indiana.[34] Even worse, his leadership skills were minimal and his combat ability was untested. Despite such handicaps, Carrington was ordered to protect the Bozeman Trail, a new route for miners and other emigrants on their way to Montana.[35]

As instructed, Carrington built an imposing fort. He saw his mission as primarily defensive, however, and did little to disturb the movements of Red Cloud or other hostile Indians in the area. Carrington was also lax in enforcing discipline, which led to disturbances among the troops and dissension among the officers. Finally, Carrington did not drill his troops, even though many were raw recruits.[36] In Carrington's defense, it is true that he had fewer troops than he requested and, at least for a time, too little ammunition to engage in proper training.[37] Nevertheless, when the time came to fight Indians, Carrington and his men were ill-prepared for the challenge.

The tribes of the Powder River country were angry about the fort from the start, but they knew it was foolish to attack the fort directly. Instead, they stole horses grazing outside the fort and harassed the soldiers whenever they left the compound, especially the woodcutters who worked in a "pinery" a few miles away. Almost daily during the fall of 1866, a few Indians would attack the wood crew and the soldiers from the fort would rush to their aid. The Indians would then retreat, only to repeat the exercise another day.

From the army's point of view, this was an irritating strategy. Too many horses were being lost and the Indian raiders roamed at will. General Philip St. George Cooke, Carrington's superior, ordered Carrington to take the offensive, an order that found immediate favor with a new officer at the post, Brevet Lt. Col. William J. Fetterman.[38] Fetterman, a Civil War veteran, had arrived at the fort only weeks earlier. From the start, he was contemptuous of Carrington's leadership and was eager to fight the Sioux. Cheyenne historian George Grinnell claimed that some of Carrington's officers "seemed to regard the Indians as a sort of game to be hunted for sport."[39] Fetterman himself boasted, "With eighty men I could ride through the Sioux nation,"[40] a prediction that soon took a darkly grim turn.

The new aggressiveness of the soldiers was a welcome opportunity for the Sioux and Cheyenne. They decided to try a decoy and ambush tactic: attack the wood crew with a small band, let the army pursue, and then ambush them with an overwhelming force. It almost worked on 6 December, but some of the eager warriors attacked too soon and Carrington, Fetterman, and their men reunited in time to thwart the ambush. The Indians tried again on 19 December, again without success. On 21 December, however, Fetterman rode headlong into the trap.

A great part of the blame can be assigned to Fetterman, who disobeyed Carrington's orders not to pursue the Indians beyond a nearby ridge. Unaware of the trap and sensing an opportunity to cut off the Indian retreat, Fetterman led eighty men into the ambush. About two thousand Indians swooped down from the hills and killed them all in about thirty minutes. Carrington sent reinforcements when he heard shooting beyond the ridge, but it was too late. The relief column returned late in the day, its wagons heavy with the dead. That night, Carrington composed a report on the fight and engaged messengers to take the news to his superiors.

Unfortunately, the press soon bungled a great many aspects of this story. The first news of the disaster in most dailies was a short AP dispatch from New York based on Carrington's original report. Thus the first news of the disaster was essentially correct in its details if not in its overall implications. The initial story correctly identified the three officers killed in the fight, Brevet Lt. Col. Fetterman, Captain Brown, and Lieutenant Grummond, although Grummond's name appeared both as "Drummond"[41] and "Grammond."[42] The dispatch was also accurate as to the two military units involved in the battle. The report put the casualties at ninety, different from Carrington's figure of ninety-four but closer to the actual number of eighty-one.

On the other hand, both the New York *Times* and the New York *Tribune* headlined the location of the ambush incorrectly, referring to a "Terrible Massacre at Fort Laramie."[43] Actually, the ambush occurred outside Fort Phil Kearney, as the dispatch made clear. The *Times* and the *Tribune*, however, distorted western geography by confusing the two forts. In fact, they were 235 miles apart.[44]

More important than such details were the implications of the word "massacre" in the initial news dispatch. Carrington's report, which was the basis for the original Fort Laramie dispatch, did not contain the word[45] and it seems likely that the massacre label was attached at Fort Laramie, possibly by General Cooke whose first telegram on the incident did use the term.[46] In any event, the newspapers hardly needed prompting; Indian attacks of various kinds were frequently called massacres. In Denver, it was a simple "Indian Massacre," while the Chicago *Tribune* emphasized the obvious: "Horrible Indian Massacre."[47] Thus even before full details of the fight became known to the press, the ambush was labeled a massacre.

In a simple sense, it was a massacre—because the term was a newspaper cliché readily applied to successful Indian attacks on whites, even when only a few whites were killed.[48] Although the term was used here in con-

nection with the army, it was also widely used by the press to describe
Indian raids on non-combatants, such as settlers and their families. For that
reason, the word had highly dramatic—even inflammatory—connotations,
stirring up images of savage Indian butchers annihilating civilized, peace-
loving whites. Sometimes that was the case. But much of the most newsworthy violence between Indians and whites in the 1860s and 1870s involved soldiers on official missions to kill or subjugate Indians. These
missions frequently grew out of long-standing disputes over such issues
as hunting rights, trading policies, and white and native land claims. The
Fetterman ambush, in fact, could be explained in just such terms. But
neither the army nor the press had a serious interest in the background of
the ambush or motives of the Indians, especially after the death of eighty-
one soldiers. Thus the attack on Fetterman was automatically cast as a
massacre caused by savages with no motive other than their own racial
deficiencies and a lust for white blood.

The emotional response to the "massacre" story was soon apparent in
the press, especially in the western press. The *Daily Rocky Mountain News,*
for example, condemned both the Indians and the government in an editorial published along with the first news of the battle, well before the facts
were clear. According to the *News* editorial—though not its news columns—
the massacre was carried out by "the same red devils who were furnished
with rations, blankets and even ammunition . . . by the United States Commissioners, at Fort Laramie last summer."[49] This charge was untrue; these
were not the same Indians.[50] Nevertheless, the *News* completed its analysis by attacking both the old Noble Savage idea as well as the misplaced idealism of the Peace Commissioners: "When will government learn to take
these Indians as they are, and get rid of the fearfully foolish idea that native nobility and integrity is a part of the Indian character."[51] Like the "massacre" label, premature editorial conclusions revealed a continuing tendency
in the press to dramatize and oversimplify the long-standing problems of
western settlement and the pacification of the Indians.

From the Indian point of view, for example, the victory over Fetterman
was an attempt to drive Federal troops out of the Powder River region, the
heart of Sioux and Cheyenne hunting grounds. The Indians had even
warned Colonel Carrington personally that they had no intention of tol-
erating his new fort[52] and their continuous harassment of Phil Kearney was
no surprise to Carrington or his superiors. Indeed, their ambush of
Fetterman was predictable, especially after the earlier near-misses on the
sixth and twenty-first of December. But such background was not the stuff

of headlines and no newspaper made an attempt to explain the ambush from the Indian point of view. Thus the widespread use of the term "massacre" did as much to obscure the details of the Fetterman ambush as it did to explain it. Still, the "massacre" label came easily to journalists and readers alike and its widespread use in the press reinforced this interpretation of the event. Within a week of the battle, the Fetterman massacre was on its way to becoming a notorious "fact" of western lore, one that held a special place in the American imagination for a decade, when it was overshadowed by Custer's reckless charge near the Little Bighorn.[53]

The press reconstruction of the fight began 28 December, the day after the first news of the disaster. A new dispatch from Fort Laramie confirmed the story but gave no new details about it. Instead, the dispatch claimed that the Indians had organized "a grand coalition of twelve tribes" to combat the whites. The press was somewhat skeptical of this claim, however, the New York *Tribune* noting, "The number of warriors is estimated at 11,000, but this report must be received with caution."[54] The *Daily Rocky Mountain News* published the same report in January but, in an apparent typographical error, put the number of Indians at "71,000."[55]

In the absence of new facts about the massacre, the *Tribune* speculated on the details of the disaster. For some reason, the *Tribune* believed that Fort Kearney itself had been captured, a fact that contradicted the report the paper had published only a day earlier. Despite this inconsistency, the paper concluded: "It is supposed that the post was captured by treachery, and it seems hardly possible that it could have been captured by Indian assault. On the other hand, the savages have so constantly manifested their hostility that it is difficult to see how the troops could have been beguiled into any relaxation of compliance."[56] "It is supposed" was the paper's disclaimer, because there was no evidence in the story that the Indians had captured Fort Kearney. Nevertheless, this early report implied fault on the army's part, a charge that—with the press's help—soon fell on the beleaguered shoulders of Colonel Carrington. Somewhat belatedly, the story went on to admit that the facts were not yet known: "We hope to have more particulars soon."[57]

Another dispatch from Fort Laramie provided a more accurate picture of the massacre. This NYAP dispatch summed up the tragedy in one fact-filled paragraph: "The troops were gradually drawn on until at a point four miles from the fort they were surrounded and slaughtered. Not a man escaped to tell the story of the disaster. The bodies were stripped of every article of clothing, scalped and mutilated. Thirty bodies were found in a space not larger than a good sized room. Nearly all the bodies were recovered and buried in the fort."[58] This report carried a "massacre" headline in the New York *Times* as well as the New Orleans *Picayune,* but the story itself, though chilling, was free from speculation or hysteria. In addition, this story reported that the fight took place four miles from the fort and that the troops "were gradually drawn on" into the ambush. This telegraph dispatch, like the initial Fort Laramie report, gave a reasonably accurate account of the Fetterman disaster.

Predictably, however, the facts about the Fetterman massacre soon gave way to a variety of speculation and wishful thinking. In Denver, the *Daily Rocky Mountain News,* citing a report in the Omaha *Herald,* reported that the fight was of "unprecedented severity and desperation," though it offered no support for this conclusion.[59] The story also noted, correctly, that the number of warriors "greatly exceeded that of the troops." But the *News* wondered how the troops came to be ambushed: "It is not stated how the command happened to be beyond the shelter of the fort, but they were probably marching to some other point." This was untrue, but such speculation helped position the soldiers in a more sympathetic light and explain the attack to an audience skeptical of Indian prowess against a force of army regulars.

This mixture of facts and speculation demonstrates how the initial press image of the Fetterman massacre grew out of a two-step news-making process. The first step involved brief telegraph reports from the West, reports that were generally accurate in their details. But these reports were too brief to satisfy either the papers or the public. This opened the way for the second step of the process. At this level, news of the Fetterman disaster was the product of press speculation. In the absence of the full story, the papers attempted to explain why and how the massacre could have occurred based on a standard set of emotional and one-sided ideas about Indian fighting in the West. Thus the defeat of Fetterman was a "massacre," not an ambush and certainly not an Indian victory. Thus the fort was "captured by treachery," not securely protected by a force of army regulars. Thus the troops "were probably marching to some other point," not pursuing the Indian raiders. All of these "facts" were wrong but they served the needs of the press and public by explaining the telegraph reports in ways that agreed with popular, preconceived notions about Indian fighting on the plains.

In terms of technology, this analysis shows that the telegraph—which had conquered the vastness of the continent—had done little to ensure the accuracy or thoroughness of subsequent press reports. Instead, the initial telegraph reports, too brief to answer many of the obvious news questions, helped create a news vacuum that the press quickly proceeded to fill with speculation. The Fetterman story demonstrates, in fact, that the telegraph was sometimes a detriment to accurate news gathering, its speed overtaking its ability to provide sufficient details to satisfy fact-hungry editors and their readers.

The Power of Unofficial News

The Fetterman massacre continued to make news for several weeks, as letters from the frontier began arriving in the East. Unlike the original telegraph dispatches, these reports provided a fuller and more human picture of the tragedy. Yet many of the writers were nowhere near Phil Kearney and their reports sometimes repeated errors and hearsay. A letter from Fort Laramie written on 27 December, for example, put the number of dead at ninety-four, the original but incorrect number reported by Carrington. The letter also claimed, incorrectly, that five civilians survived the massacre because they were "in the rear some distance, and thereby avoided the ambuscade." Finally, the writer himself, a soldier at Fort Laramie, admitted that reports of the fight were unconfirmed: "We are anxiously awaiting the full particulars, and hope that the report is exaggerated and unfounded. It may be so, and it may not; we trust the latter."[60]

A more alarming letter from Fort Phil Kearney was published in the Boise, Idaho, *Tri-Weekly Statesman* in early February 1867. This unidentified writer noted that he was not at Phil Kearney at the time of the massacre but added, "I give you the particulars as I get them here."[61] This writer was particularly concerned with the Indian mutilation, describing some victims as burned, some with their hearts cut out "and some—but I spare you the painful recital." Still, the author could not resist the horror of one final death, a civilian found "with sixty-four arrows and one spear in his body." In contrast to other reports from the West, this writer also described the Indians who destroyed Fetterman's command. He estimated the attacking force at two to four thousand Sioux and Arapahos and said that their chief was Red Cloud, generally accurate information.[62]

Yet the Indians were largely absent from the news coverage of the Fetterman massacre. Except for occasional references to their "treachery" and estimates of their superior numbers, the Sioux, Cheyenne, and Arapahos who attacked Fetterman were rarely discussed in any significant way.

Most notably, news stories of the massacre did not provide any reason for the Indian ambush. Indian complaints against whites in general or with the establishment of Fort Phil Kearney in particular were not made clear. The fact that Red Cloud and other Indians had warned the army not to enter the Powder River country months before was not mentioned in reports about the Fetterman attack. The Powder River Indians got no explanation at all in the news columns; the fact that they were Indians was explanation enough for their acts of savagery. Such an emphasis helped reinforce a standard newspaper identity for Indians of the northern plains—an identity that focused on violence, hostility, and ruthlessness.

This is hardly surprising, of course, given that the Plains Indians made news almost exclusively in the context of violence and conflict. If there were peaceful members of these tribes and instances of Indian-white cooperation—which there were—they did not make much news and they certainly did not warrant sensational headlines. By ignoring peaceful Indians and covering the hostile ones in an emotional and superficial way, even the "evil Indian" became a one-dimensional figure in the Fetterman story.

The editorial pages also reflected this one-dimensional view. A few days after the Fetterman story broke, the New Orleans *Picayune* ran an excited commentary under the headline "Indians! Indians!!"[63] It began: "We cannot open a paper from any of our exposed States or Territories, without reading frightful accounts of Indian massacres and Indian maraudings." The editorial noted that the Fetterman murders "were accompanied by the most horrible mutilations, which the prairie savages ever consider appropriate sauce and trimmings to their feast of blood." Finally, the editorial attacked the concept of treaty-making, claiming that a "treaty with any tribe of prairie Indians is worse than a farce—it is, ever has been, and ever will be a direct bid and incentive for fresh murders and depredations." Perhaps temperate remarks were too much to expect, but the *Picayune* had declared unconditional war. Such sentiments, however, only obscured the "Indian problem" and provided no insights into long-standing conflicts over western expansion.

Perhaps the most complete and thoughtful newspaper report about the massacre came from a soldier who had ample sources of information because he was stationed at Phil Kearney. Horace Vankirk of Janesville, Wisconsin, described the events of 21 December in a long letter to his father published by the Janesville *Gazette* and reprinted in the Chicago *Tribune* in February 1867.[64] Although Vankirk did not leave the fort that day, he witnessed the action there and provided a good account of troop movements and other activities before and after the battle. He described the mangled bodies of the dead and the anxious state of the post following the tragedy. And unlike most headline writers, Vankirk never referred to the ambush as a massacre.

Vankirk's writing was sometimes moving and sometimes graphic. But he was careful in his judgments and did not profess to know why or how Fetterman stumbled into the ambush. "Colonel Fetterman's party kept on, and finally disappeared over the hills toward the Peno Creek Valley, and shortly after heavy firing was heard in that direction," he wrote.[65] This, in a sentence, was as much as any white man knew of the Fetterman fight. Vankirk's letter provided a rare glimpse inside the fort during the long night following the attack. "There was not much sleep that night, everything quiet, men talking in squads in low voices, guessing if some wounded man had not made his escape and one man left to tell the tale; but none has yet appeared and all hope is given up."[66] This evocative writing marked the best on-the-scene reporting to come out of the Fetterman fight. Significantly, it came not from the AP or from official telegraphic reports from the West, but from a soldier's private letter. Like news about Indian removal and Sand Creek, the most complete and accurate story of the Fetterman disaster bypassed the formal news-making process.

Writing a Massacre

The lack of reliable information did not stop some newspapers from telling the Fetterman story. For an audience used to the drama and gore of Civil War reporting, some papers served up a healthy dose of Indian sensation and misinformation. The worst offenders were the illustrated papers that featured wood engravings of Fetterman's doomed command. Less than a month after the battle, *Frank Leslie's Illustrated Newspaper* ran an engraving and a story that misstated the facts of the fight. The story, for instance, repeated the charge that Carrington would be tried for carelessness for his role in the Fetterman massacre.[67]

Harper's Weekly, another illustrated paper, waited three months before running its Fetterman report, but the time lag did not improve the accuracy of its engraving or its story. The engraving showed a horde of spear-carrying Indians, most on horseback, dramatically closing in on a few remaining soldiers. A mounted Indian spears a soldier on the left, while three other soldiers in the center fend off attacking warriors. Three dead or dying soldiers appear in the foreground, along with a wild-haired warrior and a terrified cavalry horse. A high mountain range looms in the background, much grander in *Harper's* than at the battlefield itself.[68]

Though the illustration was overly dramatic, it did not portray the more sensational horrors of scalping or mutilation. And given the fact that the artist made up the details, the illustration was at least plausible. It was also generic, however, with little to distinguish it from any other army engagement with Indians on the high plains. As Colonel Carrington's wife Margaret later observed, "There was certainly no difficulty as to historical precedents or illustrations of Indian warfare from which to combine a proper sketch."[69] In other words, illustrators saw little difference between one Indian fight and another and, until Custer was killed, there was little motive to differentiate their drawings. Even with Custer, illustrations tended to be more similar than different, so much so that one of Charles Russell's Custer drawings was often mistitled as *The Last of the Fetterman Command.*[70]

Harper's more blatant problems turned up in the text. Despite ample time to clarify the details and investigate the background of the massacre, the *Harper's* account was even more error-ridden and sensational than the early newspaper stories. The story did not even correct the number of men killed in the ambush, referring to ninety victims instead of eighty-one. More seriously, the account claimed to be the eyewitness report of surgeon C. M. Hines, who was, according to *Harper's,* "within 250 yards of the fight, in the thick undergrowth."[71] The paper claimed that Hines was out early on a morning botanical excursion when he encountered hostile Indians. Thus Hines "was obliged to be an unwilling spectator of the greatest massacre known on the plains." About the surgeon's heroic ordeal, *Harper's* concluded: "Had it not been for him we would not have known a single word about the affair, as not a single participant in the fight was left to tell the tale."

The *Harper's* story itself was accurate in some respects, but it provided many details that no white man could substantiate. The final actions of Captain Brown, for instance, were described in great detail, including the dramatic news that he had saved his last pistol shot for himself, "preferring death to torture at their hands."[72] Such details made an exciting story, though much of it was unsupported by the facts. Hines himself, for example, did not claim to be a witness to the massacre and it is clear from all accounts that he was at the fort when Fetterman's troops began their fatal pursuit.[73] The account in *Harper's Weekly* seems to have been compiled from previous news reports, exaggerated comments from Hines, and the fertile imagination of the paper's staff writers. In short, the Fetterman massacre as it appeared in *Harper's Weekly* owed as much to the imagination of the writers in New York as it did to the actual battle. The writers, in turn, created an exciting tale for a public all too willing to believe in the grit and glory of Indian warfare in the West.

Even before *Harper's* twisted the Fetterman story, news of the incident was being shaped by forces far from the Powder River. To an audience grown accustomed to Union victories over the powerful forces of Robert E. Lee, the massacre of Fetterman and his men by a rag-tag band of warriors appeared to be a national scandal. And in a country where Indians were on the margins of national consciousness, the massacre headlines were an abrupt awakening to the War of the Plains. Something had to be done. Thus news of the Fetterman massacre produced a wide range of political and bureaucratic opinion, most of which further clouded the Fetterman story.

One of the loudest voices in the debate was Lewis V. Bogy, the commissioner of Indian Affairs. Bogy was an influential source, with access to the Washington press. He was hardly impartial, however, a fact that soon became evident in his comments about the Fetterman disaster. Still, he had agents in the West and, although they were not at Phil Kearney, they provided Bogy with information about the Fetterman fight. A 1 January story in the New York *Tribune,* for example, was attributed to a telegram received by Bogy. The story confirmed the previously published details and named seven tribes that participated in the attack.[74] Three days later, Bogy made news again, calling for an investigation into the causes of the massacre. According to the *Tribune,* Bogy warned that a failure to investigate "would bring on a general Indian war in that territory. . . . If properly investigated these consequences may be averted."[75]

By early February 1867, Bogy offered his own explanation for the massacre.[76] The Phil Kearney hostilities, he said, were the result of army policies, especially General Cooke's order forbidding traders from dealing arms and ammunition to the Indians. This order, Bogy claimed, only alienated the friendly Indians in the region and undermined the efforts of the Indian Bureau to pacify the hostile tribes. "Indians are men, and when hungry will, like us, resort to any means to obtain food," he noted.[77] Bogy also claimed, without evidence, that the Indians who attacked Fetterman were friendly and had approached the fort "desiring to communicate with the commanding officer, to get the order refusing them guns and ammunition rescinded, so that they might be able to procure their winter supply of buffalo."[78]

Finally, Bogy disputed Carrington's insistent reports of Indian harassment near the fort. Bogy believed that reports of the 6 December battle were exaggerated. "To claim that a wagon train was attacked by three hundred Indians, and yet no one killed, is simply ridiculous," Bogy said. Bogy also disputed the number of Indians involved in the Fetterman attack and blamed Carrington for precipitating the massacre: "It has been currently reported that some 3,000 to 5,000 warriors were assembled to invest this fort. This is not, and cannot by any possibility be true. . . . This number of Indians is not there. The whole is an exaggeration; and although I regret the unfortunate death of so many soldiers, yet there can be no doubt that it is owing to the foolish and rash management of the officer in command of that post."[79]

Bogy's statement was the first significant attempt to explain and defend the actions of the Indians. But Bogy's explanation was faulty in many important respects. Although he accurately noted the presence of friendly Indians in the Powder River region, Bogy grossly understated the threat posed by hostile Sioux and Cheyenne as well as the military power of these warriors.

Bogy's explanation did not find favor with the army or with their allies in the press. The *Army and Navy Journal,* for example, defended the army and attacked the Indian Bureau's policy of providing arms to Indians.[80] But Bogy had political and personal motives for discrediting the army. Blaming the army helped undermine the idea, popular after the Fetterman disaster, that Indian affairs should be removed from the Interior Department and turned over to the War Department.[81] More pointedly, Bogy himself was under investigation for financial irregularities in the Indian Affairs Office[82] and an army scandal could divert attention from his case. Whatever the case, Bogy's charges were widely published and they helped shape the public debate over the Fetterman massacre.[83]

Bogy was not the only official who blamed Colonel Carrington for the debacle. C. M. Hines, the surgeon at Phil Kearney, was an enemy of Carrington's and one source for complaints about his leadership.[84] More importantly, General Cooke had little faith in Carrington's ability. A day after he learned of the massacre, Cooke reported that Carrington "has not maintained discipline, and that his officers have no confidence in him."[85] Before long, such charges surfaced in the papers. About two weeks after the battle, the *Daily Rocky Mountain News* ran a Washington story that said that Carrington "has been relieved and will probably be ordered under arrest, for trial, on charges of carelessness, in performance of his duty."[86] No source for this information was given. But the charge was only partially true at best and highly misleading at worst. Carrington was relieved of command shortly after the massacre, but he was not arrested or tried for carelessness. Moreover, the implication that he was relieved of command at Phil Kearney *because* of the Fetterman disaster was also untrue since his transfer from the fort had been arranged well before the events of 21 December.[87] Months later, the commission investigating the Fetterman affair cleared Carrington of wrongdoing. Nevertheless, the *News* and other papers perpetuated the popular notion that the army had removed Carrington for incompetence in the Fetterman ambush.[88]

Both in the East and the West, the papers published rumors and politically motivated details about the Fetterman fight with little apparent skepticism. Even contradictions and other obvious mistakes were not corrected. More importantly, no newspaper made an attempt to sort out rumors from facts or to explain the full context of the massacre, even after the details became clear. Instead, the papers moved on to new topics, leaving the Fetterman story incomplete and awash in a sea of misinformation. But if the details were murky, one theme remained constant: the Fetterman fight was a "massacre" of American soldiers carried out by hostile Indians. No newspaper questioned that fact or challenged the idea that the Plains Indians were anything more than another band of worthless savages.

Newspaper coverage of the incident was criticized some years later by Margaret Irvin Carrington, Colonel Carrington's wife, who had been at Phil Kearney during the fall of 1866. She devoted an entire chapter of her memoirs to the "Comedy of Errors" perpetuated by the press and eagerly absorbed by the public. Her attack opened with a rhetorical question: "Has any military event in history . . . immediately after its occurrence called forth more elaborate and general explanation, and involved more contradictory and absurd criticism, all 'founded upon fact,' than the massacre near Fort Phil Kearney, December 21st, 1866?"[89] The problem, Mrs. Carrington believed, was due in large measure to the American public's lust for information. Could the public wait for the truth about the massacre? No, she said, "They must know exactly and fully all the particulars for perusal while coffee was cooling at the next morning's breakfast-table."[90] The press blatantly exploited this weakness, Mrs. Carrington claimed.

> It could not be expected, in the urgent demand for particulars, that truth and justice would be essential features of the whole; and the sensation had

to be used just at the time, or somebody's paper or somebody's friend would suppose that somebody else, who was regularly compensated to cater to the popular passion for the startling and novel, was ignorant of that of which he knew nothing. So it happened that numberless journals *obtained, at last, the true version of that sad affair.*[91]

Mrs. Carrington took particular aim at attempts by the press to make secondhand information sound more credible, noting the proliferation of "special artists," "actual observers," and "special correspondents" in the illustrated papers. "Even the metropolitan papers of New York and Washington could not possibly wait, but discharged their shafts, regardless of character or truth," she added.[92]

Some of the distortions, she said, were the fault of misinformed Indian agents who "knew just how the massacre occurred—viz., that the poor, hungry, starving women of the Sioux had come to beg." Mrs. Carrington also singled out the Albany *Argus* for its stirring report on the battle. According to the *Argus,* some survivors of Fetterman's command made their way back to the fort, pursued by hostiles. But Colonel Carrington, afraid to lose the entire fort, refused to open the gates and left the hapless survivors to their fate. Again, a highly dramatic tale—but a complete fabrication. Concluded Mrs. Carrington: "Every conceivable hypothesis but the correct one was adopted, and everybody *guessed,* without seeming to think that possibly the authorities of the fort itself knew something of the affair."[93]

Lieutenant Grummond's widow, Frances, also had harsh words for the press. When eastern papers arrived at Phil Kearney by courier, she wrote: "It was marvelous to see how enterprising and original certain news editors could be, when removed from all access to real facts, when they set their brains to work." She continued, "General news, already stale in the States, was remarkably fresh to us, and certainly very novel, as concerning ourselves."[94]

Even before the massacre, Mrs. Grummond noted the gap between the reality of the Indian frontier and the official version of that reality. When the mail finally came in November and she learned that the Laramie Peace Commission had announced a "satisfactory treaty with all the Indians of the Northwest," she noted the ironic timing of the news. "This reached Phil. Kearney in the midst of some of the most trying hours of danger and concern."[95] After the massacre, Mrs. Grummond blamed publicity given the Laramie Treaty for placating the public with regard to the Northwest Indians and causing the Fetterman news to be even more sensational than it was. The result of this misconception, she noted, brought "a burst of hateful criticism upon all the survivors of the fight, because of the surprise for which the public was unprepared."[96]

Like Mrs. Carrington, Mrs. Grummond took some of the misinformation personally. She took exception to the charge that Colonel Carrington had given powder to the Indians and that "the ladies of the garrison were in the habit of throwing packages of sugar and powder over the stockade to the squaws." She blamed the pictorial papers and their illustrations for such distortions. And she added, "We wondered if there had not been some other similar fight somewhere else of which we had no knowledge."[97]

Neither Mrs. Carrington nor Mrs. Grummond was a neutral party in the Fetterman story. Both had reasons to protect their point of view, especially in books written years after the fact. But they also had firsthand knowledge of events at Phil Kearney and both women saw how rumors were published as facts, how Washington sources manipulated the story, and how the press simplified and distorted the "massacre" for the sake of competition and sensationalism. For all these reasons, as both women complained, the full story of the Fetterman massacre did not emerge in the newspapers.

Indian News as a Pattern

The Fetterman massacre provides a useful case study of Indian warfare as it was portrayed in the press. What makes the Fetterman example even more interesting are the news parallels between it and a number of later Indian fights. Perhaps many Indian fights were alike, or perhaps many of them just seemed alike to journalists and illustrators far from the scene. Either way, the press began to look for and find similar characteristics in Indian battles, a framing practice that fostered the development of a standardized series of "facts"—that is, myths—about Indian "massacres." Thus many details of the Fetterman fight turned up in the news again as details in Custer's defeat at the Little Bighorn. In this way, the Fetterman massacre helped establish a "model" Indian fight out of which the press could explain and make sense of future Indian battles.

Only a few months after the Fetterman fight, in fact, news of another big massacre appeared in the press. This event, called the Fort Buford Massacre, had a number of similarities to the Phil Kearney disaster. It was, as *Harper's Weekly* put it, "another terrible Indian massacre."[98] The New York *Times* ran it at the top of page one, under headlines that read, "MORE INDIAN MASSACRES," "Fort Buford Captured and the Garrison Slaughtered," and "Eighty Officers and Men Butchered in Cold Blood."[99] According to an AP story from Washington published in the New York *Semi-Weekly Tribune*, one "Colonel Rankin, his wife, one child and the entire garrison were slaughtered, in all about eighty souls."[100] Like the Fetterman fight, Rankin had been overwhelmed by several thousand Indians and had inflicted heavy casualties on his attackers, killing three hundred and wounding one thousand. And in a dramatic touch, the report concluded with this detail: "It is generally supposed he [Rankin] shot his wife to save her from falling into the hands of the Indians," a detail reminiscent of Captain Brown's suicide in the Fetterman attack. All this information was attributed to a letter "from the wife of a distinguished army officer at St. Louis."

The New York *Times* published the same AP report. But the *Times* story also included a second letter from the West and this account offered a different version of the Fort Buford affair. Notably, this writer opened with a reference to the "stirring of excitement in this part of the country with the redskins. I suppose you know of the Fort Kearny affair also." As for Fort Buford, the writer confirmed that the Indians had indeed overrun the fort and killed the defenders. Unlike the first account, however, this letter made no mention of Colonel Rankin killing his wife. Instead, it offered a more horrible fate for the couple: torture and rape. It was a painful scene: "They then took them a few yards from the post, and having built a fire, tied the Colonel's hands and feet and put him in the fire, while his wife was compelled to see him burning. After that was done they mistreated her in a shameful manner, and having rolled her up in a buffalo robe, they fastened her on a wild horse and turned him loose. God only knows how long she was on the prarie [*sic*]."[101]

The key problem with the Fort Buford Massacre was not its sensational details—details by now standard in Indian war news—but its truth. Although there was a real Colonel Rankin in command at Fort Buford, the Fort Buford Massacre was a fabrication, as the *Tribune* eventually admitted. Journalism historian Elmo Scott Watson, who investigated the story, attributed the hoax to "some idle rumor to which were added some of the known details of the disaster to Fetterman's command . . . plus a liberal amount of imagination on the part of some New York reporter or rewrite man."[102] Watson also noted that neither *Harper's Weekly* nor *Frank Leslie's* ever retracted the story.

In fact, the press wanted to believe the story, even in the face of conflicting reports. On 10 April, eight days after its first Fort Buford story and one day after a new dispatch questioned the Buford report, the New York *Times* expressed faith in the original story. Significantly, the *Times* made its argument with reference to the Fetterman massacre. After reviewing all of its dispatches on the matter and discussing the general military situation in the West, the *Times* editorial concluded, "In view of all the circumstances, and the fact that there has been no official denial of the massacre, there is every reason to fear that the detailed account printed is substantially correct, and that all the horrors of the Fort Phil Kearny massacre have been repeated in an aggravated form at Fort Buford."[103] The *Times* was wrong. More significantly, it was wrong because it relied on the Fetterman massacre to make assumptions about a new Indian massacre. Assumptions and rumors, Indian butchery and torture—these were the exciting and erroneous elements of the Fort Buford story. Unfortunately, this pattern of rumor and misinformation occurred many times in news coverage of the Indian wars.

The most famous case of misinformation grew out of the Custer campaign in 1876, ten years after Fetterman. The events surrounding "Custer's Last Stand" long ago passed from fact into myth, as a number of other scholars have documented.[104] But the links between the Fetterman story and the Custer myth have not been fully explored. Although the differences between the two events are substantial, the similarities are significant enough to suggest that the press reconstruction of the Fetterman fight was a small rehearsal for the large and powerful myth-making forces unleashed by Custer's final campaign. In both cases, news from the battlefield was often independent of the facts because the stories had obvious epic qualities that were too important to be tied to issues of truth or fact, both of which required unobtainable supporting evidence.

Newspaper accounts of both the Fetterman and the Custer fights, for example, perpetuated the idea of eyewitnesses who lived to tell the world of the final heroic moments of the attack. A Chicago *Tribune* report published shortly after the Fetterman ambush claimed that the entire command was destroyed, "except [for] five citizens, who were in the rear some distance, and thereby avoided the ambuscade."[105] This group was Dr. Hines's party, which did avoid the ambush but was cut off and did not witness the battle.[106] The more exaggerated claim was the one noted earlier in *Harper's Weekly,* which identified Dr. Hines as a witness to the Fetterman massacre. This "fact" appears to have been manufactured to add credibility to the *Harper's* report.

The myth of the surviving witness surfaced more vigorously after the Little Bighorn, propelled by the instant notoriety of Custer's defeat. One of the most famous survivors was a Crow scout named Curley. Bruce Rosenberg, who studied the "lone witness" legend in detail, noted that Curley, unlike other survivors of Custer's command, "never claimed to have seen the battle, or to have been in it, or to have survived—at least at first."[107] How then did the Curley legend originate? Rosenberg writes: "Most stories were invented for him, usually by imaginative newspaper reporters, and ascribed to him for 'authenticity,' although after a while there is some indication that he did tell white interviewers what he thought they wanted to hear."[108] Rosenberg also notes the longevity of the "lone survivor" myth following the Little Bighorn. One of the first such stories appeared in the St. Paul *Pioneer-Press and Tribune* within weeks of the battle. Such stories persisted well into the twentieth century, when a number of other men offered similar tales, all holding out the promise of the real story of Custer's Last Stand. All of these stories were false.

In the months following the Custer battle, press and public interest in the matter easily overrode the press's commitment to the truth. As Rosenberg put it, "Newspapers in those days would publish almost any story bearing on the Custer disaster."[109] The truth is that no white man survived either the Fetterman or Custer battles and that the information vacuum created by this fact was too great a temptation for the press—and for some professional liars—to resist.[110]

Suicide in the face of certain death was another fictionalized aspect of both the Fetterman and Custer battles. According to Rosenberg, the "save the last bullet for yourself" idea was an unwritten law of Indian fighting.[111] Law or not, such suicides did occur. In the Fetterman case, *Harper's Weekly* reported that Captain Brown "held the muzzle to his forehead and blew out his brains."[112] The report was not quite accurate, but it was based on evidence that indicated that Colonel Fetterman and Captain Brown, in a desperate suicide pact, had shot each other in the head.[113] A slightly different version of the death-before-capture story surfaced in the faked reports of the Fort Buford Massacre, when Colonel Rankin was said to have killed his wife to prevent her capture and torture.

At the Little Bighorn, it was widely reported that Custer committed suicide, an act that was variously interpreted either as an act of defiant heroism—capture being worse than death—or cowardice. In fact, as Rosenberg makes clear, it is highly unlikely that Custer, who was right-handed, was able to shoot himself both in the left side of his torso and then in the left temple while under fire from hundreds of Indians. In short, Custer's suicide was another manufactured detail of the Little Bighorn disaster that had roots at least as far back as the Fetterman massacre.

The Fetterman disaster prefigured the Custer defeat in another respect as well. In both cases the press and public demanded a scapegoat. At Phil Kearney, that was Carrington, who did deserve some of the blame for the disaster. No one blamed the arrogant Fetterman—even though it seems clear that he disobeyed orders and hastened his command's demise. Although Carrington was eventually cleared by investigators, he never outlived the rumors and misconceptions associated with Fetterman's defeat. Blame also fell on Captain Tenodor Ten Eyck, the man Carrington sent to rescue Fetterman. Ten Eyck took an indirect route to the battlefield, which left him open to charges that he could have saved Fetterman. In truth, Fetterman's command was already lost before Ten Eyck arrived and his route was a prudent one that probably prevented another Indian ambush.[114] Nevertheless, Ten Eyck joined Carrington as a scapegoat for the Fetterman massacre.

Similarly, Custer's defeat on the Little Bighorn was not blamed on Custer, despite a wealth of evidence that he could have saved his command had he broken off his attack. Instead, the press and the public found a convenient scapegoat in Major Marcus Reno, who did break off his attack in the face of overwhelming Indian forces. This act saved most of Reno's men. Following the battle, however, Reno was subjected to a barrage of charges for this perceived failure. Like Carrington, Reno was later cleared by military investigators but the perception remained that he was responsible for Custer's fate.[115]

Significantly, too, the search for scapegoats in both cases tended to ignore the Indians, as if they were incapable of military victories without major mistakes on the part of the army. In the Fetterman fight, the press discussed the Indians most prominently in terms of their overwhelming numbers, which was true enough. But as perpetrators of a "massacre," the Powder River Indians got no sympathy and little explanation from the press. Their mutilation of the dead, for example, was a horrible fact of the Fetterman fight and a prominent part of some press reports. But no paper attempted to explain this practice from the Indian point of view. If they had, readers would have learned that the Indians cut the muscles of the dead ritually, as a way of punishing the dead in the afterlife.[116] Such knowledge would not have made the practice any more acceptable, but it would have shown that mutilation was based on something other than simple blood lust, which was the impression one got from the news.

The facts of the Fetterman and Custer campaigns were tragic enough without any amplification or exaggeration by the press. Yet more important than the fabrications themselves was the social and political need for these inventions. At this level, it is clear that the press played an important role in defining the Indian wars in ways that justified the fighting. In the popular mind, Indians had to be brutal savages and slain soldiers had to be heroes. This emphasis reinforced the "good vs. evil" mythology of western expansion and made clear the national need for the subjugation and dispossession of hostile western tribes. Thus the press used both the Fetterman and Custer affairs to create popular western melodramas in which the Indians and the cavalry were locked in a powerful, but ultimately predetermined, struggle over the conquest of the West. With such dramatic material at hand, it is no wonder that the press emphasized action and conflict over the background details of Indian conflicts, treaty rights, and the like. Fetterman and Custer were identifiable martyrs and the press simplified—and glorified—Indian fighting by creating and supporting a set of myths about martyred heroes, even when the facts underlying those myths had to be invented. And although Fetterman was not the gallant Custer and the Phil Kearney ambush was not the Little Bighorn, the press reconstruction of the Fetterman massacre in 1866 helped create and sustain the myth of glory and danger in the West that reached its apex a decade later at Custer's Last Stand.

As the preceding pages have shown, the Indian wars grew out of a complex set of conflicts between whites and Indians in the West. But these problems were not a major part of the daily journalism produced by the Indian wars. Instead, the press used these battles to tell a simple, more colorful, and more reader-pleasing story of the West, a story in which the Indian was a natural and dangerous enemy. The telegraph helped oversimplify this story, the AP helped standardize it, and the post–Civil War competition between rival reporters helped promote the natural drama and adventure of the conflict. Thus the very definition of Indian news from the frontier came to be centered on conflict, so that peaceful Indians were automatically excluded from the papers while the violence and treachery of hostile Indians was automatically emphasized. By such means, even the "facts" of Indian battles were made to fit popular journalistic expectations. The result of such practices was a distorted image of the Plains Indian as a blood-thirsty savage, intent on murdering every white man, woman, and child who crossed the prairie. There was truth to this image, of course, but it was an incomplete truth, and the consequences of this idea were greater racial hostility and suffering on both sides.

Finally, the newspapers used the hostile tribes of the West as part of the evolving national myth of white dominance and manifest destiny.

Editors as well as readers saw that the conquest of the continent was never in doubt. Yet in storytelling terms, this tale of conquest and danger required both heroes and villains and the Indians made ideal villains, all the better for their apparent inhumanity and savagery. Starting with Colonel Fetterman, the heroes became those unfortunate soldiers killed in the West. By the time of the Little Bighorn, both the newspapers and the national consciousness were prepared for a more mythic hero and, for this role, there was no greater candidate than the self-promoting and swashbuckling "boy general" himself, George Armstrong Custer.

Notes

1. New Orleans *Picayune,* 27 Dec. 1866, 1.

2. Ibid.

3. Quoted in Oliver Gramling, *AP: The Story of News* (New York: Farrar and Rinehart, 1940), 62–63.

4. *Harper's Weekly,* 31 Oct. 1863, 693.

5. Ibid., 695.

6. For example, Theodore Davis, a special artist for *Harper's,* illustrated various "Indian troubles" (including Custer's attack on Black Kettle's camp on the Washita) in 1868, months after he had returned East. See Robert Taft, *Artists and Illustrators of the Old West, 1850–1900* (New York: Charles Scribner's Sons, 1953), 69.

7. Shirley A. Leckie, *Elizabeth Bacon Custer and the Making of a Myth* (Norman: University of Oklahoma Press, 1993), 31. See also William E. Huntzicker, "Custer's Pictorial Images: Heroism and Racism in the Illustrated Press," ms.

8. William E. Huntzicker, "The Illustrated West: Foreseen and Unforeseen Consequences," paper presented at the Western History Association meeting, Oct. 1993, Tulsa, Okla., 17–18. See also L. G. Moses, *Wild West Shows and the Images of American Indians* (Albuquerque: University of New Mexico Press, 1996), 169. Moses notes that one of the most popular parts of Buffalo Bill's Wild West show at the turn of the century was the Indian attack on the Deadwood Stage, an event very much like the one drawn by Davis.

9. "The first war to be adequately and comprehensively reported in the daily press was the conflict of 1846 and 1847 between the United States and Mexico." George Wilkins Kendall of the New Orleans *Picayune* was the most famous correspondent in the Mexican War. See F. Lauriston Bullard, *Famous War Correspondents* (Boston: Little, Brown, 1914), 351.

10. Frank Luther Mott, *American Journalism,* 3d ed. (New York: Macmillan, 1962), 329.

11. Ibid., 334.

12. J. Cutler Andrews, *The North Reports the Civil War* (Pittsburgh: University of Pittsburgh Press, 1955), 640.

13. Ibid., 647.

14. Oliver Knight, *Following the Indian Wars* (Norman: University of Oklahoma Press, 1960), 32.

15. Ibid., 29.

16. Ibid.

17. Charles Sanford Diehl, *The Staff Correspondent* (San Antonio: Clegg, 1931), 83.

18. Ibid., 9.

19. Ibid., 89.

20. Ibid., 20.

21. Ibid., 19.

22. Ibid., 15.

23. Ibid.

24. Quoted in Knight, *Following the Indian Wars,* 44.

25. Ibid.

26. John F. Finerty, *War-Path and Bivouac* (1890; rpt., Norman: University of Oklahoma Press, 1961), xvii.

27. Ibid.

28. Oliver Knight, "Introduction," in Finerty, *War-Path and Bivouac,* xv.

29. Finerty, *War-Path and Bivouac,* 69.

30. Robert F. Berkhofer Jr., *The White Man's Indian* (New York: Vintage Books, 1978), 4–7.

31. Finerty, *War-Path and Bivouac,* 69.

32. Ibid.

33. The fort was named after Gen. Philip Kearny, a Civil War hero, but the spelling often followed the spelling of Gen. Stephen W. Kearney, who had a Nebraska fort named after him in 1848. This chapter uses the extra "e" because it was so widely used in the press of the day. See Dee Brown, *Fort Phil Kearny* (New York: G. P. Putnam's Sons, 1962), 17.

34. Robert A. Murray, "Commentaries on the Col. Henry B. Carrington Image," *Denver Westerners Monthly Roundup* 24.3 (Mar. 1968): 4.

35. The events at Fort Kearney and the Fetterman fight have been the subject of considerable investigation. A good number of primary documents are in Senate Ex. Docs., 40th Cong., 1st Sess., no. 13. Secondary sources include Brown, *Fort Phil Kearny;* Robert A. Murray, *Military Posts in the Powder River Country of Wyoming, 1865–1894* (Lincoln: University of Nebraska Press, 1968), 74–86; Robert M. Utley, *Frontier Regulars* (New York: Macmillan, 1973), 93–110; and J. W. Vaughn, *Indian Fights* (Norman: University of Oklahoma Press, 1966), 14–90. The Indian side of the battle is told in George E. Hyde, *Red Cloud's Folk* (Norman: University of Oklahoma Press, 1937), 134–61.

36. Testimony taken by the Sanborn Commission that investigated the Fetterman ambush; quoted in Vaughn, *Indian Fights,* 25–28. See also Utley, *Frontier Regulars,* 102.

37. Murray, *Military Posts,* 77–79.

38. Utley, *Frontier Regulars,* 103.

39. George Bird Grinnell, *The Fighting Cheyennes* (1915; rpt., Norman: University of Oklahoma Press, 1956).

40. Brown, *Fort Phil Kearny,* 150.

41. New Orleans *Picayune,* 27 Dec. 1866, 1.

42. New York *Times,* 27 Dec. 1866, 4; New York *Tribune,* 27 Dec. 1866, 1; Chicago *Tribune,* 27 Dec. 1866, 1.

43. New York *Times,* 27 Dec. 1866, 4; New York *Tribune,* 27 Dec. 1866.

44. Brown, *Fort Phil Kearny,* 13.

45. The full text of Carrington's first report on the ambush is quoted in Senate Ex. Docs., 40th Cong., 1st Sess., no. 13, p. 26.

46. Ibid., 27.

47. *Daily Rocky Mountain News,* 28 Dec. 1866, 1.; Chicago *Tribune,* 27 Dec. 1866, 4.

48. For example, the Chicago *Tribune* in 1876 used "massacre" to describe Indian attacks in which as few as two and four men were killed. Bruce A. Rosenberg, *Custer and the Epic of Defeat* (University Park: Pennsylvania State University Press, 1974), 22–23.

49. *Daily Rocky Mountain News* (hereafter *DRMN*), 28 Dec. 1866, 4.

50. Hyde, *Red Cloud's Folks,* 138–40; Utley, *Frontier Regulars,* 99.

51. *DRMN,* 28 Dec. 1866, 4.

52. Hyde, *Red Cloud's Folks,* 139–40.

53. Brown, *Fort Phil Kearny,* 11; also Grinnell, *Fighting Cheyennes,* 230.

54. New York *Tribune,* 28 Dec. 1866, 5.

55. *DRMN,* 5 Jan. 1867, 4.

56. New York *Tribune,* 28 Dec. 1866, 5.

57. Ibid.

58. New York *Times,* 28 Dec. 1866, 1; also published in the New Orleans *Picayune,* 29 Dec. 1866, 8.

59. *DRMN,* 2 Jan. 1867, 1.

60. Columbus (Ohio) *Journal,* quoted in the Chicago *Tribune,* 16 Jan. 1867, 1.

61. Idaho *Tri-Weekly Statesman,* 2 Feb. 1867, 1.

62. Brown puts the number of Indians at two thousand. Cheyennes were also involved in the Fetterman ambush. The presence of Red Cloud at the scene has not been established, but he was one of several leaders of Indian hostilities in the Fort Kearney area during the closing months of 1866. See Brown, *Fort Phil Kearny,* 173–74.

63. New Orleans *Evening Picayune,* 31 Dec. 1866, 2.

64. Chicago *Tribune,* 2 Feb. 1867, 2.

65. Ibid.

66. Ibid.

67. *Frank Leslie's Illustrated Newspaper,* 19 Jan. 1867, cited in Elmo Scott Watson, "The Indian Wars and the Press, 1866–1867," *Journalism Quarterly* 17.4 (Sept. 1943): 307–8.

68. Three photos of the Fetterman battlefield appear in Vaughn, *Indian Fights,* following p. 80. The landscape in these photos is very different from the landscape depicted in *Harper's Weekly,* 23 Mar. 1867, 180.

69. Henry B. Carrington, *Ab-Sa-Ra-Ka, Land of Massacre,* 5th ed. (Philadelphia: J. B. Lippincott, 1879), 219. This book was originally the work of Margaret Carrington. It was published under Colonel Carrington's name in subsequent editions because of supplemental material he added to the manuscript.

70. Brian W. Dippie, *Custer's Last Stand: The Anatomy of an American Myth* (Missoula: University of Montana Publications in History, 1976), 33, 42.

71. *Harper's Weekly,* 23 Mar. 1867, 189.

72. Ibid.

73. See, for example, Dr. Hines's letter of 1 Jan. 1867 in Senate Ex. Docs., 40th Cong., 1st Sess., no. 13, p. 15.

74. New York *Tribune,* 1 Jan. 1867, 1.

75. Ibid., 4 Jan. 1867, 4.

76. Report of the Commissioner of Indian Affairs, Senate Ex. Docs., 40th Cong., 1st Sess., no. 13, pp. 7–11.

77. Ibid., 8.

78. Ibid., 9.

79. Ibid.

80. *Army and Navy Journal,* 9 Feb. 1867, 397, cited in Brown, *Fort Phil Kearny,* 215.

81. This idea was editorially endorsed by several papers in the wake of the Fetterman ambush. See, for example, the New York *Times,* 10 Jan. 1867, 4.

82. This investigation also made news in January 1867. See the New York *Tribune,* 14 Jan. 1867, 1; 16 Jan. 1867, 1.

83. Bogy's statements appeared in the Leavenworth *Daily Times* and the Philadelphia *Press,* among other papers. See Robert G. Athearn, *William Tecumseh Sherman and the Settlement of the West* (Norman: University of Oklahoma Press, 1956), 110.

84. Senate Ex. Docs., 40th Cong., 1st Sess., no. 13, p. 15. See also Brown, *Fort Phil Kearny,* 218.

85. Senate Ex. Docs., 40th Cong., 1st Sess., no. 13, p. 29.

86. *DRMN,* 5 Jan. 1867, 1.

87. Murray, *Military Posts,* 85–86.

88. *DRMN,* 11 Jan. 1867, 4.

89. Carrington, *Ab-Sa-Ra-Ka, Land of Massacre,* 218.

90. Ibid.

91. Ibid., 220.

92. Ibid., 222.

93. Ibid., 224.

94. Frances C. Carrington, *My Army Life on the Plains* (Philadelphia: J. B. Lippincott, 1910), 176. Like Margaret Carrington, Frances Grummond was protective of Colonel Carrington's reputation. They were married after Margaret's death.

95. Ibid., 126.

96. Ibid., 160.

97. Ibid., 177.

98. *Harper's Weekly,* 13 Apr. 1867, 227.

99. New York *Times,* 2 Apr. 1867, 1.

100. New York *Semi-Weekly Tribune,* 5 Apr. 1867, quoted in Watson, "Indian Wars and the Press," 308.

101. New York *Times,* 2 Apr. 1867, 1.

102. Watson, "Indian Wars and the Press," 309.

103. New York *Times,* 10 Apr. 1867, 4.

104. The secondary material on the Battle of the Little Bighorn and the Custer legend is voluminous. Among the best studies of the mythic aspects of the affair are Rosenberg's *Custer and the Epic of Defeat* and Dippie's *Custer's Last Stand.* See also Richard Slotkin, *The Fatal Environment* (New York: Atheneum, 1985), esp. chaps. 16–20; Kent Ladd Steckmesser, *The Western Hero in History and Legend* (Norman: University of Oklahoma Press, 1965), esp. 163–237.

105. Chicago *Tribune,* 16 Jan. 1867, 2.

106. Vaughn, *Indian Fights,* 49; also Brown, *Fort Phil Kearny,* 184.

107. Rosenberg, *Custer and the Epic of Defeat,* 77.

108. Ibid.

109. Ibid., 74.

110. Ibid., 76.

111. Ibid., 16.

112. *Harper's Weekly,* 23 Mar. 1867, 189.

113. Brown, *Fort Phil Kearny,* 181.

114. Vaughn, *Indian Fights,* 63–67.

115. Evan S. Connell, *Son of the Morning Star* (New York: Perennial Library, 1985), 5–10. This "novelistic" history of the Custer campaign reviews these matters in some detail. See also Edgar I. Stewart, *Custer's Luck* (Norman: University of Oklahoma Press, 1955), for a discussion of Reno's actions during the fight.

116. Brown, *Fort Phil Kearny,* 198; also Col. Richard Irving Dodge, *Our Wild Indians* (1882; rpt., New York: Archer House, 1959), 180–81.

The Making of an Indian Villain:
Sitting Bull in War and Peace

SITTING Bull was one of the most famous Native Americans who ever lived, a brave, fierce, determined Lakota leader who defended his people against the invasion of the northern plains and the destruction of the Lakota way of life. But Sitting Bull was known in his lifetime largely through newspaper representations, ideas and images that routinely obscured the character, accomplishments, and failings of the man himself, creating a native identity that owed more to rumor, racial ideology, and expansionist myth-making than to truth or historical fact. Was Sitting Bull "an extremely savage type, betraying that bloodthirstiness and brutality for which he has so long been notorious," as the New York *Times* reported after the Battle of the Little Bighorn?[1] Or was he a more peaceful man, fighting only when provoked, as the Chicago *Times* reported in 1877? "I do not want to go to war with anybody," Sitting Bull told the newspaper.[2] Or perhaps Sitting Bull was simply a con artist, an undistinguished warrior who was willing to play the great chief for Buffalo Bill's Wild West show in 1885. That image turned up in the Boston *Evening Transcript* after Sitting Bull's death: "He has never been a chief, nor even a warrior of high order," said an army officer who was supposed to know.[3] The contradictions, confusions, and outright lies that surround Sitting Bull reveal the active part the press played in creating his public personality during his lifetime and after his death. And it is that Sitting Bull—the man imagined and created in the press—who became for most Americans the most famous Native American in United States history.

Sitting Bull as Man and Myth

Sitting Bull's personality and life as a Lakota leader was the subject of irregular press attention and criticism from 1871 until his death in 1890. But Sitting Bull attracted considerable press attention at three times in his life: the Battle of the Little Bighorn in 1876, on tour as a "living exhibit" in 1884 and 1885, and at his arrest and murder in 1890. These incidents gave the press an opportunity to construct competing newspaper versions of Sitting Bull to meet the needs of each moment. First and foremost, Sitting Bull was identified as "Custer's killer," a role that emphasized his "natural" brutality. Later, when the Indian threat subsided, Sitting Bull could be imagined more humanely. In New York and elsewhere, he became an object of considerable curiosity, a safe but unsophisticated relic from a once-proud but now hapless race. Still later, when the Ghost Dance movement seemed to pose a new threat to white dominance in the West, Sitting Bull's savage identity surfaced again. This pattern of competing public identities repeated the long-standing American ambivalence over Indians. Hostile Indians were created in print in ways that emphasized their natural barbarity. Similarly, friendly or nonthreatening Indians were imagined as people who simply needed some education and civilization to make them "normal." In short, the shifts in the language, themes, and meanings attached to Sitting Bull at each of these moments reveal the powerful racial assumptions at work in the press as it attempted to make sense of Indians in the final decades of the nineteenth century.

One of the continuing features of Indian news during these years was its fundamental lack of understanding of native people and their cultures. Despite the appearance of reporters in the West, most newsmen knew little about native life and saw Indians as strange, mysterious, and often dangerous people. Newspaper representations of Indians were driven by several compelling ideological forces, including the racial superiority of European Americans and the vision of a progressive, technologically advanced American empire. From the perspective of the individual reporter covering the end of the Indian wars and the closing of the frontier, Indians remained backward people, members of societies far down on the evolutionary ladder. According to Spencerian notions of American social progress, humans had evolved from savagery to civilization and the beliefs and behavior of Native Americans showed that they were closer to savagery than to civilization. No wonder, then, that Sitting Bull was the subject of erroneous and exaggerated reports—he was perceived as a leading savage whose untamed ways and violent tendencies challenged the underlying ideology of economic and social progress.

In the case of particular native leaders, the outsider status of Indians became personal. Indian leaders were judged less on who they were than on their relations to whites; "good" chiefs were those who adopted civilization or gave in to white demands, "bad" chiefs were those who did not. For Sitting Bull in particular—a man known for his hostility to whites and their ways—a fair or balanced presentation in the papers was probably impossible. Yet the coverage of Sitting Bull is an important measure of the ways the press understood "savage" Indians and made sense of Indian enemies. As we shall see, the coverage of Sitting Bull varied, but he was almost always imagined as an outsider, a man of some skill and courage but a man naturally and fundamentally hostile to important American values.

Sitting Bull and His Culture

Sitting Bull was born in the early 1830s on the Missouri River.[4] His family was a distinguished member of the Hunkpapas, a small band within the Lakota confederacy on the northern plains. Although his original name was Jumping Badger, he was known as a child for "his willful and deliberate ways [which] earned him the nickname Hunkesni, or 'Slow.'"[5] At ten, Slow killed his first buffalo, gaining status within the tribe as a hunter. Many years later, Sitting Bull told a reporter that he specialized in buffalo calves and gave the calves to the poor. "Giving away the fruits of his hunts foreshadowed one of Slow's most pronounced traits—generosity," biographer Robert Utley concluded.[6]

Slow's first success as a warrior came at fourteen, when he counted his first coup in a raid against the Crows. This honor earned him his father's name, Sitting Bull, an animal known to sit on its haunches when attacked and fight to the death. Throughout his teenage years, Sitting Bull continued to distinguish himself as a warrior, proving himself a brave and skilled fighter in what Utley describes as "one of the world's most highly developed warrior societies."[7]

Sitting Bull also became known among the Hunkpapas as a holy man, achieving distinction as a healer, singer, and composer. His tribe also considered him a prophet. When he pointed his pipe to the four winds as part of the pipe ceremony, his nephew One Bull said, Sitting Bull "could foretell anything."[8] Sitting Bull was humble both in dress and deportment, making no effort to indicate his status within the tribe. Utley also notes that Sitting Bull possessed "none of the arrogance or insolence that some chiefs assumed."[9]

The Sitting Bull that emerges from Utley's research is a remarkable individual, "the Hunkpapa incarnate, epitome of the four cardinal virtues of bravery, fortitude, generosity, and wisdom."[10] But Utley wonders if this portrait is too good, a likeness from the point of view of his family and devoted friends. The evidence might be slanted in Sitting Bull's favor, Utley writes, but not enough to alter the reality of the man's achievements. Sitting Bull emerges, Utley concludes, "as a towering figure in his or any other culture."[11]

To his own people, the people who knew him best and understood his life, Sitting Bull was a complex and powerful man. Utley highlights three distinct personalities: warrior and huntsman, holy man, good tribesman. But this is a historian's portrait, painstakingly developed after years of reading and research. Such a portrait of Sitting Bull was not possible in nineteenth-century white America and certainly not in the newspapers. In the ongoing story of Indian-white conflict, Sitting Bull represented the enemy; he was the military leader of a fierce and primitive people. Sitting Bull might impress the newspapermen as an exceptionally clever Indian, but that in no way changed the fact that Indians were from a barbaric and inferior culture, ill-equipped to adjust to the demands of a growing market and industrial economy.

Sitting Bull as Custer's Killer

Sitting Bull became known in the press as a hostile Sioux chief as early as 1871.[12] But he was not the most famous or feared chief of the early 1870s—that distinction probably goes to Red Cloud—nor was he vilified for his leadership, military prowess, or cruelty. Even in early 1876, as Custer, Crook, and Terry mounted their new campaign against the northern tribes, Sitting Bull was not always the subject of great press attention. The Bismarck *Tribune,* for example, carried many reports of the Indian campaign in early 1876, most of which did not even mention the Sioux, referring simply to "Indians." The *Tribune's* Mark Kellogg, the only newsman to follow Custer and die at the Little Bighorn, published several long letters from the campaign in May and June, none of which mentioned Sitting Bull.[13] The expansionist, rabidly anti-Indian New York *Herald,* however, was more precise, identifying both Sitting Bull and Crazy Horse as objects of the army's summer campaign.[14]

If he was not yet a major villain, Sitting Bull was becoming increasingly well known as a dangerous Indian. He was named in the Bismarck *Tribune* in January 1876, for example, as leader of a band of "hostile Sioux" who had stolen thirty horses from a Gros Venture camp near Fort Berthold. The writer, William Courtnay, blamed the Sioux for undermining the efforts of the Rees to become civilized. And he identified Sitting Bull as leader of an especially hostile group of Sioux warriors:

> Will the Government never undertake the chastisement of Sitting Bull and his band of murderers, refugees and outlaws? His camp is the home of the worst Indians in the Northwest; Rain in the Face, the escaped murderer from Fort A. Lincoln; Long Dog, who a short time ago burned two or three white men at the stake, at Muscleshell; and Black Moon, whom I know to have killed a number of white men—these, with their followers, are a few of the Indian outcasts and ruffians who compose this Indian alsotia—this camp of cut throats who for years have indulged with impunity in rapine and murder and laughed at the Government.[15]

Despite this angry report, no follow-up stories or *Tribune* editorials appeared condemning the Sioux, Sitting Bull, or any other warrior. It is notable too that Courtnay's piece appeared not on page one but on page eight, a sign of the routine nature of such charges in early 1876. A more telling story was tucked away on the last page of the same issue. It said that Custer and Crook were planning "to give the northern Indians under Sitting Bull some bad medicine."[16] As this story suggests, Sitting Bull was a "bad" Indian before his encounter with Custer. But until that battle, Sitting Bull was one of a number of hostile chiefs, a "formidable foe," as the New York *Herald* put it,[17] but one who posed little serious threat to the U.S. Army. Besides, as progressive ideology dictated and the public clearly understood, the days of the renegade Indians on the plains would soon be ended.

The sensational victory over Custer and the Seventh Cavalry changed Sitting Bull's status forever: he became an Indian icon, a major symbol of native savagery and resistance. Sitting Bull became "the Indian outlaw Sitting Bull,"[18] chief organizer of the "red devils,"[19] who "caught [Custer] in an ambuscade"[20] and had proven himself "the equal of the great Indian fighter, Crook."[21] Indeed, Sitting Bull soon took on near-mythic qualities, an explanatory frame that helped the press and public understand his seemingly impossible victory over the gallant Custer. "His Education French, and His 'Idees' Napoleonic," explained a Chicago *Tribune* headline three weeks after the battle. The *Tribune*'s James William Howard (writing as "Phocion"), reported that Sitting Bull had been taught French by Father De Smet, a Jesuit priest. Howard also referred to a steamboat captain named McGarry who "says he knows that Sitting Bull has read the French history of Napoleon's wars, and [McGarry] believes that he modeled his generalship after the little Corsican Corporal."[22] Other reports circulated that Sitting Bull was really white, a Sandwich Islander, and that he had graduated from West Point.[23] Still other stories claimed that whites in the Indian camp directed the victory.[24] Like the exploits of Osceola nearly forty years earlier,[25] Sitting Bull's military training—and his race—had to be invented by the press (and others) in order to explain the seemingly impossible Indian victory over Custer and his men.

The truth, of course, was very different. Sitting Bull did not read French, did not know Napoleon's tactics, was not a general, and had not killed Custer. He did not even fight in the major actions of the battle, leaving that task to younger men and, at forty-five, assuming his role as a protector of the women and children.[26] Nevertheless, Sitting Bull had been a forceful presence at the Little Bighorn. He provided, as Utley put it, "a leadership so wise and powerful that it drew and held together a muscular coalition of tribes, one so infused with his defiant cast of mind that it could rout Three Stars [Gen. George Crook at the Battle of Rosebud Creek] and annihilate Long Hair."[27]

Custer's killer—this was the Sitting Bull the public wanted and the press provided. Following the Little Bighorn, Sitting Bull became "public enemy number one," demonized as the most dangerous Indian on the northern plains. It was the first, the most hostile, and the most enduring of Sitting Bull's public identities. One source of error and vitriol was the New York *Herald*, a Democratic-leaning paper then under the leadership of James Gordon Bennett Jr. The *Herald* had long been an expansionist journal and the elder Bennett was a prominent Custer supporter during the Civil War.[28] Thus Custer's demise was a natural and symbolically powerful weapon to use against President Grant and his Indian policies. Even before the Little Bighorn, when news of Rosebud Creek broke, the *Herald* criticized Grant and praised "that superb Indian fighter Custer." Had Grant put Custer in the field earlier, the paper said about Rosebud Creek, "we should not now be mourning ten dead and twenty wounded soldiers."[29] As for Sitting Bull, the paper was unrelentingly negative after the Little

Bighorn, using racist generalizations to ensure that he was seen as an evil chief from an evil tribe. Sitting Bull was "a warrior who has never accepted a favor at the hands of the white man," the *Herald* said, and the Sioux were a "war loving tribe."[30]

More dramatically, the *Herald* used a collection of Sitting Bull's autobiographical drawings, completed at Fort Buford in 1870, as direct evidence of Sioux cruelty. These drawings, fifty-five in all, showed the "notable and praiseworthy deeds" of Sitting Bull's life, the paper said. The *Herald* continued: "Whether it be the scalping of a soldier in battle, the killing of a Crow squaw, counting 'coup' upon an adversary, that is striking him, killing and scalping a white woodchopper, lancing a Crow Indian, or the sly theft of a mule, he brags equally of his prowess in his curious autobiography."[31] The paper supported its claims by publishing a two-column engraving based on a Sitting Bull sketch. It showed Sitting Bull and another warrior on horseback attacking an armed soldier. The *Herald* explained, "This sketch has been selected as it is the most representative in the series and as best illustrating the history which Sitting Bull narrates in his rude and primeval way."[32] The same issue included a bitter editorial that made clear the *Herald*'s interpretation of Sitting Bull's drawings. Each drawing recounts "some deed of bloodshed, cruelty, theft or inhumanity," the paper noted. Together, the drawings "make up the life of the model savage, whom our philanthropists love to feed, the child of nature whom the Indian Ring is never weary of praising or swindling." For savages such as Sitting Bull, "everything that is cruel and vicious is a matter of ostentation and pride."

The *Herald* also made much of the violence in Sitting Bull's drawings. "No record is made of the kindly or of the good; it is only the base or the brutal that they think worthy of telling." Turning to Indians generally, the editorial concluded with a reference to the old "vices and virtues idea" and the gospel of hard work: "There is no room here for discussing whether the rough-shod march of our civilization has not made a race of simple savages a race of savage demons; but we do know that in numberless instances they have opposed a stolid score to efforts at their advancement, and, rejecting the ways of civilization, have turned again and again to the wild, rather than, as General Sherman said the other day at West Point, 'earn their bread by the sweat of their brow.' "[33] In the *Herald,* at least, Sitting Bull was the chief murderer of a murderous, obstinate, and lazy race, people so depraved and alien they might require extermination.

What stands out about the *Herald*'s image of Sitting Bull is its racial determinism. As a "model savage," Sitting Bull was naturally violent and depraved; as his drawings showed, he was actually proud of his barbarity. In addition, the *Herald* emphasized the fact that the Sioux had steadfastly rejected the gift of American progress and the lesson of hard work; these were savage people incapable of recognizing or appreciating the benefits of a civilized life. Finally, the *Herald* did its best to link Sitting Bull to other disruptive elements in American society (such as French Catholics who taught him Napoleonic tactics) and to radical Republican philanthropists (such as Wendell Phillips, who protected him and his tribe).[34] By making such connections, Bennett presented Custer's Last Stand as a major symbol in the ideological war between the civilized and the savage forces in American life. Custer, of course, was the heroic defender of civilization; his demise could be blamed on the incompetence of Grant, the corrupt traders and bureaucrats of the so-called Indian Ring, and soft-hearted Republicans. The immediate enemy was Sitting Bull and the Sioux, though these were not the only "savages" that threatened Bennett's version of American progress. As Richard Slotkin has pointed out, the *Herald* also had other enemies in mind, especially the working classes and former slaves then threatening the dominance of capitalists like Bennett. Thus Indians, African Americans, radicals, Catholics, foreigners, and lower-class whites were all connected in the *Herald*'s rehash of Custer and the Little Bighorn, so much so that Sitting Bull's persona became a part of the paper's ongoing explanation of election year issues. Less than a month after the Little Bighorn, for example, the *Herald* commented on a racial conflict in South Carolina by referring to Sitting Bull's supposed satisfaction at the spread of "Sioux Civilization" in the South, where poor whites and blacks were adopting savage ways.[35] Thanks to the Indian triumph over Custer, Sitting Bull's public identity could be transformed into a potent metaphor for a host of threats to the New York *Herald*'s self-serving vision of American order and economic progress.

Ironically, the first news reports of Custer's death and the defeat of the Seventh Cavalry were not linked to Sitting Bull. An early report based on rumors of the battle appeared in the Chicago *Tribune* on 4 July. It did not mention either Sitting Bull or the Sioux: "Rumors prevail that Custer has since had a battle with the Indians."[36] The first Little Bighorn story in the New York *Times* ran under the headline "Massacre Of Our Troops," and reported that the massacre occurred at a "large camp of savages." No individual Indian or specific tribe was named.[37] Sitting Bull was also absent from early reports in the Bismarck *Tribune*. The *Tribune*'s initial stories referred numerous times to "the Indians," once to the "red devils," and only once to "the Sioux."[38] Bennett's *Herald*, a paper that had identified Sitting Bull as the principal enemy chief, included Sitting Bull's name in a headline over its first Little Bighorn report, though the story was sketchy and offered no supporting details.[39]

By the next day, however, Sitting Bull became part of the growing sensation that became Custer's Last Stand. In the *Times*, Custer's killers were now identified as "Sitting Bull's force" and their village was "Sitting Bull's main camp."[40] The chief culprits were the Sioux; no mention was made of the Cheyenne warriors who fought in the battle. The second-day news also offered a host of horrid details, including Indian mutilation of bodies (though not Custer's). Another second-day story in the *Times* contrasted the "wild Sioux" of the plains with southern Indians, calling the Sioux "a distinct race of men." The *Times* continued, citing Cooper's famous novel not for its romantic Indians but for its savage warriors: "The Sioux live by the chase and feed chiefly upon flesh. The southern Indians are farmers and eat fruits and vegetables, the latter are at their worst cruel, cowardly robbers. The former are as much like the brave and war-like red men represented by *The Last of the Mohicans* as ever existed outside the covers of fiction and romance. The difference between the foes in the North and South-west seems not to have been well counted upon."[41] This paragraph demonstrates the way some papers made sense of Indians beyond the "bad" Indian stereotype. Not all Indians were alike; some southern tribes were merely "cruel" and "cowardly." The Sioux, however, were "brave and war-like," qualities that made them true savages. Custer should have made this distinction, the *Times* noted. Instead, "he foolishly attempted to cut his way through and punish the red devils." The *Times* was a moderate Republican paper, much less inflammatory than the Democratic *Herald* and other anti-Grant journals, and willing to criticize Custer for his foolishness at the Little Bighorn. But even the *Times* recognized that Indian savagery had to be punished.

The first *Times* editorial on the battle made this clear. Some Indians were still in a "wild or semi-subdued state," the *Times* declared, and the Custer disaster was a reminder of their terrible power.[42] "Sitting Bull's band of Sioux left their reservation with hostile intent," the *Times* said. "They refused negotiations for peace. They defied the power and authority of the United States. They invited war." The *Times* did not speculate about Sitting Bull's personality or his motives, perhaps because they knew too little about him. But the paper was convinced that Sitting Bull's Sioux had to be punished, a position that further reinforced the distinction between "good" Indians and "bad" ones.

The native press itself also made this distinction. The *Indian Journal,* an intertribal paper published in Eufaula, Indian Territory (now Oklahoma), defended the Sioux in mild language both before and after the battle. But editor William Potter Ross also made it clear that the five tribes of Indian Territory—the Creek, Cherokee, Chickasaw, Choctaw, and Seminole—were significantly more civilized than the Sioux.[43] Another native editor, William Penn Boudinot of the *Cherokee Advocate,* explained that Custer's battle plans were flawed because he "made the mistake so often made of confounding all Indians alike. The mistake cost him his life if not his reputation."[44] Partisan politics also shaped the debate over the Little Bighorn in the Indian Territory press. The *Advocate,* for example, republished an editorial from the Democratic New York *Sun* following the battle. Unsurprisingly, the *Sun* blamed the Grant administration for the Sioux troubles, difficulties it said "originated in schemes of plunder for the benefit of the notorious Indian Ring, which has had its headquarters in the Interior Department from almost the beginning of Grant's administration."[45]

Sitting Bull's notoriety grew quickly after the Battle of the Little Bighorn and the papers scrambled for information about the mysterious chief. The New York *Times,* for example, featured an interview with J. D. Keller, a former clerk at Standing Rock who had known Sitting Bull. Predictably, the report emphasized Sitting Bull's "savage" qualities and, in the words of a subhead, the "peculiarities of [the Sioux] tribe when on the war path."[46] Keller described Sitting Bull as five feet tall with a large head, eyes, and nose. "His countenance is of an extremely savage type, betraying that bloodthirstiness and brutality for which he has been so long notorious," the story continued. The people of Montana were well aware of Sitting Bull and his "ferocious nature, some of his worst deeds having been perpetuated in that Territory." The story ended with Keller's erroneous speculation about how the Sioux managed to trick the Seventh Cavalry: "My idea of the Custer slaughter is that the Indians had no women and children in their lodges, and had parapets dug under the lodges out of sight. Custer, thinking it was a family camp, rushed in the centre of their fort, where resistance would necessarily prove fatal."[47] This story, complete with its biases and errors, illustrates a type of racial determinism prominent during the Indian wars. As the leader of the notorious Sioux and the man blamed for killing Custer, Sitting Bull was portrayed as *naturally* savage and evil. Following this reasoning, he was described as "an extremely savage type" with a "ferocious nature," a characteristic of the "hostile Sioux."

The aftermath of the Little Bighorn raised new questions about the true character of Native Americans. Despite the predominance of the "evil Indian," the issue remained unresolved in many papers. The New York *Herald* produced a story asking, "Can the Indians Be Trusted?" Predictably, the *Herald* was skeptical when it came to the Sioux. The story consisted of an interview with a veteran army officer who had been training a group of young Indian men for several months. Captain Charles McDonald reported modest success with his charges. His one Modoc warrior was "stolid, indifferent, seeming to live within a world all his own"—a situation McDonald did not appreciate. But all the other men had learned to read and write so enthusiastically that they had "never missed a mail in writing to their friends and relatives at home." And McDonald assured the *Herald* reporter that his trainees could be trusted. "They are friendly and truthful. They never disobey an order and are strictly temperate. If I wanted one to watch for three nights I could rely upon any one of them for it."[48]

Yet McDonald was unwilling to claim too much. His Comanche man was "very apt and bright. He speaks good English, reads well, and is in every way a noble fellow." Here was McDonald's "good" Indian, good precisely because he had given up his own ways for civilized ways. But the Sioux member of McDonald's party elicited a very different response, in part because the Sioux were Indians of a different order. McDonald explained: "The Sioux is a puzzle. Subtle in thought, full of nervous cunning and tricks, he will laugh in your face, and at the same moment take every advantage of you. As a nation, they are the most dangerous of Indian tribes."[49] Like many others, McDonald recognized both good and bad Indians and put the Sioux among the latter. But there was hope, McDonald believed, if white Americans changed their ways. "The American Indians have been imposed upon and misrepresented until they have become maniacal in their despair." Like the *Herald* and other commentators, McDonald blamed dishonest agents and traders: "Stop the villainous robberies and unholy murders by white scoundrels among the Indians and you will stop the Indian wars."[50]

Not surprisingly, the savagery of the Plains Indians and the need for retribution was a popular theme in the western press following the Little Bighorn. The Bismarck *Tribune* ran headlines emphasizing the seriousness of the cause: "NOW IT'S BUSINESS, NO MORE FOOLISHNESS."[51] C. A. Lounsberry, the editor of the *Tribune* and an old friend of Custer's, wrote a dramatic editorial on the Indian situation, asking "WHAT WILL BE DONE ABOUT IT?" Lounsberry's answer was, in a word, revenge.

Let that christian philanthropy which weeps over the death of a lazy, lousy, lying and stealing red skin, whose hands are still reeking with the blood of defenceless women and children, slain on the frontier, and who are ever ready to apologize for these murderers, take a back seat. Invite the soldier to the front and sustain him while he causes the Indians to realize the power, and those that still live to respect the white man. Wipe out all treaties, rub out all agencies and reservations, and treat the Indians as they are, criminals and paupers.[52]

This sweeping indictment of Indians represented the anger felt by many whites, East and West, in response to Custer's defeat. It was also a personal response for Lounsberry, a Michigan native (like Custer) who had known Armstrong since the Civil War. In fact, Lounsberry had planned to accompany Custer as a correspondent for his paper and Bennett's New York *Herald.* When a family illness caused his cancellation, the assignment went to his employee, Mark Kellogg. Like the *Herald,* Lounsberry criticized Indians for their laziness, an important sign of their hostility to civilized ways. Lounsberry also named western pioneers as Indian victims— "defenceless women and children"—instead of Custer and his soldiers, a strategy that broadened the charge against the Sioux well beyond the Little Bighorn, where Custer was the aggressor. The only thing these "murderers" and "criminals" will understand, Lounsberry added, is brute force.

Lounsberry claimed, incredibly, that he was not an Indian hater. But he did not hesitate to condemn those who defended Indians, as well as the Indians themselves. His 12 July editorial did not mention Sitting Bull by name, but he did single out the Sioux: "Men and means will not be lacking to so thoroughly wipe out the Sioux that there will be only a few old men, women and children left to mourn over the slain. Let there be no captures, but send all caught with arms in their hands, whether professedly friendly or known to be hostile, to the happy hunting grounds of their fathers' by a short cut."[53] The call for the near-extermination of the Sioux was not uncommon in the western press following Custer's death. But it was an extreme position, marked by a general racial hatred. The hatred extended to all Sioux—the eastern Santees, the "middle" tribes known as Yanktons and Yanktonai, and the seven western Lakota bands such as the Oglala, Brule, and Sans Arc—as if they were all Custer's killers. In the Bismarck *Tribune,* the death of Custer and his command called for retribution against the evil Sioux, whatever the subtleties of tribal identity or the actual make-up of Sitting Bull's camp.

News of the Custer campaign echoed in the press throughout the fall of 1876. The newspapers were full of stories and editorials asking who was to blame for the Custer disaster. President Grant, his appointees, and his policies were frequent targets of the papers, especially the Democratic press. Yet the Sioux emerged as primary villains and many stories about the western campaign after Custer's death were headlined simply "The Sioux War."[54] As the campaign continued, Sitting Bull became increasingly well known, literally a household name. A few weeks after the battle, for example, the Bismarck *Tribune* appropriated Sitting Bull's hostile identity for use in an editorial "puff." "If Sitting Bull were to try a glass of lager at the Gem Saloon he would be entirely willing to surrender his arms and his ponies and be good all the rest of his life," the paper said.[55] The following week the *Tribune* portrayed a more sinister Sioux leader in its political endorsement of a Democratic candidate: "If any Republican throws rocks at him personally, he ought to be scalped by Sitting Bull."[56] This usage made Sitting Bull out to be the national boogeyman, an imaginary source of retribution for wayward voters.

Sitting Bull's name also appeared regularly in military reports from the West. In fact, a number of Sioux campaign reports in the Bismarck *Tribune* ran under the headline "Sitting Bull," even when he was not a significant part of the story. This was the case in early October when the *Tribune* reported on contact between some Gros Venture and Sioux warriors. The story included numerous references to army actions along the frontier, but Sitting Bull, the man named in the headline, was mentioned only in a note that he and his band "properly belonged" at the Standing Rock agency. This story—and others like it[57]—shows that Sitting Bull had become the most notorious leader of hostile Sioux. In the pages of this western paper, Sitting Bull's name was used to represent all the "evil" Indians of the day.

Some of the most dramatic rhetoric following Custer's defeat turned up in the press in the form of speeches, poems, and satires. A long speech by Jefferson Kidder, Dakota Territory's Congressional representative, took up a full page in the Bismarck *Tribune* three weeks after the battle. Kidder blasted Indian sympathizers for their misplaced "Christian philanthropy," criticized the fictions of Cooper and Longfellow for their "purely imaginary and meretricious" Indian nobility, and singled out the Sioux for "continually murdering innocent men, women and children."[58]

A week later, the *Tribune* ran a gory story attributed to the New York *Herald* about a wounded Sioux warrior discovered by a group of Crows.

The Crows "all chattered as wildly together as the South American monkeys" at this discovery, the story noted. The warriors proceeded to shoot the wounded man six times and mutilate his body "until there was nothing recognizable as human." "Infamies too shameful and disgusting to record completed the ghastly climax," the writer noted, adding that the Sioux themselves "practice even more refined barbarities." True to its anti-Indian form, the *Tribune's* headline was powerfully ironic: "The Gentle Savage."[59]

Adjacent to this story in the *Tribune* was a poem taken from the *Golden Era,* a California newspaper. Titled "A White Man's Lament," the five-stanza poem portrayed Indians as pampered leeches, stealing and killing with one hand while taking government largess with the other. The second stanza is representative:

> I want to be an Indian—
>   A "warrior of the plains";
> I want to wield a tomahawk
>   And scoop out people's brains.
> I want to build a campfire
>   On a human being's breast,
> And watch his writhing agony
>   With a "noble savage's" zest.[60]

The poem did not mention the Sioux, though it did name the Modocs, a tribe infamous in California for the Captain Jack affair, as well as the Utes and Cheyennes, two other tribes known for their conflicts with whites. The poem provides a vivid example of how narrow the Indian identity had become following Custer's defeat. Many Indians in 1876 were peaceful; some in Indian Territory were considered civilized. But those Indians were not interesting or relevant in the aftermath of the Little Bighorn. The lesson of that debacle, many papers made clear, was that renegade Indians—still dangerously wild and uncontrolled—must be tamed and brought to justice with maximum force. And the single Indian most identified with this untamed and savage identity was Sitting Bull.

As the most infamous Indian in late 1876, Sitting Bull was regularly lampooned by western editorialists. A column in the Bismarck *Tribune,* for instance, claimed to provide "Sitting Bull's True Pedigree." "Gen. S. Bull," the columnist said, was born on "Cow Island" and was named for his habit of "*setting* down on lonesome subjects of the American Republic whenever an Indian agent 'kicked'" (italics in original). He measures "standing up, 7 ft. 5 in. or lying down 7 in. 5 ft.," the paper said. He has six fingers on one hand, five on the other. More pointedly, Sitting Bull's "one leg is a little longer than the other or the other is a little shorter, I forget which— this deformity sorter bothers the military, as it gives him an uncertain warbling gait, and they can't tell whether he is bound for the Big Horn mountains or the British Possessions."[61] Finally, the satirist, identified as "Bismarck, Jr.," said that the chief had a limited education, but "he can cypher a government contract down as close as a Q. M. [Quartermaster] clerk." In any case, "he don't care whether Uncle Sammy pays off the boys in hard or soft money as the traders take either in pay for war material." This last barb was the most serious, because it emphasized that Sitting Bull was still at war.[62]

Another satirical account of Sitting Bull's life was published in the Minneapolis *Tribune*. This story, allegedly from a schoolmate, told how "we used to give him [Sitting Bull] a truthful little hatchet and butcher knife and the old yellow cat to play with." The writer went on, tongue firmly in cheek: "I should judge that he must have scalped that old cat as much as sixteen or seventeen hundred times before he was three years old. It was beautifully touching to observe what an interest that child took in dumb animals."[63] The writer also raised the issue of government handouts, now a familiar complaint against Sitting Bull. Even as a child, the story claimed, Sitting Bull would draw rations and blankets "just in play." The writer imagined this childhood scene: "Why I have seen him walk around the tepee hour after hour and every time he would come up and answer to a different name and [imagine] acorns for rations and burdock leaves for blankets and fish bones for scalping knives."[64] This is an ironic charge to make against Sitting Bull, a man who was well known for his hostility to agency life and his independence from the ration system. Nevertheless, this portrait of young Sitting Bull as a cruel and naturally manipulative government dependent fit the ideology of the post–Little Bighorn era; that is, it portrayed this most dangerous Indian as a petty thief, too dishonest and cowardly to be a serious threat to American life.

Months after the Little Bighorn, Sitting Bull was still represented as the most vicious of Indian leaders. When a warrior named Kill Eagle surrendered at Standing Rock in September 1876, he provided the Bismarck *Tribune* yet another account of the battle. Kill Eagle said that he and his band arrived in Sitting Bull's village innocently, where they were duped into joining the planned hostilities. As Kill Eagle told it, he and his band were "unable to escape from the meshes of the net the wily Sitting Bull

[had] woven around them."[65] Kill Eagle also denied rumors that there were white men in Sitting Bull's camp—a popular explanation for the Indian success over Custer—and he denied that Sitting Bull himself was white or a half breed. This was a helpful public correction, though the truth about the battle was so muddled in the press that no newspaper reader could be sure what to believe.

Sitting Bull's position as the most infamous hostile Indian was also evident a year after the Little Bighorn when the U.S. government organized a peace commission, the so-called Sitting Bull Commission. This meeting took place at Fort Walsh in Canada's Northwest Territories, where Sitting Bull and his band had fled in May 1877. One of the reporters who covered the meeting and met Sitting Bull was Charles Diehl of the Chicago *Times,* a talented reporter destined to become head of the Associated Press. His reports and a subsequent interview with Sitting Bull provide evidence of Sitting Bull's new status as a public person. The headlines over Diehl's first report from Fort Walsh show that Sitting Bull and the Sioux were still hostile. "THE SAUCY SIOUX," the main headline read, summarizing Sitting Bull's refusal to agree to the commissioners' terms. "That Child of Nature Coolly Invites the Government Agents to 'Go to the Devil,'" a secondary headline said.[66] The following day the main headline again identified Sitting Bull as a contemptuous native: "THE SAVAGE'S SCORN."[67]

Nevertheless, Diehl provided a fair summary of Sitting Bull's position, including the chief's complaint that the Americans had come to capture and kill him. Diehl also provided a more accurate and sensitive portrait of Sitting Bull himself, taking pains to contradict "all of the twaddle which has been published about him." Sitting Bull was a "pure-blooded savage" who was "splendidly proportioned," Diehl wrote. His almost Roman features, Diehl noted romantically, "[heighten] his air of intelligence and [add] to the almost judicial gravity of his countenance." Diehl added: "I had heard that Sitting Bull was club-footed, a scholar, a half-breed, a graduate of West Point. He is none of these; he is an untutored savage, and, as Indians go, a very fine-looking and more than usually intelligent one."[68] This was faint praise, but within the ideology of the day, it was an honest attempt to see beyond the clichés of Sitting Bull's identity and to recognize his merits as a human being and tribal leader.

Diehl went on to provide an account of Sitting Bull's reply to General Terry's demands. This press account provided one of the few opportunities for Sitting Bull and other chiefs to air their grievances publicly. Sitting Bull's speech also gave Diehl a chance to describe the man's power as a speaker. Sitting Bull began in "a sharp, vindictive manner," Diehl wrote. The reporter was impressed: "As I watched . . . and saw his mobile face light up as he spoke of the great wrongs [done to] his people, and uttered his contempt and hatred for the American nation, I could not help but admire the natural oratory which enabled him to speak so strongly. Every thought was expressed in a gesture more powerful than his words could possibly be framed to read."[69] Diehl was less impressed with Sitting Bull's stubbornness and his hostility in the official negotiations. Still, these firsthand reports provided a fuller and more humane portrait of Sitting Bull than most of the rumor and invective published since the victory over Custer. Ever so slowly, Sitting Bull was beginning to emerge from the demon's role.

Sitting Bull's new, more favorable identity was the result of two factors. One was the skill and honesty of Charles Diehl, a reporter more interested in facts than in rumor, hyperbole, and political grandstanding. More importantly, Sitting Bull could be sympathetically portrayed because he was now living peacefully in Canada and was no longer perceived as an immediate threat to the frontier. Not only that, Sitting Bull was not fighting but *talking,* passionately and sensibly from the Sioux point of view, about his tribe's long-running battle with the U.S. government. In short, Sitting Bull's new identity grew out of perceived "good Indian" qualities that could be praised in some American papers.

A turning point in the rebuilding of Sitting Bull's identity occurred with the publication of two newspaper interviews Sitting Bull gave at the Canadian talks. For the first time, Utley concluded, Sitting Bull became a fully formed public figure. Charles Diehl's interview in the Chicago *Times* appeared under the headline, "THE SIOUX'S SAVIOR."[70] As before, Diehl supplied his readers with details that made Sitting Bull more human. In conversation, Diehl wrote, Sitting Bull "looked at the person addressed fairly in the eye, and when he laughs, he does so heartily, and all the stoicism of the savage is gone." The interview also gave Sitting Bull a chance to deny his identity as a war chief and white-hater. Questioned about returning to the United States, Sitting Bull said, "I will not start any fight. Every time I have had any trouble with them [the Americans], they struck me first. I want to live in peace." Sitting Bull even denied his role as a chief or as a head soldier, saying that he was once a chief, "but the Americans killed my people and broke up my tribe." Why do the people still look up to him, Diehl asked. "It is because I am poor," Sitting Bull answered, a reply that made sense in Lakota culture but must have struck most readers as disingenuous.

Despite such confusions, Sitting Bull was speaking for himself here and Diehl was a perceptive reporter. The result was a more detailed and expansive portrait of Sitting Bull, one certainly more accurate than the stream of errors that followed the Little Bighorn. More than a year after the battle, Sitting Bull began to emerge in some papers as an intelligent and powerful Sioux leader, one who was still a savage, but now a savage with motives for his actions and an ability to carry out his wishes. And as Custer had found out, such an Indian was a force to be reckoned with.

It seems unlikely that Diehl's more complex portrait of Sitting Bull changed public opinion to any significant degree. For most of the press and public, Sitting Bull was still Custer's killer, a fierce, war-like leader of the wild and hostile Sioux and a bitter enemy of American civilization. This was not a hard case to make. Sitting Bull was, after all, on the wrong side of the most sensational and disputed Indian battle in American history. And Sitting Bull was, symbolically at least, Custer's killer and George Armstrong Custer, the self-promoting Civil War hero, "boy general," and gallant golden-haired cavalry officer, was well on his way to becoming the nation's most famous military martyr. All that clouded the public's view of Sitting Bull for years to come.

Sitting Bull Goes to Town

In 1884, eight years after the Battle of the Little Bighorn, Sitting Bull was living at the Standing Rock Agency, farming a bit and at peace. After years of exile in Canada, he had surrendered in 1881, no longer able to find sufficient buffalo or supplies to sustain his people. Moreover, many of his fellow chiefs had already surrendered, leaving Sitting Bull with fewer tribesmen willing or able to resist.[71] Arriving at Fort Buford in July 1881, Sitting Bull experienced for the first time his new role as an uncertain celebrity, widely vilified but also acclaimed for his victory over Custer. Curious crowds lined up to see the infamous chief and Sitting Bull embarked on a new life, one that included visits to Bismarck, St. Paul, Washington, and New York City. These encounters introduced him to the customs and technologies of late nineteenth-century American life. One of the early lessons Sitting Bull learned in his new world was commercial; whites would pay good money for his autograph and personal items. Entrepreneurs also saw profits in Sitting Bull's fame and before long several men, including Buffalo Bill Cody, were interested in Sitting Bull's crowd-drawing abilities.

Sitting Bull's first trip to the city was in March 1884, when agent James McLaughlin took the chief to Minneapolis and St. Paul. There Sitting Bull toured the city's industrial warehouses and factories. He visited the *Pioneer Press,* a school, and the city fire department, where the firemen demonstrated their firefighting skills. The arrival of Sitting Bull in "polite" society gave the press a chance to focus on him as a man, not as a demon, and to contrast Sitting Bull's "Indianness" with the features and customs of 1880s city life. Sitting Bull was almost always found deficient in such comparisons, but the press had no other logical way to make sense of the man than to make these ethnocentric comparisons. In other words, reports about Sitting Bull in the city were informal measurements of native life, a catalog of what it meant to be both civilized and savage. Thus the press showed an extraordinary interest in Sitting Bull's dress, speech, table manners, and the like. Such details would not be a newsworthy topic for "normal" citizens in the press, but no newspaper treated Sitting Bull in that way.

In St. Paul's *Pioneer Press,* for example, Sitting Bull and his nephew One Bull attracted a crowd. "Pushing, jostling, eager, unappeasable, the people crowded into the [hotel] corridors" to see the men "in their picturesque garb." The men were celebrities, the paper made clear, and the scene was "exactly similar to the manifestations when Sullivan, the slugger, was at the Merchants [Hotel]." The *Press* also reported that Sitting Bull had gained weight since his surrender—he was no longer "the thin and ragged warrior"—a comment on Sitting Bull's improved condition as a government ward. Sitting Bull's hosts showed him the city's cultural and technical marvels and the chief was suitably impressed. "The telephone broke him all up," the paper reported. Sitting Bull was also impressed with the city's houses. "Your tepees are very big and very high. I never saw any so big before," he told the paper. Sitting Bull also said that he hoped for a good corn crop this year. "Last year the corn grew high, but didn't amount to anything," he lamented.[72]

The most remarkable thing about this representation of Sitting Bull was its lack of rancor. The *Pioneer Press* had apparently wiped the slate clean, omitting all references to Sitting Bull's well-known "savage" characteristics: his "bloodthirstiness," his "ferocious nature," and the like. In fact, the story did not mention either Custer or the Little Bighorn, the event most closely associated with Sitting Bull's popular identity. Eight years after the battle, the *Press* seemed to forgive the old chief. An explanation for this attitude can be seen in the story's emphasis on Sitting Bull's positive response to civilization. In the city, removed from his dangerous natural habitat, Sitting Bull could be seen as someone trying to move from savagery to civilization. The story itself provided evidence of this transition, noting his wonder at the telephone, his praise of big houses, and his comments on farming. Two days later, another story summarized Sitting Bull's fire station visit, where he was asked what he liked best. "All of it, like everything," he told the paper.[73] In these stories, the *Press* presented a benign Sitting Bull and implied an optimistic Indian future where native traditions would be replaced by civilized habits and modern technology. After all, if the most hostile chief of the Sioux could be converted, then surely others could be. But the paper did not recognize the complexity of such a conversion. Sitting Bull was impressed by the technical achievements and material wealth of the city, but neither he nor the many other Indians who went to town ever said they would cease to be Indians. As historian L. G. Moses has noted, Native Americans could learn to live like whites, but they would remain Indians. It was a message few nineteenth-century Americans ever understood.[74]

In any event, Sitting Bull could not escape the shadow of the Little Bighorn for long. He could be perceived as momentarily harmless, but he was still a "bad Indian" and his violent past could not be forgotten, especially when he was uncooperative about his role at the Little Bighorn. In an editorial, the *Pioneer Press* denigrated Sitting Bull's leadership and described him as a "plotter," a quality the editor said explained his "reticence in regard to Custer's death." The editorialist continued: "A white man in fear of death for that deed would sooner or later trip himself, and let fall some clue to his guilt. I hope Sitting Bull on his death-bed, when there can be no fear of earthly punishment before his eyes, will tell all he knows of that fearful and heroic struggle."[75] In St. Paul, Sitting Bull was still accountable for Custer's death and the *Press* wanted the man to acknowledge his guilt. Without such an admission, Sitting Bull remained an "evil Indian" whose absolution could go only so far.

Back in Bismarck, Sitting Bull's trip to Minnesota was not favorably reviewed. As it was after the Little Bighorn, the *Tribune* was highly critical of Sitting Bull and skeptical about the trip's benefits. Spring was coming, the paper noted, and "the old chief's thoughts would *naturally* turn toward the war path and new deeds of petty larceny and manslaughter" (emphasis added).[76] When Sitting Bull visited the Franklin school, the *Tribune* mocked Indian education, which "consisted principally in acquiring a dexterity in making successful sneaks on the smoke houses of the intrepid settlers of the Missouri slope." Again, the paper saw this a natural part of Sitting Bull's character: "This wasn't right, but he was so educated and couldn't help it."

The *Tribune*'s attack also had a notable moral element; Indian life was portrayed as evil while life in the city offered redemption. Thus Sitting Bull was called an "old impenitent sinner" and the editor hoped that the attractions of the city might "lure the old man from the path of sin and iniquity."[77] Indeed, the *Tribune* claimed that officials had organized the trip in order to expose Sitting Bull to "a little civilization, hoping that it might wean him from his thirst for the gore of the frontiersman." In contrast to the optimistic *Pioneer Press,* however, the *Tribune* viewed the civilizing effects of the trip as mere folly: "Filling his bronze system full of pie and Milwaukee beer," the paper said, might convince the chief to "cheerfully repent of his sins and exchange his classical breech cloth for the pants of the dude and his scalping knife for show tickets."[78] The article ended with the wish that "high living may get the bulge on his untutored stomach and throw him into dyspepsia . . . but even that is a slender hope and should not be too fondly cherished."

The tone and language of this characterization reveal a great deal about the popular understanding of Indians in the western press in the last decades of the century. Indians in general and Sitting Bull in particular were still imagined as naturally savage; thus "petty larceny," "manslaughter," "thirst for gore," "a love for cussedness," and the like were inbred in the Indian character, a character so deficient that it cried out for ridicule. This portrait also perpetuated the notion that Sitting Bull and other Indians acted rashly and, even worse, that violence was for them mere sport. Sitting Bull, the paper claimed, "has been royally entertained, and asserts that he hasn't had so much fun since the Custer massacre." Finally, the *Tribune*'s bitter attack on Sitting Bull was notable for its lack of explanation or context. Sitting Bull was a leading warrior and had killed many men, both white and native. More famously, he was "Custer's killer," a fact not mentioned but well understood in Bismarck. Yet the *Tribune* argued that this violence was a natural result of the savage life—"he was so educated and couldn't help it"—ignoring more complex cultural or historical explanations for Lakota behavior. Significantly, too, the paper made no reference to the army, the U.S. government, business interests, or the actions of white speculators in the Dakotas as a way to understand Sitting Bull or his actions. This omission, of course, ignored the major forces in recent Lakota life, forces that could have made Sitting Bull's violence more understandable. In Bismarck, however, Sitting Bull's savagery did not merit an explanation—he was just evil.

Later in 1884, with the approval of agent McLaughlin, Sitting Bull and several other chiefs and their wives were organized by a showman named Alvaren Allen into "Sitting Bull's Combination." The troupe traveled to New York City in the late summer and appeared at the Eden Musée, a wax museum, as a living exhibit of native life from the plains.[79] Newspaper ads in New York built up the appearance as "a great novelty" and "a historically correct picture of frontier life" featuring "no less a personage than the original living and celebrated Sioux Chief SITTING BULL."[80] The two-week appearance was a huge success, and it gave the New York *Times* a chance to make its own cultural comparisons.

The *Times* began with a comment on native speech and appearance: "Low, guttural sounds emanating from capacious chests signaled the entrance of a singular-looking crowd yesterday noon." The reporter then listed the English and native names of each of the Indians, taking the opportunity to comment on the strangeness of the Lakota language. Sitting Bull was listed as simply "alias Tatank Iyotonka," but the listing quickly degenerated into ridicule for others in the party when "alias" was replaced by "familiarly known as," "dubbed by the boys," "usually called to dinner by," "rejoices also in the sobriquet," "humorously saluted as," "affectionately called," and "hilariously christened."[81] This string of descriptors was probably amusing to the *Times'* readers, but the language also indicates the low status accorded native naming practices.

The *Times* went on to comment on Sitting Bull's manners and appearance. He was a "powerfully built fellow," the paper noted, though when approached by a reporter proved to be "as modest as a maid." The reporter described Sitting Bull's braids in detail, but noted that his unorthodox table manners caused the most sensation. "He used the toothpicks for chopsticks to spear the chicken croquettes, which he mistook for potatoes," the *Times* reported. Sitting Bull is "reputed to be ignorant of English," though the paper pointed out that he had no trouble understanding the offer of a whiskey cocktail. Like the Bismarck *Tribune,* this account overlooked Sitting Bull's career as a warrior and provided no hint of Custer or other military exploits. Having come to the city as a popular attraction, the *Times* held to that line. Nevertheless, the newspaper's lampooning of Lakota names and its emphasis on inappropriate behavior made plain the fact that Sitting Bull and his fellow chiefs were still rude savages, far removed from grace or true civilization.

Sitting Bull's next major encounter with urban America was in 1885, when he signed on for a season with Buffalo Bill Cody's Wild West show. He was cast as the villain in the show and was often hissed when he appeared.[82] But he was undoubtedly a draw. Newspaper advertisements for the show featured his name prominently—"The Renowned Sioux Chief SITTING BULL"—and, to the chagrin of the Bismarck *Tribune* and like-minded papers, he was often greeted by public officials and other prominent citizens.

A large ad in the Washington *Post* in 1885 revealed America's western movement as Buffalo Bill imagined it. The left side of the illustration showed a bearded rider resembling Buffalo Bill watching covered wagons track across the plains toward the Rockies. The right side of the illustration showed an Indian on horse back, observing an encampment of tipis. In the middle of this tableau—symbolically linking the Indian past with the white future—was a large bust of Buffalo Bill himself, facing the Indian, eyes scanning the horizon. "Buffalo Bill's Wild West," said the headline over the picture. Below the picture: "America's National Entertainment," and beneath that, Sitting Bull's name, also in headlines. In the design of this ad—and, more importantly, in the mythic tale that Cody was telling—Sitting Bull was a central (though secondary and villainous) character in "America's National Entertainment."[83] In his Wild West show, Buffalo Bill was consciously selling the nation's most triumphant tale, the epic story of western expansion and conquest. It was a compelling and popular story, one that needed heroes as well as villains—and for that job, no one was more qualified than Sitting Bull.

Sitting Bull was particularly acclaimed in Canada, where he met members of Parliament and "stole the show," according to historian Don Russell.[84] The Wild West show appeared in Montreal, Ottawa, Kingston, Toronto, and Hamilton; everywhere Sitting Bull "was honored by mayors and members of Parliament," Russell wrote.[85] The Toronto *Globe,* for example, praised the Wild West show without referring to "Indian treachery" or similar terms. The paper treated Sitting Bull respectfully, pointing out his intelligence and pleasant demeanor. The *Globe* highlighted Sitting Bull's generosity—"The old man, as was his custom, invariably fed all the hungry members of his tribe . . . whenever he had rations"—but criticized this habit as "most unpractical."[86] The *Globe* also emphasized Sitting Bull's loyalty, noting his fast friendships with several white and native Canadians. Based on this report, Toronto readers could reasonably conclude that Sitting Bull was less the threatening savage of Little Bighorn fame than a colorful, if somewhat curious, native leader.

In the United States, however, Sitting Bull's reception was substantially more ambivalent. In Washington, Sitting Bull and fifteen chiefs met with President Grover Cleveland and other officials, including their old battlefield foe, General Phil Sheridan. Whatever the import of the meeting, the Washington *Post* focused again on dress and manners. "The Indians wore their war costumes," the paper said. "Their faces were embellished with red and yellow paint and on their heads they wore immense single feathers." Sitting Bull, in contrast, wore "a number of feathers of large size," though he did not impress the *Post* reporter. "Sitting Bull gave an occasional grunt when spoken to by an Indian companion," the reporter noted. "He paid but little attention to his surroundings." Other Indians, however, were amused by a buffalo scene hanging on the wall, talking and laughing among themselves. No interaction or conversation between Sitting Bull or General Sheridan was reported. As for meeting with the president, the *Post* produced only four lines of type, mentioning simply that the chief "gave the President a letter in the Indian language."[87]

A somewhat more revealing *Post* story appeared a few days later, when the paper published a review of Buffalo Bill's show. The subhead referred to one of the event's highlights, in which "A Group of Howling Savages Pursue a Defenseless Stage Coach." The story described the attack in detail, naming the driver, John Higby, and recounting his efforts to elude the attackers. "Nearer and nearer came the Indians, yelling like mad and exchanging rapid shots with the passengers," the paper said. Suddenly, Buffalo Bill and his men appeared, driving off the Indians. The *Post* as well as the public apparently believed this bit of theater: "The thrilling act ended in a blaze of Grecian fire from the interior of the vehicle in a realistic manner peculiar to the original genius of the West. The other features of the 'Wild West' show were greeted with equal enthusiasm and proved greatly entertaining."[88] Despite his headline billing, Sitting Bull was not named in this story. Instead, *Post* readers caught a glimpse of the West as spectacle, complete with "defenseless" passengers, a daring stage driver, howling savages, and of course, a rescuer named Buffalo Bill. Whatever his real fame as a warrior and chief, Sitting Bull could not be the hero of this tale.

Sitting Bull's more notorious identity was resurrected when the show appeared in Michigan, Custer's home state. A day before the show opened in Detroit, the lead editorial in the *Evening Journal,* "A Shameless Enterprise," introduced the chief as "head butcher of the Sioux."[89] Not coincidentally, Sitting Bull was compared to Henry Wirz, the Confederate commandant of the infamous Andersonville prison who was tried and executed for war crimes by a Union military commission.[90] "What would have been thought of the men who only nine years after Wirz's savage deeds should have taken him through the country as a money-making curiosity, and what would have become of Wirz if such a thing had been attempted?" the *Journal* asked.[91] The paper supplied no answer nor did it criticize Buffalo Bill by name. But the editorial took direct aim at Sitting Bull and the massacre—"not a battle"—at the Little Bighorn: "Sitting Bull's warfare was characteristic of a bloodthirsty, ferocious, bestial bushwhacker. And the murderous barbarity displayed by him in the ambush where the gallant Custer and his brave comrades lost their lives is his chief claim to the distinction which makes it a good speculation to carry him through the country for exhibition."[92] The paper reminded readers that nine Michigan men died with Custer and that the people of the state could feel only "morbid curiosity" to see Sitting Bull and "be gratified at the sight of his brutish face." Despite this warning, the paper stopped short of directly threatening Sitting Bull and ended with this lukewarm admonition: "Unless the memory of these things [the Little Bighorn] is dead Michigan ought not to be a good state for Sitting Bull to visit."

Two days later, the *Evening Journal* published an interview and another editorial on Sitting Bull. Under a headline identifying him (erroneously) as "ONE OF GEN CUSTER'S MURDERERS," Sitting Bull was described in negative, but somewhat ambivalent, terms. He was the "notorious chief" and "noted murderer" but also the "great chieftain." The reporter described Sitting Bull's appearance, his clothes, and jewelry, noting "a very dirty pin" and gold buttons that "yearned for cleaning." But the man's face impressed the Detroit writer; it reminded him of portraits of Daniel Webster. The reporter concluded with an ironic note: "Sitting Bull is one of the finest looking Indians who ever committed murder."[93]

The interview itself included details of Sitting Bull's early life, Indian horsemanship, and travels in Canada. The reporter noticed that Sitting Bull spoke slowly, with great deliberation. "His tones are quiet and unassuming, though he gesticulates a great deal," the reporter wrote. The story concluded with a bare mention of the show itself: "It was similar to previous entertainments given by the combination here last spring, and was witnessed by an immense crowd of highly delighted spectators."[94]

The editorial on the same page was more forceful. Sitting Bull was now "that dirty savage," "the murderer of the heroic Custer," and an "unpunished criminal." The *Journal* criticized those unidentified prominent citizens—including a "once warm friend" of Custer—who "bowed before him as if he were an august potentate instead of a red-handed brute." The lesson here, the *Journal* claimed, was for murderers to make sure their victims were the bravest and best. Such a criminal will then, like Sitting Bull, "cease to become a murderer and become an honored warrior killing for some noble object."[95]

In most of the cities where he appeared, Sitting Bull was an object of both admiration and fear. The Indian wars were over, it seemed, and the Wild West battles were strictly for sport. As sport, or more accurately, as spectacle, Sitting Bull could be celebrated as the greatest Indian of them all, a living relic of American's westward quest. He was the quintessential Indian warrior but he was also real, his name and his body available to complete the story of American adventure and destiny. The crowds consistently turned out to see Custer's nemesis, now tame enough to "play Indian" and sell his autograph. In the papers, Sitting Bull was an easy target for ridicule, his manners, speech, and dress still distinctly at odds with the fashions of the day. That was good sport too, though the continuing emphasis on differences helped obscure a more complete portrait of Sitting Bull or the Sioux.

But in Detroit, the events of 1876 were still too fresh to make Sitting Bull a neutral figure. He might be a great chief and the object of some misplaced attention, but he was still the man most responsible for the death of Michigan's most honored native son, a fact that could not be easily forgiven. In Michigan, nine years was not enough time to erase Sitting Bull's identity as the most treacherous Indian in the West.

The Press and Sitting Bull's Murder

Sitting Bull made the front pages again in late 1890 when, in a response to the Ghost Dance movement then sweeping the northern plains, army officials ordered his arrest. The arrest and murder of Sitting Bull on 15 December was one of the many tragic and unnecessary events associated with the rumored rise of an Indian messiah and the Ghost Dance, a spiritual movement that promised its believers a native utopia, ripe with buffalo and free from whites. Inspired by a Paiute holy man named Wovoka, the Ghost Dance was a seductive if unrealistic vision, producing a number of true believers among the Lakota as well as a fierce response from government and military officials. The press played a harmful and amplifying role in the perception of the Ghost Dance movement, sensationalizing its dangers and routinely referring to its effects as the "Messiah craze," a "religious craze," or simply "the craze."[96] The Ghost Dance hysteria culminated near Wounded Knee Creek on the Pine Ridge reservation on 29 December, when soldiers attempted to disarm a Miniconjous band led by Big Foot. Some of the warriors resisted, believing that their ghost shirts would render them invincible to army bullets. The confrontation quickly escalated into a massacre, leaving Big Foot and scores of women and children dead. Several soldiers were also killed and rumors spread among the tribes and in the press about a new Indian war.[97]

Sitting Bull was not a true believer. But he had been open to some of the Ghost Dance ideas and invited a Miniconjou man named Kicking Bear to Standing Rock to make his case. To agent McLaughlin and the army, this was an openly provocative act, one the government could not ignore. Although McLaughlin and the army were often at odds over the details, they began planning Sitting Bull's arrest. This action, they hoped, would undermine the messiah movement and, not coincidentally, muzzle Sitting Bull, whose presence was always seen as a threat. In the early hours of 15 December, some forty Indian policemen surrounded Sitting Bull's cabin and quickly apprehended the sleeping chief. He agreed to go, then hesitated. A crowd gathered, urging resistance and shouting taunts at the police. Suddenly one of Sitting Bull's men fired at a policeman named Bull Head, who, falling, fired at Sitting Bull, hitting him in the chest. The next minutes were chaotic, but when the shooting stopped, Sitting Bull and several others on both sides lay dead.[98]

Sitting Bull's murder gave the papers one more chance to define the man and tell his story. Unfortunately, the newspaper response to Sitting Bull's death became another opportunity to recycle the old clichés and reinforce the racial ideology of the day. In death, Sitting Bull's life was reduced to his most hostile characteristics. In the overheated atmosphere of the messiah craze, the press relied on "official" sources and the language of difference to make sure Sitting Bull was once again known as the cruel savage who killed the gallant Custer.

Sitting Bull's death was big news, even in the East. The New York *Times,* for example, published several page-one stories, including one supplied by agent McLaughlin and said to be "the last visit paid by a white man to Sitting Bull's camp prior to the tragic events." The note introducing McLaughlin's report said, "The narrative throws a flood of light on the old chief's wily character," and McLaughlin reported on his efforts to undermine the disaffected Indians. "Knowing the Indians as I do, I am confident that I can . . . settle the Messiah craze at this agency, and thus break up the power of Sitting Bull, without trouble and with but little excitement," he wrote. This report revealed McLaughlin as far too optimistic, but it also laid the blame for Sitting Bull's murder on the "very obstinate" chief himself.[99]

A more hostile *Times* story was the page-one profile of Sitting Bull published under the headlines, "THE DESPERATE CHIEF'S CAREER" and "A BITTER FOE OF THE WHITES, SAGACIOUS, CRUEL, AND BLOODTHIRSTY." The lead paragraph neatly but erroneously summed up Sitting Bull's infamous public identity: "Sitting Bull, of all the Indians, was the most unrelenting, the most hostile, the most sagacious, the most cruel, and the most desperate foe of any chief of modern times. He never assented to the control of the United States Government over his people, but persistently fought the troops whenever they came in his way."[100] This statement recognized Sitting Bull as the ultimate Indian enemy, hardly surprising in the continuing Ghost Dance paranoia. But like most press reviews of his life, this characterization oversimplified Sitting Bull's hostility and overlooked the more peaceful aspects of his relationship to whites. Even in 1890, the public needed an "evil Indian" and the *Times* obliged, creating a Sitting Bull who was every bit as cruel and stubborn as the public imaged him to be. On the occasion of his death, such a portrait reinforced Sitting Bull's most evil identity and justified his murder to millions of American readers.

The *Times* editorial emphasized these points. The paper attached a string of unfavorable descriptors to Sitting Bull's name. He was "mischievous and turbulent," "bumptious and bombinating," "distinguished for his impracticality and apparent motivelessness," and known for his "pure cussedness." The *Times* recalled that the "old savage" had once escaped to Canada, where he "openly practiced polygamy, free trade, and other revolting vices at which we were aiming moral and patriotic legislation." The editorial also blamed "the old reprobate" for the Ghost Dance troubles. The *Times* concluded with this colorful comparison: "The announcement of his death is not calculated to arouse any other emotions than those excited the other day by the slaying of a 'rogue' elephant in Cincinnati, though no quadruped ever did do much widely extended and long continued mischief as Sitting Bull."[101] The editorial's explanation of Sitting Bull focused on his racial identity—his "Indianness." Other people were "mischievous" as well as "bumptious," but Sitting Bull was portrayed this way mainly because he was an Indian. That racial logic accounts for this passage:

Bull would undoubtedly have been a much more comfortable old savage if he had settled down under the aegis of the United States to draw his rations and to lament loudly whenever he found them deficient in quantity, for it is inconceivable that the red man should reject anything edible on the score of its quality. He has, however, persistently been of the opinion that

"One crowded hour of glorious life
Is worth an age without a name,"

and in his time he has had many crowded hours in setting traps for the United States troops, or in fighting them, or in running away from them.[102]

This was Sitting Bull's editorial send-off in the *Times:* the "savage red man" in his truest and most dangerous form.

Farther west, the St. Louis *Post-Dispatch* opened its report with an accurate but hostile assessment: "Sitting Bull, the famous old chief, who has for so long been a source of trouble and annoyance, is dead."[103] Editorially, the paper was harsher, pointing out Sitting Bull's reputation as a "restless, unscrupulous Indian" and a hater of whites. Predictably, the *Post-Dispatch* named Sitting Bull as one of those responsible for Custer's death and a dangerous leader of the "unsatisfied Sioux." His death, the paper said, "removes one of the greatest obstacles to the maintenance of permanent peace among the Northwestern Indians."[104] More pointedly, a one-sentence editorial in the paper the following day summed up the paper's attitude toward Sitting Bull: "Even his worst enemies admit now that Sitting Bull is a good Indian."[105]

The Chicago *Times* ran the news of Sitting Bull's death on page one. But unlike other papers, the *Times* had a writer who had met Sitting Bull, the Indian war correspondent John Finerty. Finerty provided the paper with a more complex characterization of the fallen chief. "Sitting Bull was a striking personality," Finerty recalled. He described Sitting Bull's facial features, labeling him "the perfect specimen of the fast-dying race." Despite this "perfection," Finerty was no fan of Sitting Bull. The man was undistinguished in war, Finerty claimed, though he was a prime example of the "sagacity and cunning that have always been considered among the chief attributes of the red man's character."[106] Despite Finerty's errors and personal misgivings about Sitting Bull, his brief profile in the Chicago *Times* offered a more meaningful portrait of Sitting Bull than most of the other reports published at his death.

Boston's largest newspaper, the 150,000 circulation *Daily Globe,* also carried Sitting Bull's story on page one accompanied by several sidebars and a long profile of the chief.[107] Although the reports were factual, Sitting Bull was roundly criticized as an enemy of whites and their civilization. Like the *Times,* the *Globe* resorted to clichés to explain Sitting Bull's life story. One headline referred to him as a "Wily Savage" while another summarized his life, declaring simply "Sitting Bull Was Bad."[108] The profile built up the chief as a "remarkable representative of the Red Man's race" and "the most famous of his kind." But these were hardly compliments, since Sitting Bull's fame was based on his "craftiness and cruelty" and his "savage nature."

Given this savagery, the *Globe* was unable to praise Sitting Bull forthrightly. Instead of saying, "Sitting Bull had several good qualities," the paper struck a carefully qualified negative pose: "Sitting Bull was not devoid of some good qualities." One of these qualities, the paper explained, was Sitting Bull's devotion to his tribe, a fact no one was likely to dispute. Despite a host of fair and accurate assessments of Sitting Bull, the profile painted a picture of an untrustworthy and mean-spirited man. Even as a youth, the paper claimed, he was "not given to any of those boyish sports which Fenimore Cooper has set up as a standard." In addition, "He was lazy and vicious and never told the truth when a lie would serve better."

These were harsh comments, especially in Boston, a city with many Indian activists and a long history of sympathy toward Native Americans. Such sympathy might have existed, but it was clearly not a factor at the *Globe.* This was underscored by two editorial comments on Sitting Bull's murder. The day the news broke, the Boston editorialist—like his St. Louis colleague— quipped: "If Sitting Bull is really dead the impossible has come to pass. He has become a good Indian."[109] The following day, the *Globe* returned—sarcastically—to a theme they perceived to be lacking in the late chief: honesty. "If the parents of SITTING BULL had named him LYING BULL they would have hit nearer the mark. There is no authentic record of any occasion on which the late distinguished Sioux statesman ever told the truth if he was sober," the *Globe* said.[110]

The Boston *Evening Transcript* was more sympathetic toward the Sioux, though this was not always obvious. One early dispatch about Sitting Bull's death, a wire story carried in a number of major papers, quoted Lt. Col. Henry Corbin. Sitting Bull was a "mischief-maker," Corbin said. "He has never been a chief, nor even a warrior of high order," Corbin added. At the Little Bighorn, Corbin said, he "skipped out with his people and got away from danger."[111] The following day, a story from Standing Rock opened with a quote from Sitting Bull himself: "I'll fight and die before any white man can make me an agency Indian"—an accurate quote, perhaps, but one that neglected his last nine years as a peaceful farmer at Standing Rock. The story also referred to the Sioux chief as "probably one of the brainiest Indians that ever lived, one of the most picturesque and characteristic incidents of American history" and cited his "oft-expressed wish to be remembered as the last Indian on the continent to give up his rifle."[112]

The *Transcript*'s editorials picked up on these ideas, recognizing Sitting Bull's ferocity and stubbornness but not his leadership abilities. Commenting on Sitting Bull's role as a statesman, the *Transcript* conceded that he has "a great deal of craft and cunning"—two terms often associated with successful chiefs—but that he was not "on a level with such forest statesmen as King Philip, or Pontiac, or Tecumseh." The editorial concluded, "Great in war, daring in design, wise in counsel, Philip, Pontiac, and Tecumseh were chiefs whose deeds justified Cooper's delineation of 'the noble redman.'"[113] Even in death, Sitting Bull did not meet Cooper's or the *Transcript*'s measure of the "noble" Indian.

In spite of the errors and the lingering hostility toward Sitting Bull, the *Transcript* was not close-minded on Indian issues. This became clear after the Wounded Knee massacre of 29 December. In the aftermath of this new bloodshed, the *Transcript* published a long and sympathetic review of Indian policy that offered an alternative to the official view of the "Indian Problem." In contrast to news and editorials just three weeks earlier, this article cited reports that Sitting Bull "was wantonly murdered at the beginning of the present outbreak."[114] The bulk of the article was a recounting of wrongs done to the tribes, from the "holocaust" at Gnadenhutten, Pennsylvania, in 1779, to Chivington and the Sand Creek massacre in 1864 and the Camp Grant massacre of 1871. The writer, Thomas Addison, cited Helen Hunt Jackson, Gen. O. O. Howard, and others to make his case that Indians were honest and decent people. The most significant aspect of the article was its articulation of the Indian viewpoint and its pointed challenge to the status quo. Addison wrote: "Not only have we dispossessed [the Indian] of his lands; not only have we paid him pauper prices for it; not only have we driven him into regions where the utmost industry fails to extract a living from the soil; but we have sought to annul his traditional customs, to confine and hem him in by force in sections of country that are as unattractive as can well be imagined. The Israelites had the whole desert to wander in, but the Indian has not even that sorry privilege."[115] This remarkable passage captures the reform spirit one might expect in Boston. But it took the terrible tragedy at Wounded Knee Creek for the paper to offer an alternative view, and then it was a contribution from a Boston activist. Like much of the American press, the *Transcript* itself offered no editorial on Wounded Knee.

As this chapter demonstrates, the themes of Sitting Bull's press identity traced an arc from violence and hostility after the Little Bighorn to ridicule and curiosity during his exhibition years and then to fear and hostility again in the Ghost Dance movement. In each of these phases, Sitting Bull was narrowly portrayed, his personal qualities, his abilities as a Lakota leader, and his hopes for his people barely glimpsed and rarely understood. For most of his public life, Sitting Bull was known as a notorious enemy of American progress and expansion, so demonized that he could not be accurately represented in the press. When it became clear that Sitting Bull's camp was responsible for the massacre of Custer and his men, the public demanded and the press provided an appropriate Indian villain— Sitting Bull. But this was a newspaper Indian whose identity owed more to the needs of a vindictive nation than to the actual man known as Sitting Bull. Sitting Bull's identity shifted dramatically as his perceived power diminished and he surrendered; then he could be imagined as a plains bumpkin impressed by city life and, with Buffalo Bill's showmanship, as a popular living relic of the mythic West. Finally, in the violence and hysteria surrounding his death, Sitting Bull's identity returned again to the most familiar native theme: savagery.

Despite the variations of his identity, most of the things Americans knew about Sitting Bull were either wrong or incomplete. Sitting Bull's life and death were reported by the press in ways that reinforced the expansionist ideology of Manifest Destiny and gave almost no credence to native responses to that ideology. In his most humane public identity, such as the one created by Charles Sanford Diehl, Sitting Bull emerged more fully as an individual but he remained a stranger, his life and culture so primitive and removed from civilization that it could not be fully understood. Even when he got the rare opportunity to speak for himself in interviews or speeches, Sitting Bull could not control the headlines, editing, and themes of the stories that contained his words. In short, Sitting Bull's popular identity was always in the hands of people who knew little about him— but assumed they knew enough. The Sitting Bull of the papers and the man himself were often worlds apart.

Though the military war against the Indians was ending and the end of the frontier was near, Native Americans in 1890 remained subject to the ideology of progress and civilization. It was that ideology that infused the newspapers and that kept Indians firmly identified as an inferior people, in need of language, religion, manners, job skills, and personal habits necessary to enter the American mainstream. To the press and most of the public, there was no place for the "old" Indian in the new century. Those days were gone. Now more than ever, American ideology required that Indians change. Sitting Bull had not changed and that cost him his life.

Sitting Bull's popular identity is significant because of his enduring popularity in American culture. Of the thousands of native leaders who achieved prominence in American history, only a handful—Geronimo, Crazy Horse, Squanto, Sequoyah, Pocahontas, Cochise, Sacagawea, and a few others—have made a permanent mark on the popular mind. Of these few, Sitting Bull stands out, linked forever to the victory over Custer at the Little Bighorn. With that claim to immortality and the promotional genius of Buffalo Bill, the Sioux themselves came to represent all American Indians, regardless of the differences between tribes.[116] As a leading Sioux warrior, always imagined in war paint, with full bonnet astride his horse, Sitting Bull became known as the greatest Sioux, the archetype of the American Indian, the one man in whom all the myths and tales of native life could be projected. This was a hopelessly simple way of imagining American Indians, but simplicity was also its greatest strength because simple, one-dimensional Indians could be easily portrayed and easily understood by the press and public alike.

Notes

1. New York *Times,* 10 July 1876, 5.
2. Chicago *Times,* 14 Nov. 1877, 5.
3. Boston *Evening Transcript,* 16 Dec. 1890, 1.
4. The account is drawn from Robert M. Utley's acclaimed recent biography, *The Lance and the Shield: The Life and Times of Sitting Bull* (New York: Ballantine Books, 1993), 3.
5. Ibid., 6
6. Ibid., 11.
7. Ibid., 16.
8. Ibid., 33.
9. Ibid., 35.
10. Ibid.
11. Ibid., 36.

12. See, for example, the New York *Times*, 1 July 1876, 1. This story stated that Red Cloud's influence had waned and that Sitting Bull had assumed control of Red Cloud's band of Teton Sioux.

13. See Kellogg's reports, signed "Frontier," on 17 May 1876, 1; 14 June 1876, 2; and 21 June 1876, 1.

14. New York *Herald*, 21 June 1876, 6–7.

15. Bismarck *Tribune*, 19 Jan. 1876, 8. "Alsotia" is apparently a misspelling of "Alsatia," defined in the *OED* as the precinct of White Friars in London that was once "an asylum for criminals."

16. Ibid., 23 Feb. 1876, 8.

17. New York *Herald*, 24 June 1876, 4. The *Herald* did make Sitting Bull the object of news and editorial attention following the Battle of Rosebud Creek. See, for example, 25 June 1876, 5. These stories, however, provide little information about Sitting Bull other than to identify him as leader of "hostile reds."

18. Chicago *Tribune*, 8 July 1876, 4.

19. Bismarck *Tribune*, 12 July 1876, 1. Also see Chicago *Tribune*, 1 Nov. 1876, 1, which claims that Sitting Bull "planned the entire Indian campaign."

20. Chicago *Tribune*, 7 July 1876, 1.

21. Ibid., 4.

22. Ibid., 15 July 1876, 6.

23. Some of these claims are mentioned in a satirical letter from "Bismarck, Jr.," Bismarck *Tribune*, 30 Aug. 1876, 4. See also Shirley A. Leckie, *Elizabeth Bacon Custer and the Making of a Myth* (Norman: University of Oklahoma Press, 1993), 202.

24. Bismarck *Tribune*, 12 July 1876, 2.

25. Osceola was also reputed to have studied at West Point and to have up to three-quarters white blood. See Richard A. Grounds, "Tallahassee and the Name Game" (Ph.D. diss., Princeton Theological Seminary, 1994), 137.

26. Utley, *Lance and the Shield*, 162–63.

27. Ibid., 164.

28. Richard Slotkin, *The Fatal Environment* (New York: HarperPerennial, 1985), 436.

29. New York *Herald*, 25 June 1876, 8.

30. Ibid., 7 July 1876, 4.

31. Ibid., 9 July 1876, 3.

32. Ibid.

33. Ibid., 6.

34. Slotkin, *Fatal Environment*, 460.

35. Slotkin develops this connection in detail; see ibid., 463–68.

36. Chicago *Tribune*, 4 July 1876, 1.

37. New York *Times*, 6 July 1876, 1.

38. Bismarck *Tribune*, 12 July 1876, 1.

39. New York *Herald*, 6 July 1876, 5. Surprisingly, Sitting Bull was not mentioned in the *Herald*'s reports published the following day; see 7 July 1876, 3.

40. New York *Times*, 7 July 1876, 1.

41. Ibid.

42. Ibid., 4.

43. John M. Coward, "Explaining the Little Bighorn," in Frankie Hutton and Barbara Straus Reed, eds., *Outsiders in Nineteenth-Century Press History: Multicultural Perspectives* (Bowling Green, Ohio: Bowling Green State University Popular Press, 1995), 150–51.

44. *Cherokee Advocate,* 22 July 1876, 1, quoted in ibid., 152–53.

45. *Cherokee Advocate,* 22 July 1876, 2, quoted in ibid., 153.

46. New York *Times,* 10 July 1876, 5.

47. Ibid.

48. New York *Herald,* 10 July 1876, 3.

49. Ibid.

50. Ibid.

51. Bismarck *Tribune,* 12 July 1876, 1.

52. Ibid., 2.

53. Ibid., 3.

54. See, for example, the Bismarck *Tribune,* 27 Sept. 1876, 1; 1 Nov. 1876, 1.

55. Bismarck *Tribune,* 2 Aug. 1876, 4.

56. Ibid., 9 Aug. 1876, 2.

57. See, for example, the Bismarck *Tribune,* 1 Nov. 1876, 1; 15 Nov. 1876, 1.

58. Ibid., 19 July 1876, 2.

59. Ibid., 26 July 1876, 2.

60. Attributed to the (California) *Golden Era* in ibid.

61. Ibid., 30 Aug. 1876, 4.

62. Ibid., 20 Aug. 1876, 4.

63. Attributed to the Minneapolis *Tribune* in ibid., 25 Oct. 1876, 2.

64. Attributed to the Minneapolis *Tribune* in ibid.

65. Ibid., 27 Sept. 1876, 1.

66. Chicago *Times,* 22 Oct. 1877, 5.

67. Ibid., 23 Oct. 1877, 5.

68. Ibid., 6.

69. Ibid.

70. Ibid., 14 Nov. 1877, 5.

71. This summary is drawn from Utley, *Lance and the Shield,* 225–38.

72. *Pioneer Press,* 15 Mar. 1884, 8.

73. Ibid., 17 Mar. 1884, 7.

74. L. G. Moses, "Interpreting the Wild West, 1883–1914," in Margaret Connell Szasz, ed., *Between Indian and White Worlds: The Culture Broker* (Norman: University of Oklahoma Press, 1994), 170, 172.

75. *Pioneer Press,* 16 Mar. 1884, 12.

76. Bismarck *Tribune,* 21 Mar. 1884, 4.

77. Ibid.

78. Ibid.

79. Utley, *Lance and the Shield,* 262–63.

80. New York *Herald,* 14 Sept. 1884, 12. The same wording appeared in a similar ad in the New York *Times* on 14 September.

81. New York *Times,* 12 Sept. 1884, 5.

82. Don Russell, *The Lives and Legends of Buffalo Bill* (Norman: University of Oklahoma Press, 1960), 316.

83. Washington *Post,* 21 June 1885, 8.

84. Russell, *Lives and Legends of Buffalo Bill,* 316.

85. Ibid. Russell notes, however, that this warm reception was a switch for the Canadian government, which had offered a much cooler welcome when Sitting Bull and his band had taken refuge in Canada in the 1870s.

86. Toronto *Globe,* 24 Aug. 1885, 6.

87. Washington *Post,* 24 June 1885, 1.

88. Ibid., 23 June 1885, 1.

89. Detroit *Evening Journal,* 3 Sept. 1885, 2.

90. James M. McPherson, *Battle Cry of Freedom* (New York: Oxford University Press, 1988), 797.

91. Detroit *Evening Journal,* 3 Sept. 1885, 2.

92. Ibid.

93. Ibid., 5 Sept. 1885, 2.

94. Ibid.

95. Ibid.

96. See, for example, the Boston *Evening Transcript,* 16 Dec. 1890, 3; 20 Dec. 1890, 1; and the New York *Times,* 16 Dec. 1890, 1. The press role in the Wounded Knee affair is documented in Elmo Scott Watson, "The Last Indian War, 1890–91: A Study of Newspaper Jingoism," *Journalism Quarterly* 20.3 (Sept. 1943): 205–19. See also John E. Carter, "Making Pictures for a News-Hungry Nation," in Richard E. Jensen, R. Eli Paul, and John E. Carter, *Eyewitness at Wounded Knee* (Lincoln: University of Nebraska Press, 1991).

97. Watson, "Last Indian War, 1890–91," 214–15.

98. Drawn from Utley, *Lance and the Shield,* 299–302.

99. New York *Times,* 16 Dec. 1890, 1.

100. Ibid.

101. Ibid., 4.

102. Ibid.

103. St. Louis *Post-Dispatch,* 16 Dec. 1890, 3.

104. Ibid., 4.

105. Ibid.

106. Chicago *Times,* 16 Dec. 1890, 7.

107. Michael Emery and Edwin Emery, *The Press and America,* 6th ed. (Englewood Cliffs, N.J.: Prentice Hall, 1988), 195.

108. Boston *Daily Globe,* 16 Dec. 1890, 1.

109. Ibid., 4.

110. Ibid., 17 Dec. 1890, 4.

111. Boston *Evening Transcript,* 16 Dec. 1890, 1.

112. Ibid., 17 Dec. 1890, 1.

113. Ibid., 18 Dec. 1890, 4.

114. Ibid., 9 Jan. 1891, 6.

115. Ibid.

116. Phyllis Rogers, "'Buffalo Bill' and the Siouan Image," *American Indian Culture and Research Journal* 7.3 (1983): 43–53. Rogers recounts a telling moment in Poland, where she identified herself as a Navaho. This word puzzled her hosts, until they recalled the only Indians they knew, the Sioux, which they pronounced as "Sukes." For these Europeans, all Native Americans were "Sukes."

Indian Reformers and
the Idealized Indian

IN the early morning hours of 30 March 1879, Gen. George Crook came
to the newsroom of the Omaha *Daily Herald* in search of a reform-
minded editor named Thomas H. Tibbles, a former abolitionist and cir-
cuit-riding preacher. Crook told the thirty-eight-year-old assistant editor
that he was troubled by an order to return thirty Ponca Indians from Fort
Omaha to Indian Territory. The order was, the general declared, as cruel
a thing as he had ever been forced to do, punishment for a desperate and
sickly band of peaceful Indians who had been forced from their homelands
on the Niobrara River, near the Nebraska–South Dakota border. "I would
resign my commission, if that would prevent the order from being executed—but it would not," Crook admitted. "It's no use for me to protest.
Washington always orders the very opposite of what I recommend." In
Tibbles and the *Herald,* however, the general saw a possible solution. "You
have a great daily newspaper here which you can use," Crook told Tibbles.
"I ask you to go into this fight against those who are robbing these helpless people," Crook continued. "The American people, if they knew half
the truth, would send every member of the Indian Ring to prison."[1]

At seven that same morning, Tibbles walked four miles to the fort to
interview the Poncas. At first, Standing Bear, leader of the Poncas, would
not talk, fearing publicity would anger General Crook. But Tibbles had
considerable experience with Plains Indians and even claimed to have been
inducted into a secret tribal society. When he revealed the secret signs to

the chief, Standing Bear convened a council and the Ponca chiefs began to tell their sad tale to the Omaha *Herald*.[2]

News of the Ponca arrests soon reached the papers in Chicago, New York, and Boston, where, as General Crook had predicted, it found a receptive audience. Indian sympathizers, still recovering from the public uproar over the Custer disaster, saw the peaceful Poncas as an ideal vehicle for resuscitating their movement. Aided by editors like Tibbles and promoted by reformers like Episcopalian Bishop Henry Whipple, Mary Lucinda Bonney, and Helen Hunt Jackson, the Ponca controversy, like the debate over Indian Removal forty years earlier, soon became a cause célèbre among American social reformers.

The Ponca affair marked a crucial point in the post–Civil War debate over federal Indian policy. The Grant administration's Peace Policy, instituted in 1869, sent Indian agents recruited from mainstream Christian denominations to reservations across the west, a move that humanitarians thought would protect the Indians from extermination, promote their civilization, and prevent additional violence. Despite these lofty ideals, conflict and misunderstanding continued. Moreover, many humanitarians began to criticize the reservation system, believing that it perpetuated traditional communal living and prevented the kind of individualism and progress they believed was necessary for successful native assimilation. By the late 1870s, the Peace Policy was largely discredited.[3] Carl Schurz, a liberal reformer appointed Secretary of the Interior by President Rutherford Hayes in 1877, worked furiously to end corruption in the Indian Bureau, but even he was on the defensive regarding the Poncas. Thanks to Tibbles, Standing Bear and other Indians had become celebrities on the eastern lecture circuit. The publication of Helen Hunt Jackson's *A Century of Dishonor* in 1881 further cemented the gains of the revitalized reform movement and promoted the passage of the Dawes Severalty Act of 1887, a bill that promised land as well as United States citizenship to individual Indians. Little more than a decade after the tragedy on the Little Bighorn, Indian reformers looked forward to ending the reservation system, promoting assimilation, and producing a new kind of Indian, finally free from native superstitions and, with white assistance and Christian charity, well on the way to civilization.

The press played an important and ultimately crucial role in this reform process, publicizing government abuses of the Poncas and providing a platform for the humanitarians and their opponents to debate the "Indian problem." This debate was yet another chapter in the ongoing cultural process of defining the Indian. Despite decades of trying, neither the press nor the public had settled on the true nature of the Indian. Some of them—such as the Poncas—seemed virtuous and, with "proper" Christian instruction, might be saved, but others—such as the Sioux—remained barbaric and beyond the promise of civilization. For "good" Indians like the Poncas, the result was a newspaper identity that was superficially humane but fundamentally flawed—an identity that led the press to idealize them beyond their actual merits and oversimplify or overlook the very real problems that assimilation, citizenship, and land ownership would soon produce for many Native Americans.

Indians and Public Opinion in the 1870s

The newspapers in the early 1870s found Indian news all across the American West, most of it—despite the Peace Policy—violent. The Modoc War in California was typical. When a Modoc chief known as Captain Jack betrayed a peace delegation and killed an army general and a Methodist minister, the nation—and the press—was outraged. The Saint Paul *Daily Press* summed up the national mood: "The feeling of indignation against the Modoc murderers, as attested by conversations . . . in Washington, reaches a degree of intensity which no Indian treachery has ever heretofore created."[4]

The Sioux, as we have seen, made even larger and more hostile headlines, especially after the Battle of the Little Bighorn.[5] Later in the decade, the Cheyennes and the Utes were at war—and in the papers. Western papers, almost always protective of local economic interests, were easily alarmed about Indian violence and contemptuous of eastern reformers and humanitarians. Said the editor of the Montana *Post,* "It is high time the sickly sentimentalism about humane treatment and conciliatory measures should be consigned to novel writers, and if the Indians continue their barbarities, wipe them out."[6] Concerning the Utes, Denver's *Daily Rocky Mountain News* remained single-minded: "That the North American Indians are hopeless savages is the most clearly established fact in the history of man."[7] In Phoenix, C. E. McClintock, founding editor of the weekly *Salt River Herald,* devoted most of his editorial space to favorable reports on the Arizona climate, farming conditions, and mining. So when Indians intruded on McClintock's vision of Arizona, the *Herald* could not be neutral. In 1878, the paper reported, "This section of the country is alive with strange Indians, their camp fires may be seen upon many hills. They are saucy, bold and hungry."[8] Although these "strange Indians" had not attacked anyone, they had made threats against whites and the paper was taking no chances. "The people here are in arms and ready for an attack." Despite this warning, no reports of Indian violence appeared in the next several issues.

Eastern papers, too, could find reasons to distrust the Indians. In the late 1870s, the Washington *Post* ran headlines that referred to "Discontented Indians," "Redskin Murderers," "Cunning Chiefs," and the like.[9] The hostilities between whites and Utes in 1877 also received hostile coverage in the *Post*. The notorious Meeker massacre, for example, in which Ute warriors had killed Indian agent Nathan Meeker and a number of other persons, led to a series of *Post* reports on the Indian troubles in Colorado. When several Utes came before an investigating board, the *Post* headline did not pretend to be neutral: "SWEARING THE INDIANS / They Perjure Themselves Just the Same as White Men." The story, however, cited no specific perjury, though it openly challenged the testimony of a Ute named Ben Johnson.[10] In any case, such comments were not those of a sympathetic eastern press.

Yet attitudes toward the western tribes were moderating during these years. Indeed, as historian Frederick Hoxie has noted, many newspapers, both East and West, approached Indians with a new sense of fairness. Even the Meeker tragedy prompted some editorial support for Indians, Hoxie discovered. "Massacred by Utes," was the initial headline in the Chicago *Tribune*, but two days later the paper took a less sensational approach. "There are two sides to every question, even an Indian question," the *Tribune*'s editorial noted.[11] Even some western papers recognized that the Ute outbreak had roots in unfair government policies and mistreatment of the tribe. "One thing is certain," said the *Alta California* in the wake of the Meeker tragedy, "and that is that our whole Indian policy is a miserable one and a failure."[12]

Western historian Charles Rankin also found a moderate tone in the 1870s. Working independently, journalists Frederic Lockley and John Hanson Beadle described life in Indian Territory and demonstrated that peaceful Indians could be portrayed as reasonable individuals, even if they were not quite the equal of whites. Lockley, an English-born Civil War veteran living in Leavenworth, Kansas, worked as a freelance writer for the Chicago *Times*, the New York *World*, the New York *Times*, and other papers. A westerner by choice, Lockley "possessed neither the bias nor the condescension toward the West common among many Eastern commentators," Rankin noted.[13] Lockley was also an independent sort, more interested in telling the truth as he saw it than in boosting the local economy or pleasing public opinion. As a result, Lockley wrote sympathetically about the people of Indian Territory, praising many native qualities and defending the tribes against white injustice. "Can we find nothing but vice and degradation to taunt our red brother with?" Lockley asked in the Leavenworth *Commercial.* "There is a natural repugnancy between the races, but all the virtues are not on our side."[14] Despite such sympathy, Rankin discovered that Lockley, like most whites, assumed white superiority as well as the need to "save" the Indians by pushing them to accept civilization, a position that foreshadowed the efforts of the Indian reformers. Nevertheless, Rankin concluded, Lockley was not an Indian-hater and his reports offered readers "a thoroughgoing assessment of native life in the early 1870s."[15]

John Hanson Beadle held similar views. An Indiana native and, like Lockley, a Civil War veteran, Beadle went west to improve his health, financing his travels by writing for the Cincinnati *Commercial.* He visited Indian Territory in 1872, but was unimpressed at first by Indian progress: "On the road [near Muskogee] is no enterprise, no improvement, no trade of account that I can see," Beadle wrote.[16] But in the Cherokee capital of Tahlequah, Beadle happily read tribal history, concluding that the Cherokees "represent the best . . . hope of the Indian race."[17] After a few weeks among the "civilized" tribes, Beadle began to overcome his prejudices and recognize the humanity of native people: "I have seen the Indians at home and on their farms, have attended their churches and visited their schools, have talked by their hearths and slept in their cabins, 'eaten of their salt and warmed at their fires.' I have seen so much more progress than I had been led to expect."[18] Beadle, like Lockley, believed in the rightness of civilization and judged Indians by that standard. Yet he wrote honest, sensitive stories, Indian news based on firsthand observations and free from the racial stereotypes and hostility that marked so much Indian reporting. For peaceful, progressive Indians, both Beadle and Lockley showed that the Indian identity could be expanded beyond the standard clichés. Rankin concluded, in fact, that their approach to Indian issues "reflected an increasing desire on the part of many Americans to substitute facts for belief in arcane creeds and conventional wisdom."[19]

Despite this more balanced editorial tone, many Indian stories described Indians in stereotypical terms. When an Indian was executed in Oregon in 1879, for example, a one-paragraph dispatch from San Francisco ended with this sentence: "He maintained an apparently stolid indifference to the last."[20] Another Indian execution, this one in California, involved a man identified as "Indian Jack." Like other reports on Indian violence, the news story assigned Jack's alleged murder not to an explainable motive but to "pure deviltry, without the motive of passion, gain or revenge." Yet when he died, this man too became a cliché: "Jack preserved Indian stolidity and died without a struggle."[21] Even an Indian anecdote emphasized this purported Indian tendency, contrasting it with the more surprising discovery of Indian humor. "You would hardly expect to find wit among the Indians, and yet they are just as human as the rest of us, and in spite of their stoicism, indulge in a joke now and then," the Jackson [Miss.] *Weekly Clarion* reported.[22]

Such examples show a continuing tendency to represent Indians as a large but coherent race, not as individuals. Although individual Indians and some tribes were judged exceptional, popular Indian representations usually emphasized the similarities of the "Indian character," not their unique characteristics. Also, as in the past, editors used their expectations of what Indians should be as the guiding principle in describing how Indians were. Nevertheless, many post–Civil War newspapers and their readers were advocating a more complex view of Indians: they might still be "savage," but they could also be seen as innocent victims of their "degraded" state. Armed with Christian charity and progressive idealism, humanitarians and even some journalists continued to believe that Indians could be civilized—at least some of them could. By the late 1870s, the idea of the "civilized savage" was turning up in the press with increasing frequency.

The Press and the Poncas

The Ponca controversy began with a government blunder long before editor Tibbles sat down to interview Standing Bear. In 1868, the United States negotiated a treaty with the Sioux that granted that tribe twenty-two million acres in the Dakota Territory, including ninety-six thousand acres that an earlier treaty had granted to the Poncas.[23] And since the Sioux were old enemies of the Poncas and were a larger and more aggressive tribe, the Poncas soon found themselves in a dangerous situation: "penniless, homeless and surrounded by an overwhelming force of bitter enemies," as one historian put it.[24]

Having given the Ponca land to the Sioux, the government was not inclined to return it, because such a move might anger the Sioux and risk another Indian war. It was much easier to move the Poncas, who were, after all, a small and cooperative band. So in 1877, the Indian Bureau forced the Poncas from their Dakota homes and sent them south.

The move did not go well, however. To begin with, many Poncas resisted and the first removal party consisted of only a small portion of the tribe.[25] Unsatisfied with that result, the Indian Bureau redoubled its efforts and delivered an ultimatum: move voluntarily or move under force, but move. The Poncas went, enduring floods, storms, and a series of illnesses on their way to present-day Oklahoma. It was a miserable journey and a number of Poncas died along the way.[26]

The forced removal of the Poncas was not a major news story in the spring of 1877, despite the protests of some area missionaries and citizens. Nevertheless, the controversy generated some scattered publicity. On the northern plains, editorial opinion concerning Ponca removal was divided; the Niobrara [Neb.] *Pioneer* protested the removal while the Yankton *Daily Press and Dakotaian* thought the Poncas should leave.[27]

By April 1877, news of the budding Ponca controversy surfaced in government circles. A Washington dispatch published in the New York *Times* referred to the "animated contest" then in progress over the removal and noted that Congress had appropriated forty thousand dollars for the move. More significantly, the story explained the opposition to Ponca removal in pragmatic terms, noting that area settlers opposed removal because their "departure from the reservation will result in its speedy occupation by the Sioux, who are not regarded as desirable neighbors." The story ended with an allegation and a decision: "It has also been alleged that the consent of the Poncas was given under a misunderstanding, &c., but after full investigation of the subject, the [Interior] department has finally decided to press the removal; and at last advices nearly all the Indians were expected to start southward in a few days."[28] This was a fair presentation of the Ponca controversy, at least from the government's point of view. But the *Times* cited no sources in the West and did not investigate the alleged "misunderstanding, &c." surrounding the removal. Neither did the Poncas merit a *Times* editorial. Still, the *Times* was one of the few eastern papers to give the Ponca story any attention in mid-1877.

The removal itself made the *Times* two months later, although the news was more about the weather than the Poncas. A short Washington dispatch relayed word from Indian agent E. A. Howard, the leader of the removal, that a tornado had struck the Ponca camp in Nebraska, killing one person and severely injuring several others. The story did not name the dead man or describe the condition of the injured, but did note "a large amount of damage done to the supplies and other property." Finally, in a bureaucratic twist, the story offered a reassuring message concerning the purpose of the trip: "Agent Howard reports that this [tornado] will cause delay, but he will repair damages and proceed on the march as fast as possible."[29]

The Ponca story got a more significant burst of publicity in late 1877, when a tribal delegation arrived in Washington for talks with government officials. Again, the New York *Times* provided extensive coverage. The paper announced the Poncas' arrival on page one, and with a favorable headline: "PEACEFUL INDIANS AT THE CAPITAL." Although these were hardly the first Indians to visit the capital, the story described several of the men in great detail. White Eagle, the paper said, "is tall and athletic, wears a white shirt, blanket, leggings with the sides worked with beads, and moccasins."[30] The *Times* reporter was especially fascinated with the Poncas' adornments: "They seem to regard the armlets and finger rings as indispensable, and some of them have rings on every finger." More importantly, the reporter was impressed by the chiefs' peaceful declarations: "It is one of their boasts that a Ponca has never shed the blood of a white man and their interpreters claim that of all the tribes they are the best disposed."[31] The story also described the tribe's life in Dakota, where they "lived in log cabins and frame buildings, having their own horses, farming implements and schools." As for the purpose of their visit, the paper reported that the Poncas "do not express any dissatisfaction at the result [of their removal] but claim that they should be paid for their crops which were left in the ground."

The next day, however, the *Times* contradicted this statement when it reported on a meeting between the Poncas and President Rutherford Hayes, Secretary Schurz, and other officials. Four chiefs addressed the president, the paper reported, and the "one burden of each Indian's oration was an expression of dissatisfaction at their present place of residence in the Indian Territory, and their desire to remove back to their old agency."[32]

The *Times* coverage of the Poncas certainly helped their cause, though the effects of the publicity were not immediately apparent. Indeed, the visit to Washington had not won the Poncas the right to return to their old homes nor did it arouse great public or press support. Perhaps the time was not right; the Little Bighorn was still fresh in the public mind in 1877. Yet the *Times* stories had treated the Ponca claims seriously, if not sympathetically, and the paper depicted the tribe as civilized by pointing out their peaceful intentions, their agricultural successes, and their log houses. In the *Times,* at least, the treatment of the Poncas amounted to an endorsement; these were "good Indians," capable of civilization and worthy of white support. This endorsement was, in effect, part of a shift in the press's explanatory frame, a shift prompted by a revived reform spirit in American society, especially among Protestant church men and women in Boston, New York, Philadelphia, and other eastern cities. While some Indians could still be characterized as "wild" and "uncivilized," the *Times* editors recognized the Poncas as peaceful, progressive Indians, willing to change their ways to live in modern America. This view helped set the stage for a public reconsideration of the Ponca cause.

Ponca News in 1879

The Ponca troubles did not cease when the tribe arrived in Indian Territory in mid-1877. The Indian Bureau had no housing prepared for the tribe and the land was damp and unhealthy for these northern Indians. By the end of their second year in Indian Territory, seventy-one Poncas had died of malaria.[33] Standing Bear, who had lost several family members during the move, lost his only son to illness in 1878. Before he died, however, the younger man asked his father to bury him on their Dakota homeland. In early 1879, Standing Bear and several dozen other Poncas began the long walk home.

When the Indian Bureau learned of Standing Bear's journey, it dispatched soldiers to return the Poncas to Indian Territory. Thanks to General Crook, word of their confinement and the order to return them to Indian Territory reached the Omaha *Herald* and the Poncas soon became the objects of great attention. Tibbles was nearly an ideal propagandist for the Poncas. Born in rural Ohio and raised in western Illinois, Tibbles had strong convictions and considerable public relations skill. As a young man, he was involved in anti-slavery hostilities in Kansas. In 1856 he spent three years at Mount Union College in Ohio, and then served as a soldier and newspaper correspondent during the Civil War. As a minister in rural Missouri and Nebraska, he witnessed the devastation of the grasshopper invasion of 1874 and was active in efforts to relieve the suffering of prairie farmers and their families. It was the famine, in fact, that gave Tibbles the opportunity to test his public relations abilities as he traveled east to raise money for the needy. Although his efforts were derided by some Nebraska politicians and newspapers, Tibbles succeeded in collecting several thousand dollars to aid famine victims.[34] By 1879, Tibbles had retired from the ministry and risen to assistant editor of the *Herald,* where he had numerous contacts with Nebraska reformers. With General Crook's cooperation, Tibbles helped organize a group of Omaha ministers and other Indian sympathizers on behalf of the Poncas. The group engaged two prominent Nebraska lawyers, who then proceeded to sue for a writ of habeas corpus in federal court in Omaha. The case, known as *Standing Bear vs. Crook,* paid off in late May 1879. Judge Elmer Dundy ruled that the Poncas had a right to bring suit and he ordered the release of Standing Bear and his band. Perhaps more importantly, the lawsuit and Judge Dundy's decision focused new attention on the government's misdealings with the Poncas and added more fuel to the fires of Indian reform.

The first reports of the Ponca controversy in 1879 involved the army's apprehension of the runaway Indians. A New York *Times* dispatch from Omaha published on 31 March reported the arrest of six Poncas who were attempting to return to Dakota. The story also dramatized the woes of the travelers. "During their march they were forced to endure all kinds of hardship, and when they arrived at the reservation they were in extreme need."[35] The article paraphrased the comments of a Ponca named Long Runner, who "said with vehemence that his people would die before they would return to Indian Territory." Despite this potentially sympathetic information, the headline in the New York *Times* referred to "Hostile Poncas" and claimed, incorrectly, that they had been "Forced Back To The Indian Territory."[36]

A few days later another Omaha dispatch put the Ponca suffering in more dramatic terms. Ponca leaders, the story said, met recently with General Crook: "Standing Bear and Buffalo Chips drew a dismal picture of their sufferings, wrongs, and misfortunes, and protested against being sent south." The Indians also "acknowledged that they must obey and go" back to Indian Territory, the *Times* reported. "They only asked that Gen. Crook furnish the money to bury those of their number who must die on the way of fatigue and unaccustomed heat." Finally, the report ended on an ominous note: "Five Poncas now here are already ill."[37]

These dispatches were routine news reports and were not overtly sympathetic to the Poncas. Yet in keeping with the reform spirit in Omaha and in the East, both stories acknowledged the suffering of the Indians and presented their hardships in terms that white readers could understand. The presentation of such facts in the *Times* underscored the idea of the "civilized savage." In contrast to new reports about the Sioux, the Poncas were not referred to as "savages." Moreover, they were portrayed as reasonable persons, willing to submit to government authority. They simply wanted to return to their homes. The Poncas suffered and died, these stories implied, not because they were barbarians, but because they had a fierce attachment to their homeland. Thus the Poncas, by virtue of their reasonable demeanor and their obvious suffering, were identifiable as "good Indians," people worthy of a fuller, more sympathetic portrayal in the eastern press.

Explaining the Ponca Decision

When the Ponca case went to trial in early May, the New York *Times* put the news on page one. The story, a dispatch from Omaha, portrayed the case as "very important" and ended by emphasizing its uniqueness: "This is said to be the first case of the kind ever brought before a United States court, and excites unusual interest."[38] The *Times* followed up the next day, publishing a one-paragraph summary of the proceedings.

The Ponca trial did not make page one in the Chicago *Tribune,* but the paper was openly sympathetic to the tribe. "THE PONCAS," was the *Tribune*'s main headline, but its secondary head was more revealing, even though the writer fell back on stereotypical labels: "Probability that Justice May Be Done These Unhappy Savages."[39] Unlike the *Times,* the *Tribune* story provided some details about testimony given before Judge Dundy. W. W. Hamilton, for instance, a clerk at the trader's store on the Omaha Reservation, testified that the Poncas "had tried to break away from Indian habits, and follow the habits and pursuits of civilized whites." More significantly, the story contained a short summary of Standing Bear's remarks, including this touching quote: "My son . . . asked me when he was dying, to take him back and bury him [in Dakota Territory], and I have his bones in a box with me now. I want to live there the rest of my life, and to be buried there." The story ended with a prediction that the Indians would carry the day, although this position was unsupported by any evidence.

Four days later, the *Tribune* offered its own opinion of the Ponca case. The editorial opened by reviewing the history of the controversy and praising the tribe's advancement toward civilization. Significantly, the paper also noted the tribe's obedience to the rule of law: "The order of the Government . . . was by no means cordially assented to, although its binding force was recognized by them. They went as they were told,—without trouble."[40] The *Tribune* editorial painted a gripping picture of Ponca suffering during the removal. While this information was specific and credible, the paper was less certain about other aspects of the Ponca controversy. Concerning the land in Indian Territory where the tribe had settled, the paper hedged: "It is fair to suppose that the land left for the Poncas was of not much value." The paper was more convincing in its discussion of the legal merits of the case. The paper argued that Indians who severed their ties with their tribe had been—and ought to continue to be—considered citizens of the United States. In support of this position, it raised a number of thorny issues about the government's relationship to the "civilized savage":

> [The Government] claims that, under no circumstances, can the Indian be other than wards of the nation. It is important that it be known when, if ever, does this wardship cease. Is the Indian, no matter how civilized he may be, never to become a free citizen? If permitted to acquire citizenship, what degree of civilization shall he possess in order to be free from the shackles of the Indian Bureau, and to feel that he has a right to acquire property, to make a home where it pleases him, and to raise and educate his children?[41]

The editorial ended by praising the civilized condition of the Poncas and criticizing the government for mishandling the matter. The *Tribune* also contrasted the treatment received by the Poncas with the treatment of more hostile tribes: "The Government gives far more consideration to the caprices of savage tribes who make themselves feared than it does to the rights and necessities of those tribes who have for years striven to acquire the white man's habit of life."[42]

Other newspapers did not give the Ponca trial such sympathetic coverage. The New Orleans *Picayune,* for example, did not run an account of the trial in early May. The story was also absent from the pages of the *Daily Rocky Mountain News,* a long-time foe of Indian rights. Nevertheless, the papers that did report the Ponca trial added further credibility to an evolving explanatory frame for this story: innocent Poncas and a heartless Indian bureaucracy.

The Ponca victory in Omaha received considerable praise in the eastern press. Whitelaw Reid, now in charge of Greeley's New York *Tribune,* praised the Poncas, Judge Dundy, and especially Tibbles for bringing the case to court. The paper outlined the characteristics and rights of the ideal Indian: "The second century of the Republic is a late date to announce that any body of men born heirs to the soil, intelligent, moral, hard-working Christians, 'have the inalienable right to life, liberty and the pursuit of happiness as long as they obey the laws and do not trespass on forbidden ground.'"[43] The editorial ended with a call for government action: "How will the Government rectify its mistakes?" This question was addressed two weeks later by Tibbles himself. In a letter to the paper, he reviewed the wrongs inflicted upon Standing Bear and outlined plans for new legal action. Tibbles concluded with a plea for financial support: "I suppose you are well aware that lawsuits cost money. . . . To recover this land belonging to the tribe will cost at least $1,000. . . . I write to ask you if readers of THE TRIBUNE cannot help me in this fight for the natural rights of man."[44] The *Tribune* did not comment on the letter, but its headline revealed the paper's pro-Ponca bias: "T. H. Tibbles, The Nebraska Editor, Asks For Means To Continue The Fight Which He Has Bravely Begun."

The New York *Times* was much more reticent on the Ponca decision. Although the paper ran the news of Judge Dundy's decision on page one,[45] the *Times* waited three weeks to comment on the case. More significant than this delay, however, was the nature of the commentary: informed, rational, and totally bland. The editorial opened with a reference to the "full text of the important opinion" and explained legal arguments on both sides in the case as well as the high points of the decision. The closest the *Times* came to offering its own opinion on the matter was the observation that "an appeal was promptly taken, it remains to be seen whether the Supreme Court of the United States will affirm or reverse the judgment of Judge Dundy"[46]—no ringing endorsement here.

The Chicago *Tribune* used the Ponca decision to comment on the nature of the "good" Indian and the government's role in Indian affairs. The paper built its case on the fact that many Indians, including the Poncas, had demonstrated their potential for civilization and therefore deserved legal protection. "Such Indians have laid aside their savage instincts and customs, and they are now law-abiding, frugal, and industrious." What the government must do, the paper continued, is to make changes in the law that recognize this fact. "Means should be devised by which an Indian, when he has attained the necessary degree of civilization, shall be released from the arbitrary control of the Indian Bureau, and allowed all the rights and immunities of a free man."[47] The effect of such reasoning, however, was to reinforce the idea that Indians could be readily "civilized" through such simple means as farming or working as laborers. Although this was a long-standing belief among many Indian bureaucrats and Christian reformers, the process of becoming "civilized" was a much more difficult and complex process. The *Tribune* and other newspapers, however, failed to recognize these complexities and continued to advocate simple—and ultimately destructive—solutions to Indian problems.

Indian policy was also emphasized in the Atlanta *Constitution*. But in this highly partisan newspaper, Indian policy was once again embroiled in politics. The *Constitution* was a Democratic newspaper and it did not hesitate to use Indian issues to score political points against the ruling Republicans. Earlier in the year, for example, the paper used the massacre of Cheyennes at Fort Robinson to mount a forceful attack on the Republican leadership of the Indian Bureau.[48] In the Ponca case, the *Constitution* made a similar recommendation. "This decision is calculated to make Schurz and Hayt and the thieves and knaves in the employ of the Indian bureau open wide their eyes with wonder. It has been fondly supposed ever since the republicans have been in power that the red men had no rights under the law."[49] A few days later, the paper followed up with a longer editorial that reviewed the case and attacked corruption in the so-called Indian Ring.[50] Although this editorial was not openly partisan, the general response to the Poncas in the *Constitution* seemed motivated as much by politics as by humanitarian concerns.

Despite the *Constitution,* the outpouring of editorial support for the Poncas was genuine and well intentioned. The papers wanted justice for the Poncas and reforms in the Indian Bureau. Yet these were easy positions for the eastern newspapers to take; no Indians threatened their readers and the problems of the western states were readily solved on paper. Moreover, the newspapers treated the Poncas as an exceptional case, a tribe easily distinguished from less-civilized natives. The Chicago *Tribune,* for instance, enthusiastically supported the Poncas. But the language of the paper's support provides some insight into why and how the Poncas gained editorial favor. In its 6 May editorial, the *Tribune* praised the tribe for its acquiescence to government authority; even in the face of forced removal, the tribe acknowledged the power—and superiority—of the United States government. In addition, both the 6 May editorial and another published on the nineteenth praised the Poncas for their progress toward civilization, progress that was, in reality, a test of their willingness to give up their own ways and become as much like whites as possible. Indeed, the Poncas had adopted many ways of the whites. So it was easy for the Chicago *Tribune* and other reform-minded papers to praise the Poncas because they were nearly ideal Indians, at least from the white point of view. Other tribes—most notably the Sioux—were much harder to praise because they were still "savage" Indians, unwilling to be tamed and disrespectful of white authority. Viewed in this light, newspaper support for the Poncas seems more expedient than enlightened. Although the Chicago *Tribune* and other newspapers were sincere in their concern for the Poncas, their support for Indians tended to be confined to tribes most willing and able to give up their culture and "become" whites. Thus much of the newspaper sympathy for the Poncas, like the concerns expressed by the humanitarians, accepted a simple-minded version of assimilation as the ultimate solution to the "Indian problem."

Assimilation was not a solution proposed by the *Daily Rocky Mountain News*. The paper announced Judge Dundy's ruling in a Washington dispatch that was more commentary than news. The story portrayed the decision as a blow to the government, saying that it would disrupt the "present Indian system" and "prove extremely dangerous alike to whites and Indians upon their reservations."[51] The story went on to predict a worst-case scenario: "Under this decision it would seem that the Indians would become a body of tramps moving without restraint wherever they please and exposed to the attacks of frontiersmen without being able to secure any redress from government."[52]

The following day, the *News* offered a tongue-in-cheek endorsement of the Ponca ruling: "This decision of an Omaha judge that Indians are citizens is another grand triumph of great moral ideas. The more barbarians as voters the more offices for demagogues and the more burdens of misrule for the people."[53] A day later, the paper offered a new opinion on the Indian situation, this one even more hostile. "War with the Indians is cheaper than peace with them. Powder and shot makes a bad red man a quiet and inexpensive reminiscence. It would be cheaper to board them at first-class hotels, than it is to feed and protect them on reservations."[54] Although this commentary did not mention the Ponca decision, its timing suggests that the Ponca victory in court had generated new feelings of hostility at the *Daily Rocky Mountain News*.

The Ponca Debate Moves East

The attitudes expressed in Denver were not widespread, at least not in the East. But in the months following the Ponca decision, the news about the controversy began to come from two primary sources, each with an ax to grind. In Omaha, the Ponca sympathizers had been acutely aware of the need for national publicity from the start, with Tibbles using the telegraph to reach papers in New York, Chicago, and other cities shortly after his first interview with the Indians.[55] Without their own correspondents in Omaha, these papers relied on telegraphic dispatches from Ponca sympathizers for their news about the controversy. Not surprisingly, much of the information emanating from Omaha emphasized the suffering of the Poncas at the hands of the Indian Bureau. The other side of the story came from government sources in Washington and the most active newsmaker was Interior Secretary Carl Schurz. With easy access to the news columns of several major newspapers, Schurz vigorously defended the Indian Bureau and attempted to justify and explain his position on the Poncas.

One of the papers that figured prominently in this debate was the New York *Times*. In mid-1879, for example, the *Times* published an official report from the Indian Bureau that contradicted reports from Omaha about conditions at the Ponca Agency in Indian Territory. Indian Inspector John McNeil described the Ponca settlement in glowing terms: "Quite a town has grown up at the agency, having the most delightful situation of any in the whole Indian country."[56] He also noted that the government's disciplinary measures at the agency had been effective. Some wayward Indians, McNeil wrote, "have felt the power of the Government—that was lesson enough. They are now [Col. Whiteman's] best working hands." McNeil concluded by evaluating the morale of the Poncas. "The Indians are in good health and appear to have lost that morose and gloomy bearing they so uniformly exhibited last year. Work appears to have much the same effect upon the Indians as upon the white man in improving his health and his temper."[57] The *Times* published this report without editorial comment or any other explanation of its source. Yet it seems clear that the government's release of this official correspondence was intended to counter the negative image of Indian Territory described by Standing Bear and the runaway Poncas.

The dispute between Ponca supporters and Secretary Schurz became more public during the summer of 1879, when Tibbles resigned his position at the Omaha *Herald* to devote himself to the Ponca cause. He traveled East to arrange a lecture tour for Standing Bear and an educated Omaha woman named Susette LaFlesche, also known as Bright Eyes. In Boston, Tibbles's message had great appeal and several prominent citizens organized an Indian reform committee. Among the principals on this committee was D. A. Goddard, editor of the Boston *Daily Advertiser,* whose paper gave Tibbles and the Ponca cause considerable attention.[58]

But Tibbles's activities did not sit well in Washington and Schurz responded to the allegations in two open letters published in the *Advertiser* in August.[59] Also published that month was a New York *Times* story that questioned both Tibbles's facts and his motives and went on to defend the current administration. Although the story was published as news and was not identified as the work of Schurz or his staff, it was heavily biased against Tibbles and supportive of the Indian Bureau. The *Times* article admitted that the Poncas had been mistreated. Concerning the government, the article emphasized the positive: "Since 1877 everything possible has been done to promote the interests and welfare of the Poncas and if Mr. Tibbells [*sic*] knows of the existence of an Indian Ring, and will come here and indicate where it can be found to Secretary Schurz, he will accomplish more than by haranguing the people of Boston."[60] This story was clearly more editorial than news and its origins in Washington suggest a partisan source. More importantly, this story, and stories like it, further obscured the facts surrounding the Ponca controversy by reducing their condition to a series of charges and counter-charges, the truth of which remained unknown and uninvestigated in the press.

The New York *Tribune* also got involved in the Ponca dispute in response to Tibbles's message. An 11 August editorial praised Tibbles as "the heroic Editor of Omaha, who forced Justice . . . to take off her bandage and deal fairly with Standing Bear." The Poncas, the paper said, were model Indians who had an indisputable right to their land. "They had been confirmed in their ownership by three separate treaties. They had never been at war with the Government; never had once violated a treaty."[61]

According to the *Tribune,* the dispute was the result of a "few sharp dealers in Washington [who] wanted this property" and who conspired to drive the Poncas away and deprive them of their rights. The paper concluded by endorsing the Omaha court decision and advocating expanded rights for Indians. "Bring the red man under the protection of the courts and give him the ballot, and the problem is solved, and there will be an end of such wholesale rascally outrages as this of the Poncas has been."[62]

The newspaper's position was helpful to the Ponca cause, but it was not an entirely realistic assessment of the Ponca dilemma. In the first place, the paper glossed over the shortcomings of the Indians, saying only that they were "civilized; had farms, trades, good schools, churches which they built and supported." In the *Tribune*'s telling, the Poncas were model citizens who had easily adopted the ways of the whites. Significantly, the *Tribune* built a Ponca identity based on reports from Tibbles and other Ponca sympathizers, information that was hardly neutral. The paper also oversimplified the effect of expanded Indian rights, which were, as the paper claimed, "a move in the right direction." But court protection and the right to vote was not the simple solution the newspaper implied; bureaucratic incompetence and corruption, racial discrimination and cultural readjustment would confront the Poncas and other tribes for years to come.

A more informed assessment of the Poncas came from Secretary Schurz himself. In a statement released in Washington on 22 August and published in the *Tribune* the following day, Schurz defended the government's actions in the Ponca case. Although he was hardly impartial, Schurz, unlike the *Tribune,* had official reports from Ponca territory and his statement cited evidence not found in other news reports. For example, Schurz questioned the tribe's self-sufficiency in agriculture as well as their degree of civilization. "While the Poncas have always been very good Indians, they were very far removed from a civilized condition," he wrote. "The fact is, they were regularly fed by the Government. They are gradually approaching a civilized condition now, but they are certainly nearer to it at present than they have ever been before."[63] Although Schurz was much less sympathetic toward the Poncas than the *Tribune,* the paper was even-handed enough to run his statement on page one. On the other hand, Schurz's statement put an official twist on the Ponca story that the newspaper was unable to challenge. In this way, the real truth about the Poncas, their progress toward civilization, and their running dispute with government officials remained unclear.

The *Tribune*'s defense of the Poncas did not go unchallenged from its readers either. At least one New Yorker was incensed enough over the issue to write a letter attacking the paper and the status of all Native Americans. The letter challenged more than the Poncas' claim to citizenship or land; it challenged their very right to exist. The writer, identified only as "D.E.D.," opened with a few questions to the editor: "I would like to know what rights the Poncas or any other Indians have, or are entitled to?" D.E.D. also asked this extraordinary question: "What right have they to be in the country, anyhow?"[64]

Without legal standing—or moral standing, for that matter—the Indians were indefensible in D.E.D.'s eyes: "They are nothing but barbarians; they have no vote; while we are Christians and voters. Therefore, the land they occupy is unprofitable, and I for one cannot see why any white man who is a voter, and desires the land, should not make a claim to it, and if necessary, get help from the Government to obtain it."[65] The letter claimed that the government's Indian policy was a sham, a roundabout way of "killing them off by whiskey and starvation, and by employing agents, in the first place, to get them to run away, and soldiers, in the second place, to kill them under pretense of bringing them back." Finally, the writer ended with a call to patriotic values: "This is a glorious country—'the land of the free and the home of the brave'—where the oppressed of all nations may find a refuge, become naturalized and vote, providing they are white."[66]

Despite the outrageousness of the letter, the paper ran it without comment. As a racist diatribe, the letter followed a well-established pattern of thinking about Indians. They were not Christians, hence they were "barbarians" and inferior by definition. They were not voters, another sign of their inferiority (though this was a Catch-22, of course, since they were not permitted to be citizens). Moreover, they occupied "unprofitable" land, an implication that the Indians were incapable of improving it. Finally they were not white, which by itself precluded their entering the land where "the oppressed of all nations" could find safe haven. In all these ways the Indians were separated from whites and assigned to a no-man's-land of servitude and humiliation.

None of these ideas belonged to the *Tribune.* Yet the *Tribune* was not completely blameless in its portrayal of the Ponca case. Whitelaw Reid's editorials proudly supported the Poncas, but the paper did not effectively challenge the position of Secretary Schurz or the biases of D.E.D. In addition, the *Tribune* did little to inform itself and its readers of the Poncas' true condition. With no correspondent in the field, the paper provided no direct evidence about the Poncas, evidence that could have shed some needed light on the state of their civilization and their mistreatment by the government. As it was, the paper could only assert what Tibbles and other Indian sympathizers said about the Poncas and then print the other side from Schurz and more vociferous Indian-haters. Like Indian Removal news in *Niles' Weekly Register* decades earlier, this process made for a rough editorial balance or "objectivity," but it did not lead to a deeper or more informed portrait of the Poncas. Thus the actual condition of the Poncas was beyond the journalistic grasp of one of the tribe's best editorial supporters, the New York *Tribune.*

The Poncas on Tour

The war of words became even more intense when Tibbles, Standing Bear, and Bright Eyes began their lecture tour in late 1879. Tibbles's advance work quickly began to pay off as the party traveled to Chicago, Boston, and New York. "Everywhere they were received by crowded, enthusiastic houses of good folk who listened to the stories of their wrongs, were impressed by stage costumes and contributed liberally," one historian concluded.[67] The newspapers helped the cause too, publishing frequent reports on the speakers and the activities of their supporters. In New York, for example, the *Times* published a short report on a reception held for the Poncas and their supporters at a home on Fifth Avenue. The headline asked, "IS THE INDIAN A CITIZEN?" but the story was less about legal issues than about the tribe's troubled relationship with the government. The story also listed a number of prominent citizens who attended the reception, most of them New York clergymen.[68]

A few days later, the *Times* ran its account of the Ponca meeting in Steinway Hall, where a thousand people came out to see and hear the Poncas. Standing Bear was described as "an athletic savage—if such a term can be applied to a very docile Indian" and Bright Eyes was "a little woman about 20 years of age . . . of tawny complexion, pleasant features, and has a very feminine voice and manner."[69] The reporter was obviously moved by their appeal: "The story told by these people of the incredible wrongs they have suffered was simple, plain, and pathetic almost beyond the power of description."

Several speakers addressed the crowd: the Reverend Henry W. Bellows, Tibbles, Bright Eyes, and Professor Roswell D. Hitchcock. Bright Eyes, the paper said, "was listened to with great apparent interest." So great were the Ponca sufferings, she said, that sometimes she almost lost her faith in God and in justice. It crushed her, she said, "to see a little handful of poor, helpless, peaceable people oppressed by a mighty nation." Bright Eyes also did her part to show Indians as human beings, something that was frequently lacking in western press reports. "She assured her hearers that the Indians were human beings like themselves, with hopes and affections like themselves, who loved and hated as they did," the *Times* reported.[70]

The evening ended with a speech by Professor Hitchcock, who endorsed the idea of the Indian as a human being and pointed out that public opinion about Indians was constantly swinging from one extreme to the other. "We used to have in our books an ideal Indian—Logan, for example, in the speech which Thomas Jefferson put into his mouth, and King Philip, as described by Washington Irving," said Hitchcock. "Latterly we had heard that the only good Indian was a dead Indian. The pendulum had traversed its arc. The truth lies between these two extremes, one of which was sentimental, the other brutal, or worse than brutal." The Indian question, Hitchcock said, was really a moral question, "not to be settled at once, but slowly, as all moral questions have to be settled; not to-day, perhaps, nor to-morrow, but some time, and settled rightly."[71] Here, at last, was a realistic—if abstract—assessment of the identity problem confronting Native Americans. Unlike most other Indian sympathizers, including those in the press, Hitchcock was willing to admit that the Poncas were neither perfect Indians nor savage brutes but somewhere between these extremes. And Hitchcock, unlike the editorial writers, could see that equality and justice for Indians was a long-term goal that could not be achieved simply through court decisions and executive fiat.

Hitchcock's ideas, however, did not capture the imagination of the press or public. That role fell to Bright Eyes, who, unlike Standing Bear, could speak English fluently and who used her verbal abilities to dramatize and embellish her speeches for maximum effect. The number of families decimated in Indian Territory increased from sixteen to twenty-four in Bright Eyes's testimony, and a group of Ponca chiefs stranded by the Indian Bureau in 1877 had to travel, first, five hundred miles to their homes, then one thousand, and later twelve hundred.[72] More significantly, Bright Eyes was an attractive and charming presence on stage, a fact that soon affected her public image. After her speech at Steinway Hall, for example, the *Times* reporter noted, "The audience gathered about the Indian girl . . . to talk with her and shake her by the hand."[73] Notably, no such comment was made about Standing Bear, who was, by contrast, much more "Indian" than Bright Eyes. The eastern papers also contributed to Bright Eyes's image. According to her biographer, she wanted to be known by her formal name, Susette LaFlesche, but "the newspapers would not let her."[74]

Bright Eyes's fame in the East soon had concrete consequences. She was particularly popular in Boston, where she met Henry Wadsworth Longfellow, the author of *Hiawatha*. According to one account of their meeting, "The poet clasped her hand with both of his own, looked down into her eyes and after an appreciable pause, said, 'This is Minnehaha.'"[75] So began a rumor that Bright Eyes was the model for Longfellow's fictional Indian heroine, a rumor that further idealized the public image of Bright Eyes. Such sentimental notions probably helped the Ponca cause, but they did not promote a realistic view of Indians or the long-term problems they faced in the West.

A more important consequence of Bright Eyes's fame was her influence on Helen Hunt Jackson, a New England writer then living in Colorado. Mrs. Jackson, daughter of an Amherst professor and a childhood friend of Emily Dickinson, was part of a group of privileged eastern women (such as Lydia Maria Child, Mary Bonney, and Amelia Quinton) who became active "friends of the Indian" about this time.[76] Mrs. Jackson wrote sentimental verses and travel pieces for a variety of newspapers and magazines, including the New York *Evening Post,* the New York *Independent, Atlantic Monthly, Riverside Magazine for Young People, Woman's Journal,* and the *Christian Union.*[77] In early 1879, Mrs. Jackson was restless and depressed, having lost her zeal for Colorado and feeling cut off from her literary friends in the East. Bright Eyes and the Poncas soon changed all that. Returning to Boston in November 1879 for a celebration in honor of Oliver Wendell Holmes's seventieth birthday, Jackson heard the Ponca delegation speak and was immediately attracted to their cause. In fact, the treatment—that is, mistreatment—of Indians became a consuming passion for the rest of her life and resulted in her two best-known and most influential books, *A Century of Dishonor,* a history of Indian-white relations, and *Ramona,* a romantic novel about the California Mission Indians. This conversion to the Indian cause was all the more remarkable because of Jackson's previous antipathy to nineteenth-century social reforms. Unlike some other educated Christian women from the East, Jackson had not embraced the abolitionist or temperance movements, work that leading clergymen said was proper for upper- and middle-class women in their role as guardians of the home and hearth.[78] Prior to her Ponca encounter in Boston, in fact, Jackson had displayed no interest in Indians, describing those she had met on her travels as "loathsome" and "hideous."[79] But the Ponca story and the "civilized" demeanor of Bright Eyes had a powerful effect on Jackson. According to Bright Eyes's biographer, Jackson told the younger woman, "My dear, you have given me a new purpose in life. You and I will work miracles together. You will see."[80] Indeed, for the next several months, Jackson "gave her entire mind, strength, heart and soul to the Indian cause."[81] Using her literary and research skills as well as her connection to eastern editors, Jackson began her own publicity campaign on behalf of the Poncas. In December 1879, under her pseudonym "H.H.," she composed a long attack on the government's Indian policy that the New York *Tribune* published alongside a report on the most recent lecture by Tibbles, Bright Eyes, and company. Jackson did not confine herself to the Poncas, but detailed the troubles of a number of western tribes, including the Omahas (Bright Eyes's own tribe), the Nez Perce, and the White River Utes. About the latter tribe, Jackson quoted Schurz's annual report that the tribe had "no just cause for complaint." Her next sentence quoted another official report that said, "The situation of the White River Ute

Agency is the worst possible in all respects, unless it should be the intention to keep the Indians as National paupers."[82]

Secretary Schurz replied in the *Tribune* four days later. He answered "H.H." point by point, attacking her positions as incomplete and based on erroneous information. Concerning the Poncas, Schurz repeated his argument that the blame belonged to the previous administration and that he and his staff were the ones who had exposed the situation in the first place.[83] This answer did not satisfy Jackson, whose reply to Schurz's reply appeared a few days later. In this article, Jackson launched her own point-by-point rebuttal of Schurz's statements. She disputed the secretary's claim that he and the Indian Commissioner "were the first persons to bring the wrongs inflicted upon the Poncas to public notice." Somewhat grudgingly, Jackson admitted that they were "among the first," but credited Tibbles and the Omaha lawyers with the real discovery.[84]

In early 1880, Jackson's outspoken support for Indian reform started another newspaper debate, this one involving the former editor of the *Daily Rocky Mountain News,* William Byers. As events surrounding the Sand Creek massacre made clear, Byers had little use for Indians, especially those who interfered with the development of his beloved Colorado. In a defense of the Colorado Utes published in the New York *Tribune,* Jackson included a commentary on the Sand Creek massacre and the role of the *News.* "When this Colorado regiment of demons returned to Denver they were greeted with an ovation. *The Denver News* said: 'All acquitted themselves well.'" She went on to quote portions of the investigation that revealed the atrocities committed by the Colorado soldiers and then compared those misdeeds with the ones currently being used against the Utes. "Shall we sit still, warm and well fed, in our homes, while five hundred women and little children are being slowly starved in the bleak, barren wilderness of Colorado?" she asked.[85]

In response, Byers charged that Jackson had "arraigned the people of Colorado as a community of barbarians." As for Sand Creek, Byers was unrepentant. The investigation into the massacre, he said, "was made for certain selfish purposes." And as for the crimes committed by the soldiers, it was, he claimed, only a natural response to the "evidence of barbarism" the soldiers found in the Sand Creek camp.[86] Had she been in Colorado before Sand Creek, when the entire territory was threatened by Indian violence, Byers said, H.H. would have realized the necessity of that battle. "Sand Creek saved Colorado, and taught the Indians the most salutary lesson they had ever learned." The White River Utes, Byers added, deserved their fate because of recent massacres.

Byers's letter was answered by Jackson, who was followed again by Byers.[87] Like the dispute with Schurz, however, this debate shed more heat than light on the problems of Indians in the West. In her public letters and in *A Century of Dishonor*, Jackson helped enflame passions about the injustices done to the Indians, but she did not address the long-standing problems of the western tribes in specific and useful ways. Jackson's strength as an Indian reformer was identifying problems, not developing workable solutions. And despite her acquaintance with the Poncas and the inspiration of Bright Eyes, Jackson did not have a deep understanding of Indians or a firsthand knowledge of their condition. Most of the information in *A Century of Dishonor*, in fact, came not from interviews with Indians or from her observations in the West, but from research at the Astor Library in New York.[88]

For their part, Schurz and Byers showed that there were two very different sides to the Indian issue and that the problems in the West were not necessarily subject to easy solutions. Nevertheless, these debates were helpful to the Indian cause—and ultimately the national cause—because they kept the Indian problem on the public agenda in the early 1880s. At the same time, however, they sometimes obscured the real needs of Indians by focusing on trivial matters such as who first discovered the Ponca problems.

Responding to the publicity tour and continuing complaints from Helen Hunt Jackson, the *Tribune*'s Whitelaw Reid developed strong opinions about the Ponca controversy.[89] So when Congressional hearings on the matter began in early 1880, the *Tribune*'s editorial expressed no doubts; the headline was, "A QUESTION EASILY SETTLED" and the piece opened, "There is no need of prolonged discussion or argument in the case of the Poncas." After a quick review of the facts, the paper claimed that the Ponca removal "was as tyrannical and brutal an outrage as the banishment of any Russian subject to Siberia." The solution, then, was simple: "There is the land; there are the men who own it. Send them back to it. Then let us promptly see to it that such outrages are made impossible for the future."[90]

Unfortunately, such solutions were too simple, which, to its credit, the *Tribune* soon recognized. In another editorial in early 1880, the paper attempted to address the confusion and misinformation surrounding the Indian debate: "So many statements and counter-statements about the Indians fill the papers just now that the average reader is likely to thrust aside the whole matter in disgust. He would like to know the truth and deal justly. But what is the truth? How is he to be just?"[91] These were important questions and the *Tribune* attempted to answer them with three proposals. First, the paper examined the Ponca controversy and cited the need in that case for legal protection for Indians. "So long as the Indians remain without the protection of the law, we give the lie to our claim to be a Republic as much as we did when we permitted slavery," the paper said.

Second, the *Tribune* addressed the problem of the "Utes and other semi-civilized tribes." Here the problem was more difficult, because whites trespassed on Indian lands and the Indians murdered in response. The paper urged Secretary Schurz to make immediate amends with the Utes by granting them "their land in fee simple,—or sufficient land for all their needs,—making it inalienable for a generation." In addition, the paper urged immediate assimilation: "Let them have the chance they crave of education in books, in the trades and farming; recognize them in law, and then, if they deserve it, put them in jail and hang them."[92]

Finally, the paper acknowledged the power of the Indian reform movement and endorsed its efforts to advance Indians from their primitive state through education, religion, and agriculture. The *Tribune* put its faith in the reformers. "There is no doubt of the ultimate success of this movement. The justice and religious sense of the people is fully awakened."

These were worthy arguments, well meaning and certainly sensitive to the Indian cause. But they were also naive, especially in the case of the Utes, where the paper assumed that legal protection would keep Colorado settlers away from highly desirable lands and that education and agriculture would quickly put the Utes at the same social level as whites. And although the paper was correct in its assessment of the growing power of the Indian reform movement, it adopted the movement's ideas uncritically and failed to foresee the problems caused by the reformers themselves.

Nevertheless, the reform spirit generated by the Poncas and their supporters blossomed with the new decade. In March 1880 the New York *Tribune* published a positive review of *Our Indian Wards,* a reform book by George W. Maypenny, who served as Commissioner of Indian Affairs under Franklin Pierce. Although Maypenny did not mention the Poncas in his critique of Indian policy, his recommendations were similar to those advocated by the friends of the Poncas. "To begin," Maypenny wrote in his introduction, "let [the Indian] have a fixed and settled home." And in words that echoed the government's mistreatment of the Poncas, he added, "Let him be distressed no more with the fear and apprehension that this home will be taken from him."[93]

The *Tribune* also reviewed *A Century of Dishonor* upon its publication in 1881. Not surprisingly, the book was well received at the *Tribune,* although the unidentified reviewer noted the disjointed structure of the book as well as its one-sided approach to the problem of Indian-government relations. The review repeated some of the book's homilies, such as advice from Julius Seelye, president of Amherst College, who declared in the book's "Introduction" that "the only solution of the Indian problem involves the entire change of these people from a savage life to a civilized life." More critically, the reviewer pointed out that, contrary to Jackson's thesis, the government had "in many instances behaved with great generosity, and is now feeding, clothing and paying annuities to thousands of savages who will not work for a living; . . . that if the treaties with the Indians had been strictly observed all the country west of the Alleghenies would to-day be a howling wilderness; that the Indian as a rule is an ugly and vicious creature, who only behaves himself when he is afraid to rob and scalp his white neighbors."[94] All this might be said, the reviewer continued, but "it would not excuse the folly and injustice that has in many instances characterized our dealings as a nation with the aboriginal tribes." Finally the reviewer summed up the book's message as "less force and more kindness, less shooting and more teaching," and concluded that though Jackson's method was faulty, her motive was worthy. In this instance, at least, the *Tribune* recognized that the Indian reformers did not have all the answers.

The Superficial Story

The Indian reform movement that began in the 1870s culminated in 1887 with the passage of the Dawes Act, a bill designed to hasten the assimilation of the Indians by allotting individual Indians tracts of land on which they could grow crops and raise cattle, and, in time, transform themselves into ordinary United States citizens. Unfortunately, the Dawes Act also undermined the tribal structure of native life, a move that seriously eroded the strength of their cultures. Moreover, reservation land not distributed to Indians soon passed into the hands of whites, as did many of the parcels originally assigned to Indians. Eventually, millions of acres of tribal land would be lost forever. The Dawes Act, despite its Christian idealism and humanitarian aims, was a disaster for American Indians.[95]

The roots of the Dawes bill extend far back into the popular debates over the nature of Indians and the ebb and flow of the Indian reform movement. But the Ponca controversy of 1879–80 was one of the more immediate sources of the Dawes Act because it focused so dramatically on the mistakes of the Indian Bureau and the virtues of the Ponca tribe. The newspapers, as we have seen, were a major part of this controversy. Without sympathetic news coverage and supporting editorials, in fact, opposition to Ponca removal and support for Indian reform could not have attained the broad level of public support that it did.

On the surface, the newspapers deserve credit for their part in the Ponca controversy. After all, open sympathy for Indians in the news and editorial columns was a far cry from the hostility and condemnation that had long been a standard newspaper response to Native Americans. But the Poncas were almost too easy to support. They were a peaceful people with a history of friendly relations with whites. In addition, they had been clearly wronged by the Indian Bureau. As a result, the story was easily framed as a band of "good" Indians under the thumb of bungling Indian bureaucrats. Moreover, the eastern press was not taking a major editorial risk in supporting a peaceful western tribe. The Poncas, like the "civilized" Cherokees years before, were treated as an exceptional case, Indians easily distinguished from the "savage" and "semi-civilized" tribes who were still seen as lazy, heathen, and barbaric. As noted in chapter 6, the Sioux and other tribes continued to make news in unfavorable—and often exaggerated—reports from the West for years to come.[96] Yet as the perceived threats from hostile Indians declined, the public and the press were increasingly open to the idea that some western Indians were capable of "civilized" behavior and social progress. This recognition was not entirely new, but as the power of the tribes appeared to weaken across the decades, some papers emphasized a more sympathetic Native American identity.

Press coverage of the Ponca affair was also subject to the activists on both sides. As documented above, the Poncas did not become a national news story until they were promoted by Thomas H. Tibbles, who combined journalistic talent with moral indignation and the amplifying power of the telegraph to get the Ponca confinement story into several important eastern papers. Tibbles then kept the story alive by organizing the Ponca lecture tour, an event that made Bright Eyes famous, energized writer Helen Hunt Jackson, and put the Ponca story on the news agenda of the New York *Tribune* and several other important newspapers. The key figure in this public relations success was Bright Eyes, an attractive and articulate mixed-race woman who charmed both the public and the press in support of the Ponca cause. Although Bright Eyes and Standing Bear were hardly neutral parties in the debate, the publication of their speeches was a strength of the newspaper coverage because it represented one of the few opportunities for Indians themselves to address Indian issues in a sustained and serious way.

The newspapers, unfortunately, never went far beyond this point. Although Carl Schurz and others presented the government's side of the issue, the deeper problems of the Poncas and other tribes remained largely unexamined. Thanks to the telegraph, major papers could get the Ponca story without sending reporters to Nebraska. And since no eastern paper covered the Ponca controversy independently or investigated the charges and countercharges of the debate, the news agenda was set by partisans on both sides. Thus the newspapers examined here emphasized political and bureaucratic conflict over information about the actual conditions of the Poncas or the consequences of Indian policy. For all these reasons, the Poncas were portrayed generously but superficially.

A greater problem—though not widely recognized at the time—was the newspapers' easy acceptance of the reformers' assumptions about the Indian character and their ideas about assimilation and civilization. The humanitarians believed that education, religious instruction, and a plot of land on which to farm would soon lead the Indians into the mainstream of American life. Such hopes were premised on a host of doubtful assumptions about native life and culture, not to mention the intentions and activities of land-hungry western settlers. Nevertheless, these assumptions fit neatly within the reform spirit of the late nineteenth century, so neatly that papers like the New York *Tribune* believed that high ideals, allotment, and citizenship could change Poncas into "normal" Americans. The result was a reform movement that failed to recognize the devastation unleashed by the Dawes Act until years later, when the damage to native life and culture was already done.

Notes

1. Thomas Henry Tibbles, *Buckskin and Blanket Days* (Garden City, N.Y.: Doubleday and Co., 1957), 193–95.

2. Ibid. See also Thomas Henry Tibbles, *The Poncas Chiefs* (1880; rpt., Lincoln: University of Nebraska Press, 1972), 18–19.

3. Robert Winston Mardock, *The Reformers and the American Indian* (Columbia: University of Missouri Press, 1970), 151. See also Valerie Sherer Mathes, *Helen Hunt Jackson and Her Indian Reform Legacy* (Austin: University of Texas Press, 1990), 3–4.

4. Saint Paul *Daily Press,* 15 Apr. 1873, quoted in Henry E. Fritz, *The Movement*

for Indian Assimilation, 1860–1890 (Philadelphia: University of Pennsylvania Press, 1963), 171.

5. See also the summary of negative publicity in Fritz, *Movement for Indian Assimilation,* 171–78.

6. Quoted in Robert G. Athern, *William Tecumseh Sherman and the Settlement of the West* (Norman: University of Oklahoma Press, 1956), 118. See also Roger L. Nichols, "Printer's Ink and Red Skins: Western Newspapermen and the Indians," *Kansas Quarterly* 3.4 (Fall 1971): 82–88.

7. *Daily Rocky Mountain News,* 2 Mar. 1880, 4.

8. *Salt River Herald* (Phoenix, Arizona Territory), 18 May 1878, 2.

9. Washington *Post,* 8 Nov. 1877, 1; 12 Nov. 1877, 1; 19 Nov. 1877, 1.

10. Ibid., 17 Nov. 1877, 1.

11. Quoted in Frederick E. Hoxie, *A Final Promise: The Campaign to Assimilate the Indians, 1880–1920* (Lincoln: University of Nebraska Press, 1984), 6.

12. Ibid.

13. Charles E. Rankin, "Savage Journalists and Civilized Indians: A Different View," *Journalism History* 21.3 (Autumn 1995): 105.

14. Leavenworth *Commercial,* 27 Nov. 1872, 2, quoted in ibid., 106.

15. Rankin, "Savage Journalists," 106.

16. Quoted in ibid., 109.

17. Quoted in ibid.

18. Quoted in ibid., 110.

19. Ibid.

20. New Orleans *Daily Picayune,* 6 May 1879, 3.

21. Arkansas *Gazette,* 25 May 1879, 2.

22. Jackson [Miss.] *Weekly Clarion,* 9 July 1879, 1.

23. Mardock, *Reformers and the American Indian,* 169. For additional background, correspondence, and other documents related to the government's role in the Ponca controversy, see *Senate Reports,* 46th Cong., 2d Sess., vol. 6, no. 670, 31 May 1880.

24. Earl W. Hayter, "The Ponca Removal," *North Dakota Historical Review* 6.4 (July 1932): 266.

25. Fritz, *Movement for Indian Assimilation,* 189.

26. The journey is dramatically described in Dee Brown, *Bury My Heart at Wounded Knee* (New York: Bantam Books, 1972), 338–40. See also Hayter, "Ponca Removal," 268–69.

27. Stanley Clark, "Ponca Publicity," *Mississippi Valley Historical Review* 29.2 (Mar. 1943): 495–97.

28. New York *Times,* 14 Apr. 1877, 2.

29. Ibid., 12 June 1877, 1.

30. Ibid., 9 Nov. 1877, 1.

31. Ibid.

32. Ibid., 10 Nov. 1877, 8.

33. Hayter, "Ponca Removal," 271.

34. Tibbles's own account of his life is in his autobiography, *Buckskin and Blan-*

ket Days. Also see the "Publisher's Preface" to the autobiography for additional biographical details on Tibbles.

35. New York *Times,* 31 Mar. 1879, 1.
36. Ibid.
37. Ibid., 2 Apr. 1879, 5.
38. Ibid., 2 May 1879, 1.
39. Chicago *Tribune,* 2 May 1879, 3.
40. Ibid., 6 May 1879, 4.
41. Ibid.
42. Ibid.
43. New York *Tribune,* 16 May 1879, 4.
44. Ibid., 31 May 1879, 3.
45. New York *Times,* 14 May 1879, 1.
46. Ibid., 6 June 1879, 4.
47. Chicago *Tribune,* 19 May 1879, 4.
48. Atlanta *Constitution,* 16 Jan. 1879, 2.
49. Ibid., 14 May 1879, 2.
50. Ibid., 16 May 1879, 2.
51. *Daily Rocky Mountain News,* 15 May 1879, 1.
52. Ibid.
53. Ibid., 16 May 1879, 2.
54. Ibid., 17 May 1879, 2.
55. Tibbles, *Buckskin and Blanket Days,* 32–33.
56. New York *Times,* 3 July 1879, 5.
57. Ibid.
58. Clark, "Ponca Publicity," 500–502.
59. Ibid.
60. New York *Times,* 3 Aug. 1879, 3.
61. New York *Tribune,* 11 Aug. 1879, 4.
62. Ibid.
63. Ibid., 23 Aug. 1879, 1.
64. Ibid., 3.
65. Ibid.
66. Ibid.
67. Clark, "Ponca Publicity," 505.
68. New York *Times,* 9 Dec. 1879, 2.
69. Ibid., 13 Dec. 1879, 2.
70. Ibid.
71. Ibid.
72. Clark, "Ponca Publicity," 505.
73. New York *Times,* 13 Dec. 1879, 2.
74. Dorothy Clarke Wilson, *Bright Eyes* (New York: McGraw-Hill, 1974), 217.
75. Clark, "Ponca Posterity," 507. See also Wilson, *Bright Eyes,* 235, and the New York *Tribune,* 8 Dec. 1879, 1, which repeated the Minnehaha story.
76. Bonney and Quinton, with the encouragement of Mrs. John Jacob Astor,

founded the Women's National Indian Association in Philadelphia in December 1879. See Mardock, *Reformers and the American Indian,* 199.

77. Ruth Odell, *Helen Hunt Jackson* (New York: D. Appleton-Century, 1939), chap. 1. See also Odell's bibliography of Jackson's work, ibid., 249–314.

78. An overview of the civilizing role for Victorian women is in Mathes, *Helen Hunt Jackson,* 9–17.

79. Odell, *Helen Hunt Jackson,* 155.

80. Wilson, *Bright Eyes,* 233.

81. Odell, *Helen Hunt Jackson,* 164.

82. New York *Tribune,* 15 Dec. 1879, 5.

83. Ibid., 19 Dec. 1879, 5.

84. Ibid., 28 Dec. 1879, 5.

85. Ibid., 5 Feb. 1880, 5.

86. Ibid., 22 Feb. 1880, 6.

87. New York *Tribune,* 24 Feb. 1880, 2; 27 Feb. 1880, 5.

88. Rosemary Whitaker, *Helen Hunt Jackson* (Boise, Idaho: Boise State University Western Writers Series, 1987), 26. See also Andrew F. Rolle, "Introduction," in Helen Hunt Jackson, *A Century of Dishonor* (New York: Harper Torchbooks, 1965), xi.

89. Mathes, *Helen Hunt Jackson,* 25–26, documents Jackson's letters to and complaints about Reid and the *Tribune's* coverage of the Ponca affair.

90. New York *Tribune,* 15 Feb. 1879, 6.

91. Ibid., 29 Feb. 1880, 6.

92. Ibid.

93. George W. Maypenny, *Our Indian Wards* (Cincinnati: Robert Clarke and Co., 1880), xii.

94. New York *Tribune,* 4 Feb. 1881, 6.

95. For details on the effects of the Dawes Act, see Fritz, *Movement for Indian Assimilation,* 212–21. See also Brian W. Dippie, *The Vanishing American* (Middletown, Conn.: Wesleyan University Press, 1982), 174–75; Hoxie, *Final Promise,* 44.

96. Exaggerated Western news reports continued after the Ponca story ceased to make news. See, for example, Elmo Scott Watson, "The Last Indian War, 1890–91: A Study in Newspaper Jingoism," *Journalism Quarterly* 20.3 (Sept. 1943): 205–19. See also reports from the New York *Herald* in 1882 cited by Loring B. Priest, *Uncle Sam's Stepchildren* (New Brunswick, N.J.: Rutgers University Press, 1942), 91.

CONCLUSION:

THE NEWSPAPER INDIAN

ONE day in the spring of 1879, readers of the New Orleans *Evening Picayune* picked up their papers to find a short telegraph dispatch from Texas on page one. The news was not good, but the headline promised excitement: "The Spring Raids on the Border—The Kiowas Murdering and Stealing—Fears of a General Massacre." The story itself provided only a few more details: "Galveston, April 29—A special to the Galveston News from the neighborhood of the Pecos River reports that the Kiowas are killing herders and driving off stock. Mr. Beleher and one of his men were killed Saturday; another on the 23d. Fears of a general massacre are entertained. The Indians number sixty."[1] This was the complete story; no other details were provided. Yet the readers of the *Picayune* did not come to this story without some knowledge of Indians and their ways, ideas drawn at least in part from newspapers like the *Picayune*.

The *Picayune* story, unfortunately, was typical of hundreds of telegraph bulletins published in the nineteenth century. Time and again, Indians were newsworthy because they were involved in conflicts with whites. But why did this story—from the wilds of west Texas—make the front page of the New Orleans *Picayune*, over five hundred miles away? And why did the story provide such limited information, revealing the Kiowas only as thieves and murderers?

The answers to such questions reveal the complex ideological and cultural processes that shaped the Indian identity in nineteenth-century news. The story was page-one news not because it was important in New Orleans but because it was dramatic and timely information, published under the *Picayune*'s running headline, "LATEST TELEGRAPH." The telegraphic source of the story also helps explain the story's brevity; long telegraph reports were expensive. Besides, this was a simple news bulletin, not intended to give a detailed explanation of events on the Texas frontier.

Yet the story was notably lacking in information about the Kiowas. Warriors had stolen livestock and killed three men; this much seemed clear. But the story furnished no clear motive or explanation for the Kiowa actions, implying that no explanation existed. If there was an explanation— if, for example, tribal lands had been invaded—the story provided no clues. Moreover, the headline, "Spring Raids on the Border," suggested that Kiowa attacks were an annual event. Perhaps they were; the story did not say.

But the article was very clear about its expectations of Kiowa conduct: "Fears of a general massacre are entertained." Under the circumstances, this was a plausible fear. What is striking, however, is not the idea that the Kiowas would start a "general massacre" but that they were expected to. In that sense, this story reveals more about white fears than it does about Indians. The actual Kiowas, their motives and their problems, were not a significant part of the *Picayune* story. The Indians referred to here—newspaper Indians—were defined in terms of their relations to whites, relations that often centered on suspicion, violence, and fear. Thanks to the news, such fears extended all the way from the Pecos River to the narrow streets of the French Quarter and beyond.

The Ideological Indian

No single factor fully accounts for the newspaper Indian. Making sense of many individual Indians and Indian peoples under various conditions over many decades was always a complicated matter. But it does seem clear that Indian identity in the nineteenth-century press was circumscribed by an active and powerful ideology of civilization and progress, a set of ideas about history and race in which Native Americans were understood primarily as obstacles to economic growth and national development. If America was, as the ideology maintained, "the fulfillment of the progressive and liberating promises of the Renaissance, the Reformation, and the Enlightenment," then history was on the side of the advanced, civilized peoples who were destined to dominate or exterminate the weak and backward races.[2] This ideology so informed the principles and practices of American journalism (and American society generally) that Indians came to be understood as a race of primitive people unable or unwilling to become "normal," civilized citizens. This position made Native Americans readily available as symbols for a host of American aspirations. From colonial days on, Indians were seen as living examples of both natural human virtue and the dangers of unschooled barbarism. Over time, these apparently contradictory identities coalesced into a set of conventional ways of knowing and explaining native people. The themes of these stories and images varied over time, but it was always clear in the popular mind that Indians were different from whites and, more often than not, deficient.

As the preceding chapters have shown, the newspapers played a major role in creating and maintaining popular Indian identities in the nineteenth century. But the press was not alone in this process; it operated as part of a larger cultural system that had shaped beliefs and created meanings about Indians for many decades. Religion, for example, had long been used to sanction the Euro-American conquest of the continent. In colonial Virginia, the English thought God's plan would reward the colonists for bringing Christianity to the Indians. As the Reverend Samuel Purchas put it, "God in his wisedome having enriched the Savage Countries, that those riches might be attractives for Christian suters, which there may sowe spirituals and reape temporals."[3] In addition, most early Americans believed the Indians did not deserve the rich land they occupied. Despite evidence to the contrary, Indians were seen as hunters who had not improved the land in accordance with God's will—or, for that matter, John Locke's natural law. Thus the taking of Indian land was justified because both God and nature required the triumph of civilization over savagery. Moreover, popular "scientific" theories of the day held that races, like individuals, passed through stages. Just as individuals were infants, children, and eventually adults, so races began in savagery before they advanced to civilization. Since Indians were obvious savages—witness their brutality, immorality, speech, manners, and so on—in a progressive and increasingly civilized society, change was inevitable. Indians could become civilized, perhaps, especially with the help of missionaries and other humanitarians. Federal Indian policy was based on this idea. Improve their circumstances, teach them the values and skills of civilized life, and Indians too could join the march of progress. This was paternalistic, of course, but most Indian policies were intended to be a benevolent form of paternalism, something akin to a stern but understanding father who wants to protect and guide a seemingly helpless child.[4] More likely than civilization, however, was extinction. Indians would simply fade away, their cultures overmatched by the glories of progress and new technology.

In popular culture, Indian identity was filtered through the romantic imagination of eighteenth- and nineteenth-century American writers. Phillip Freneau, Cooper, Longfellow, Lydia Maria Child, and others created noble (but ultimately doomed) Indians to criticize American society or imagine its glorious future. Freneau presented Tomo-Cheeki as an alternative to the unfulfilled promise of civilization, flying "hastily through the dews of the forest," quite content—unlike civilized men—in his search for food.[5] Child created Hobomok, a friendly and positive character, and allowed him to marry a white woman after the supposed death of her beloved. But when the "dead" man returned, Hobomok surrendered his bride because he knew his place. "Hobomok will go far off among some red men in the west," Child wrote. "They will dig him a grave."[6]

Later in the century, the savage Indian returned to popular consciousness, this time as a bloodthirsty yet proud warrior. In the "dime novels" of Beadle and Adams, Ned Buntline, and others, the West was an exciting terrain where brave men could test themselves against the savages. Warring Indians were easily portrayed as "treacherous red devils," subhuman creatures who took pleasure in torture and death. In this role, the Ignoble Savage was a useful and necessary enemy, the creature whose defeat signaled the rising power of the American nation. Indians also had political uses. Disputes over their treatment and character, in fact, often devolved into partisan bickering, each side accusing the other of mishandling the "Indian problem." Indians also could be made to represent the "dangerous classes," poor whites, immigrants, and former slaves who seemed to threaten the new industrial order. James Gordon Bennett Jr. was the most vigorous proponent of this idea, using the New York *Herald*'s editorial columns to link savage Indians with savages from the underclass. Commenting on a racial incident in South Carolina shortly after Custer's defeat, Bennett wrote, "Sitting Bull is said to be profoundly gratified with the reports of the Hamburg riot. It shows that Sioux civilization and Sioux tactics are spreading."[7] But the Indian threat in the last half of the century was always more symbolic than real. Soon, in fact, the romantic (but disarmed) savage was resurrected. Sitting Bull and other Indians were now safe enough to play themselves in Buffalo Bill's reenactments of the West's glory days. In the American mind, fact and fiction seemed to merge and, significantly, the Indians always lost.

The newspaper Indian was created in this complex cultural milieu. This was not a straightforward process, however, since many of the beliefs and ideas about Indians were dynamic and contradictory. The press, however, was in a position to smooth over or ignore the contradictions. Depending on the circumstances, some Indians were "good," while others were "bad." More important than the inconsistency of this identification process, however, was its easy availability and usefulness in the creation of a larger national identity. As a subordinate racial group, Indian identity was routinely appropriated and shaped to fit the editorial or political needs of the moment. Editors and reporters, in their role as cultural mediators, were able to use various Indian identities to help articulate and comment on the kind of society they wanted. Indian representations were easily simplified too, so that presumed Indian qualities could be seen as offering support for one cause or another. The Indian as dangerous savage, for example, made clear the need for laws and other trappings of an orderly, civilized society. Further, it allowed Americans to rationalize the death and destruction of native people by presenting this as the victory of civilization over savagery.

The imagery of the "evil Indian" was (and is) so powerful that it is tempting to see the inherent racism of this figure as the major legacy of the nineteenth-century press. But the problem of Indian identity was never so simple or one-dimensional. Racism existed, of course, and it influenced Indian identity in significant ways. Yet the "good" Indian, as we have seen, was also portrayed in the papers. In this role, sympathetic editors, humanitarians, and other "friends of the Indian" promoted the idealized Indian as they battled for Indian rights and policy reforms. They emphasized the natural virtues and redeemable qualities of native people as they made their case for Christian charity and racial justice. True, much of this sympathy was paternalistic or patronizing and it often did little to advance the Indians' own interests or views. But it is also true that Native Americans could sometimes speak for themselves in the press. Elias Boudinot's editorials from the Cherokee *Phoenix,* for example, were reprinted in a number of eastern newspapers in the 1830s. Later in the century, white reporters sought out interviews with Sitting Bull, Bright Eyes, and other native leaders, allowing them a chance to tell their own stories in their own words. These opportunities were rare and Indian speakers had no control over the presentation or editing of their words, but this was probably as close as nineteenth-century American journalism could come to an honest and empathetic representation of Native Americans. The existence of these native voices also suggests that the ideology of domination and dispossession so common in the papers was not absolute or universal. Slight and incomplete though it was, Indians could sometimes represent themselves in the nineteenth-century press, a welcome development that foreshadowed a larger and more active Native American role in twentieth-century news-making.[8]

News, Technology, and Indian Identity

Ideas about civilization and progress clearly shaped news about Indians. But as we have seen, Indian representations were also influenced by a host of practical and technological factors. Over the course of the century, news gathering went from an informal, relatively personal business to an increasingly standardized and professional system. Early in the century, journalists printed news, letters, rumors, poems—whatever material they happened to have that struck their fancy. Antebellum editors were primarily passive collectors of information, dependent on the post office for news from exchange papers. Beginning in the 1830s, the penny press editors began to actively observe and investigate the world beyond the newsroom, looking for facts. The telegraph and the centralizing power of the Associated Press accelerated these changes, placing a premium on speed and promoting the development of a tighter, more fact-filled narrative style. News became increasingly commodified, an exciting product that could be sold to news-hungry readers during the Civil War and the Indian wars that followed. Reporters were now on the scene, gathering facts but also making reality more interesting by emphasizing the colorful over the mundane. Leading reporters saw themselves as adventurers, risking their lives in search of the truth. By the final decades of the century, American journalism had developed a set of professional practices that pointed toward journalistic objectivity, facts that promised a near-scientific explanation of the world.

But "objectivity" was an impossible goal, especially in cross-cultural communication. The selection and presentation of news, after all, was always arbitrary and never complete; journalistic "facts" were rarely absolute and some details were bound to be over- or under-emphasized. This was certainly the case in newspaper explanations of Indian violence against whites. One-sided and sensational reporting can be explained as the obvious response to what was seen as sensational Indian violence—ambushes, raids, mutilations, and the like. But the persistence of this theme across many decades suggests something about the particular nature of much Indian news. Violent encounters between evil Indians and innocent whites made compelling, page-one stories; peaceful relations and gentle Indians did not. Moreover, Indian-white conflicts could be easily reduced to a standard set of sensational "facts," ready-made for telegraphic transmission to every AP newspaper. Even when "good" Indians were featured in the papers, their stories lacked the vivid details necessary to capture the public imagination. Year in and year out, the press looked for—and found—simple tales of violence and evil on the Indian frontier. These stories were journalistically "true," but they were never the full story of Indian-white relations in the West. For Native Americans, already viewed as savage and uncivilized, this emphasis on violence worked to reinforce Indian inferiority and ensure that the news would continue to emphasize conflict over more benign ideas about Indians.

One of the major consequences of these news-making practices was an exaggerated sense of racial difference. Native Americans and whites were different in many ways, of course, but they were also similar, sharing the same human concerns for family, food, shelter, and safety in a sometimes hostile land. But this was not the stuff of news—or of the rumor mill that flourished on the frontier. As a result, many nineteenth-century Americans thought they knew all about Indians and the Indian threat before they ever encountered a single native person. Pioneer women, for example, traveled west in fear, fully expecting daily attacks by howling warriors. But as historian Glenda Riley has shown, most passages across the plains were peaceful and many travelers discovered that real Indians were not nearly as dangerous as the kind they read about in the papers.[9]

A Final Word

In the end, the cultural gap between white Americans and Native Americans was so fundamental and so wide that it could not be closed by nineteenth-century journalism. As the preceding chapters have shown, news gathering evolved over the decades: it became faster, more efficient, and more fact-driven. But the changes in nineteenth-century journalism were not the kind that could provide depth or insight into the complexities of Native Americans and their cultures. American journalists and readers alike believed that facts about Indians could be known and that journalism had the power to render Indians accurately and "realistically." This was a false hope. Nineteenth-century journalism was a product of its time, bound to a set of ideas about civilization and progress that could not conceive of Native Americans in a relative or pluralistic way. Nineteenth-century journalists could be sympathetic to Indians from time to time, but they could not render Native Americans as fully realized individuals from cultures as valuable and as important as their own.

Notes

1. New Orleans *Evening Picayune,* 30 Apr. 1879, 1.

2. Richard Slotkin, *The Fatal Environment* (New York: HarperPerennial, 1985), 228.

3. Quoted in Roy Harvey Pearce, *Savagism and Civilization* (Berkeley: University of California Press, 1988), 8.

4. Francis Paul Prucha, *The Indians in American Society* (Berkeley: University of California Press, 1985), 10–11.

5. Quoted in Pearce, *Savagism and Civilization,* 144.

6. Quoted in Robert S. Tilton, *Pocahontas: The Evolution of an American Narrative* (New York: Cambridge University Press, 1994), 65.

7. New York *Herald,* 15 July 1876, quoted in Slotkin, *Fatal Environment,* 465.

8. See Mary Ann Weston, *Native Americans in the News: Images of Indians in the Twentieth-Century Press* (Westport, Conn.: Greenwood Press, 1996), esp. chaps. 6–7.

9. Glenda Riley, *Women and Indians on the Frontier, 1825–1915* (Albuquerque: University of New Mexico Press, 1984), 92–98.

INDEX

John M. Coward is associate professor and chair of the faculty of communication at the University of Tulsa. His articles on Native Americans and the media have been published in *Journalism Quarterly, American Journalism,* and *Journalism History.*

The History of Communication